Longman Social Policy in Britain Series
THE PERSONAL SOCIAL SERVICES

LONGMAN SOCIAL POLICY IN BRITAIN SERIES

Series Editor:
Jo Campling

Published Titles:

Health Policy and the NHS: Towards 2000, 2E
Judith Allsop

Foundations of the Welfare State
Pat Thane

Elderly People in Modern Society 3E
Anthea Tinker

Social Work, Social Care and Social Planning:
the Personal Social Services since Seebohm
Adrian Webb and Gerald Wistow

Housing Problems and Housing Policy
Brian Lund

Forthcoming Titles:

Responding to Poverty
Saul Becker

Disabled People
Brian Oliver

Foundations of the Welfare State 2E
Pat Thane

LONGMAN SOCIAL POLICY IN BRITAIN SERIES

The Personal Social Services:
Clients, Consumers or Citizens?

Robert Adams

LONGMAN
London and New York

Addison Wesley Longman Limited,
Edinburgh Gate, Burnt Mill, Harlow,
Essex CM20 2JE, England
and Associated Companies throughout the world.

© Addison Wesley Longman Limited 1996

First published 1996

ISBN 0 582 25875 8 PPR

British Library Cataloguing-in-Publication Data

A catalogue record for this book is available from the British Library

Library of Congress Cataloguing-in-Publication Data

Adams, Robert, 1944–
  The personal social services : clients, consumers or citizens?/
Robert Adams.
  p.   c.m – (Longman social policy in Britain series)
  Includes bibliographical reference (p.   ) and index.
  ISBN 0–582–25875–8 (pbk.)
  1. Social service – Great Britain.   2. Public welfare – Great Britain.   3. Child
welfare – Great Britain.   4. Great Britain – Social policy.   I. Title.   II. Series.
HV245.A65   1996   95–49641
361.941 – dc20   CIP

Set by Fakenham Photosetting Ltd., Fakenham, Norfolk
Produced through Longman Malaysia, CLP

DEDICATION

To Pat with love, and thanks for all those debates about the personal social services.

'...whenever the British people have identified and investigated a social problem there has followed a national call for more social work and more trained social workers' (Titmuss, R., 1968, *Commitment to Welfare*, Allen and Unwin, London, p. 85).

Interviewer: Do you think the overall sense of decay that you've talked about stems from political decay or political decay stems from other powerful symptoms?

Dennis Potter: Both ... they interlace ... the press ... politics ... the commercialisation of everything means of course you're putting a commercial value upon everything and you turn yourself from a citizen into a consumer ... we're not citizens ... we're consumers and politics is a commodity to be sold.

(From an interview with Dennis Potter by Melvyn Bragg on *Without Walls*, Channel 4, 5 April 1994.)

CONTENTS

ACKNOWLEDGEMENTS

The number of people who have contributed directly or indirectly to this book is very great. I should like to acknowledge invaluable discussions with, and ideas from, Ian Aitken, Saul Becker, Ann Cleverly, Giles Darvill, Sheila Dent, Sandra Dodgson, Hugh Gault, Tony Harwood, Tom Hopkins, Brian Kay, Christine Sedgwick, Ashley Wyatt and Andy Stevens. Dilys Page and Steve Conway commented on earlier draft material and Peter Birchenall on the near-final draft; it is always helpful to clarify concepts with Terence O'Sullivan. I much appreciate the personal attention I received to my detailed queries from the National Deaf Children's Society, National Children's Homes, Terrence Higgins Trust, Michael Jarman, director of child care for Barnardo's and David Lovell, social work director of The Children's Society, Tim Newell and Eric Cullen and the following directors of social services: R.J. Lewis, Metropolitan Borough of Stockport; David Behan, Cleveland; Derek Myers, London Borough of Hounslow; Barbara Smith, acting director of Oxfordshire; and Chris Cheatle, assistant director of Essex. Sarah Caro, Jane Toettcher and Heather Harvey have helped with preparation of the manuscript and, as ever, Jo Campling has remained a constant source of advice and support. None of the above can be held responsible for the omissions and mistakes of this book, which are mine alone.

We are grateful to the following for permission to reproduce copyright material:

London Borough of Barnet for an extract from *Community Care Plan Summary 1995/96*: BASW Trading Ltd (British Association of Social Workers) for an extract from *ADVOCACY; Power to People with Disabilities* by David Brandon with A. and T. Brandon, published by Venture Press; CCETSW (Central Council for Education and Training in Social Work) for extracts from 'Purchasing and contracting skills' by David Best in *Improving Social Work Education and Training*, No. 18 and 'Back from the Wellhouse' in *CCETSW Paper 32.1* edited by Andy Stevens; Calouste Guilbenkian Foundation for extracts from *Taking Children Seriously* (1991) by Rosenbaum and Newell; the Controller of Her Majesty's Stationary Office for extracts and Tables from *National Institute for Social Work* (1988), *Children in Public Care* (1991) by Utting, extracts from *Social Services Inspectorate* (1994) and *The Report of the Enquiry into the Care and Treatment of Christopher Clunis* (1994). All Crown Copyright. Crown Copyright is reproduced with the Permission of the Controller of HMSO; Staffordshire County Council for an extract from *The Pindown Experience and the Protection of Children – Report of Staffordshire Child Care Inquiry* (1990) by Allan Levy and Barbara Kahan.

We have been unable to trace the copyright holder of *Broadmoor* by David Cohen, and would appreciate any information which would enable us to do so.

LIST OF FIGURES AND TABLES

This book sets out the major features of the personal social services in Britain and traces their past, present and possible futures. This involves studying the topography around the social and political context and the legal basis for policy and practice. It also involves examining the details of the personal social services and posing questions associated with these features. What are the personal social services? How may they be conceptualised and viewed? What are the origins, values and purposes of the personal social services? What are the major theoretical perspectives on the personal social services? How do the assumptions of the 1990s about the personal social services differ from those of the 1940s? In what demographic, social, legal and policy context do the personal social services operate? How are the personal social services organised and delivered? What are the roles of the personal social services and who does the work? What major approaches are used in various aspects of the work – with children, younger people, older people, in youth justice and criminal justice, and related areas? What are the main issues arising in these aspects of the delivery of the personal social services?

I need to say briefly why this aspect of social policy and practice remains problematic and why, in spite of the seeming straightforwardness of the book's aim set out above, the essentially contested nature of perspectives on, theories of, and practice in the personal social services make 'it so difficult, if not impossible, to realise this aim'.

The first reason lies behind the subtitle for this book and provides themes for the treatment of the subject matter of each chapter. While until the 1960s the notion of treating *clients* was taken for granted, in the 1990s the concept of empowering service users as *citizens* is prominent. I have examined in some detail in another book (Adams, 1996) the impact on social work of this shift from the client treatment paradigm to the citizen empowerment paradigm. Unfortunately for those involved in studying, practising and receiving services from the personal social services, Shakespeare's understanding of the way a youth 'crawls to maturity, wherewith being crowned crooked eclipses 'gainst his glory fight' applies all too readily to the superimposition on the treatment and empowerment paradigms alike of the consumerism of the quasi-markets in health and social care in general, and community care in particular. The value and knowledge base of social work is contested, notably by some Conservative politicians who would prefer to dispense with the ideologically challenging anti-oppressive discourse of empowerment and reduce it to a charter for *consumers* of social services.

Second, I am all too aware of the dangers of reducing complex issues to single words in this way; however, as this book is being written, empowering social work as a profession is struggling to survive. At the London School of Economics – where the first course of qualification in social work began in Britain – it became apparent in August 1995 that the Diploma in Social Work programme would close. No doubt this decision reflects not simply ideological issues of whether there is a place for the education of social workers in a two-year qualifying programme in higher education, but also issues concerning how to find the resources from current funding to run such a programme in genuine partnership with employers and students and to provide adequate agency-based practice learning opportunities, without the programme degenerating into mere training.

Third, it is not possible to write about the personal social services with the same detachment that one would apply to a subject known only from an external position. Very few people can claim to stand outside the field of the personal social services. My sister, an aunt and one parent have all been clients of the social services and in receipt of community care. These experiences have contributed to my views and prejudices, developed through my professional work as an academic. Writing and research in the field of the personal social services forms a huge and rapidly expanding bulk, and practice varies very widely from local authority to local authority. To digest all this and reflect its complexity and detail would require a bookshelf rather than this single volume. There is a tension between writing at a level of generality that glosses over the complexity of details and one that addresses specifics at the expense of general trends. While this cannot be resolved in a single book of this length, recognition can be given to the existence of irregular terrain between major landmarks. For example, I have tried to acknowledge the significant differences in the organisation and work of the personal social services in Wales, Scotland, Northern Ireland and England. In some aspects of the personal social services, the United Kingdom is anything but united: I have tried to indicate where key differences exist, while focusing on UK-wide perspectives and issues. Because Westminster dominates in so many areas of the work of the personal social services, because I have always lived in England or Wales, because I am white, middle-class and middle-aged, these factors have an inevitable impact that I have not always managed to objectify and transcend.

Structure of the book

There are problems of how to structure the subject matter of this book. The approach adopted should prove least confusing for the reader and most useful for services and service users, since Parts Two, Three and Four correspond with the ways services are organised and provided. The book falls into six parts. Part One – the first three chapters of the book – is concerned with the nature and history of the personal social services, policy-making processes and some of the major issues and problems in the organisation and delivery of personal social services. Part Two – chapters 4 and 5 – deals with services for families and children. Part Three – chapters 6, 7 and 8 – deals with community care, group care and disability, HIV/AIDS, mental health and substance misuse, while in Part Four, chapters 9 and 10, focus on criminal and youth justice respectively. Part Five – chapter 11 – looks at possible scenarios for the future of the personal social services. The final part consists of a file of extracts from relevant documents, a list of some Key Acts and inquiry reports and a selective bibliography of the major sources referred to in the book. The reader should note that some work with adults in families is dealt with in Part Two rather than Part Three, and some aspects of work with children and young people are dealt with in Part Three.

Reference

Adams, R. (1996) *Social Work and Empowerment*, Basingstoke: BASW/Macmillan.

PART ONE

Reshaping the personal social services

CHAPTER 1

Personal social services: an overview

This first chapter provides an introduction to the personal social services. It considers the changing ideologies of the personal social services in their various contexts, in the period from the universalism of the 1940s to the more specialist selectivism of the mixed economy of welfare in the 1990s. It also examines the main features of their organisation and working. It outlines the shifting emphasis of social work from the casework-treatment paradigm, which dominated in the earlier decades, to the empowerment paradigm, which became prominent in the professional literature of social work and social care by the early 1990s. In the process, it highlights tensions between empowerment and the consumerism promoted by government through legislation such as the NHS and Community Care Act 1990.

Changing context of the 'personal social services'

The formal origins of the personal social services in England and Wales lie in the Seebohm Report (Cmnd 3703). The term 'personal social services' was coined for this committee. The Seebohm report on Local Authority and Allied Personal Social Services (1968) marked the beginning of a period of dramatic turnabout in the previously relatively low profile of the personal social services; in this, it was aided by the Local Authority Social Services Act 1970, establishing local authority social services departments, the Local Government Act 1972, which led to local government reorganisation in 1974, and the impact of the inquiry into the death of Maria Colwell (HMSO 1974), one of a series of scandals highlighting the poor quality of treatment by health, social care, social work and allied professionals.

Seebohm was one outcome of a 20-year period of accumulating pressure for change in social work and social services for people in need. The values of the personal social services reflected the broader context of changes, between Beveridge's enthusing about collectivism in the 1940s (Beveridge, 1942, 1944, 1948) and the Conservative government's emphasis on voluntary provision from the 1980s. The demographic, social and economic contexts have changed in this period (see below and chapters 4 to 10 on particular aspects), and the scale of these changes raises critical questions not simply about the assumptions and theories informing them, but also about their key features and, crucially, their impact on people in the welfare industry – workers, service users and carers. Here, the focus is on the changing trajectory of social policies.

From Beveridge to Borrie

A good illustration of how dramatically the centre of gravity of assumptions about what constitutes appropriate provision in the personal social services has shifted in the second half of the twentieth century is provided by comparing the Beveridge Report of 1942 (Cmnd 6404) and the Borrie Report of 1994 (Borrie and Atkinson, 1994). One obvious difference is the contrast between the way the reports were received. The Borrie Report more or less sank into the background as the Labour Party was reorganised by its new leader, Tony Blair. The publication of the Beveridge Report produced a legendary mile-long queue outside HMSO in Holborn, London, and 635,000 immediate sales; *The Times* referred to 'a momentous document which should and must exercise a profound and immediate influence on the direction of social change in Britain, (Jacobs, 1992, p. 6).

Beveridge

Beveridge based his recommendations on three guiding principles: fundamental changes were necessary, not constrained by past experience; social insurance was a contributory part of comprehensive social policies attacking the five giants of Want, Disease, Ignorance, Squalor and Idleness; social security would be established by linking the individual and the state so as not to stifle personal initiative. The social insurance plans of Beveridge were not particularly revolutionary. Apart from the aim of providing a national minimum for all, they were based on generalising the already existing selected benefits, alongside a social security scheme for income maintenance in times of loss or interruption of earnings. Beveridge also was not revolutionary in that the social insurance plan was an insurance scheme, rather than a socialist approach maintaining everybody out of taxation according to the principle of 'from each according to means and to each according to needs'. Beveridge judged that negative feelings about the legacy of the Victorian Poor Law Amendment Act 1834 pointed to the preference of people for contributory benefits from their earnings, rather than charity handouts which discriminated between the deserving and the undeserving poor. There was general approval of the brand of universalism in Beveridge which, irrespective of income or wealth, treated everybody in the insurance scheme the same as far as payments and benefits were concerned.

Unfortunately, this meant that flat rate contributions were a heavy load on those who earned less.

Borrie

The report, published on 24 October 1994, of the Commission on Social Justice set up by the Labour Party with Sir Gordon Borrie as its chairperson marks half a century of changes in the personal social services in the second half of the twentieth century. The Commission visualises a pragmatic post-welfare state social policy to coincide with the social democratic realism of the Labour Party led by Tony Blair in the mid-1990s. The report encapsulates not just the extent of the social policy changes in this period – from the creation to what in some ways is the swan-song of the universalistic welfare state – but also a shift in the political consensus about social policy. In the 1940s, most people would have voted for the benefits of universal state provision in major areas of social policy including the personal social services. In the 1990s, whether reluctantly or not, a growing proportion of people accepted the inevitability of the declining role of the state, and increasing voluntary and private contributions to these services. Nevertheless, Tad Kubisa, president of the Association of Directors of Social Services, at its annual conference in September 1995, called for a royal commission to reconsider the role of the welfare state on a similar broad scale to that of Beveridge. Of the social services departments, he noted: 'In some ways, welfare is at the crossroads. There is a real danger that we shall wither on the vine and become a residual low-key agency, much as we were before the creation of the welfare state' (*The Guardian*, 22 September 1995).

David Marquand, one of the members of the Commission on Social Justice, identifies three significant differences between the 1940s, when Beveridge wrote his reports which played a key role in creating the welfare state, and the 1990s: first, Beveridge only had to crystallise the concept of social citizenship located in 'the robust collectivism of a nation fighting for its life'; second, thanks to Keynesian economic policies having been applied for the previous decade, Beveridge's giant of Idleness through unemployment had been dealt with before he began to tackle Want, Disease, Ignorance and Squalor; third, little remained in the 1990s of the commitment of Keynes and Beveridge to public spending by the state as a way out of economic depression and high unemployment. There was a fourth difference, which relates to the changing power relation between service providers and service users (Adams, 1996), and is implicit in the subtitle of this book, namely a shift from 'clienting' people to regarding them as consumers or, in some circumstances, as empowered citizens. 'Beveridge assumed that a beneficent mandarinate could deliver social citizenship from the top down; Keynes, that a qualified technocracy could manage the economy from the bowels of the Treasury'. But, Marquand maintains, 'social citizenship is empty unless the citizens own the institutions that embody it; economic success comes from a symbiosis between public and private power on the local as well as national level. Social capital holds the key to economic strength as well as to social justice; and social capital accumulates from the bottom up' (Marquand, 1994). Marquand typifies the absence of a critical presence in Borrie. This view is a 'managed market' position which lies between what before the 1990s could have still been described as the polarised standpoints of conservative free-marketeers and socialists (see chapter 11).

Nature of the personal social services

The personal social services have played a complex role for more than 40 years in a vital yet relatively under-appreciated sector of the welfare state. Many people, for example, confuse social work and social services departments with departments of social security. Social work has a rather weak professional identity partly because social workers deal with a large proportion of the less powerful, less influential and low status members of society; social workers practise in diverse agencies, roles and settings and, unlike lawyers, doctors and engineers for example, do not draw on a body of knowledge and expertise agreed and held in common to all in the profession. There are often uncertainties about what course of action would be most productive and there may be no agreement about this among social workers themselves, let alone among other professionals and – when a newsworthy item involves them – the mass media.

In parallel with the widespread tendency to ignore or stigmatise people on the receiving end, the personal social services are a relatively poorly understood and marginalised feature of the welfare state. There are several reasons for this. In part, it is because the personal social services lack a clear professional identity, adequate resourcing and professional power to compete with, say, medical professionals in the health service. Partly, also, it is because their role spans such a variety of preventive and interventive, caring and controlling activities: from material aid to psychological support; from administering and delivering treatment to working in partnerships; from controlling to empowering and engendering independence among service users.

The low esteem of the personal social services is ironic since in many ways they are a core part of the welfare state, in view of their role in enabling people to tackle problems, and address needs that can arise at any time of life. This low esteem is because they cater for the most vulnerable people in the community. Although sometimes intervention and control are called for, much of the more difficult and subtle work that social workers, for example, do involves facilitating people to take charge of their own circumstances and empowering them to address whatever needs and wants they identify. Nevertheless, the mainstream of social services intervention, as exemplified in the legal authority to remove a child or adult from a household in her or his best interests, is the priority responsibility for protecting people. Social workers may be associated with a recognisably Victorian attitude, which comes close to blaming people for many of their problems and doing nothing to reduce the stigma many people feel at having to be involved with 'the welfare'.

Roots of contemporary policy and practice

The personal social services over the past half century have been dominated by the tension between their traditional roles as gate-keepers of a range of custodial institutions for warehousing children, mentally ill, older and disabled people and as dispensers of welfare, care or support. Responses by the state in Britain since the late eighteenth century to unemployed, homeless, sick, mentally ill, poor or criminal people, in the past considered misfits, outcasts, deviants and otherwise unacceptable, have relied heavily on provision developed through a range of statutory, voluntary and self-help agencies, organisations and groups. Since the eighteenth century, residential institutions have played an increasingly prominent part in social policy responses to individual and societal problems, as Roy Parker describes in some detail in the introductory essay of the Wagner Report on residential care (Parker, 1988). In 1834, the Poor Law Amendment Act heralded a new era of intervention by the state, when it distinguished deserving from undeserving poor people, singling the undeserving out for relatively harsh treatment to prevent them from becoming scroungers. The mid-Victorians tended to allow paupers they regarded as deserving to have some limited access to charity, with a view to encouraging them to pull themselves up by their own bootstraps and achieve respectability, by self-help. Meanwhile, the 'undeserving poor' were segregated in the deliberately harsh conditions of the workhouse. In view of the fact that relatively small numbers of people actually went through the workhouse, it is amazing that its ghost still hangs so vividly over the contemporary picture of residential care for older people, as a conversation with many an older person will quickly reveal. Even at the peak of the use of workhouses in 1871, only 0.6% of the population were in poor law institutions, compared with 4.6%, or about a million people, getting outdoor relief.

Whatever the reality, workhouses, like prisons, have long been regarded as the ultimate punishment for poor people. In many towns and cities, former workhouses are still remembered as such by local people, even though they have for decades been converted and used as hospitals or Part III accommodation (named after Part III, Section 21 of the Act, enabling local authorities to provide accommodation) for older people under the 1948 National Assistance Act. Perhaps this is understandable, since, as Goffman found in the classic study of one mental hospital in Washington DC from which he drew a series of striking general observations (Goffman, 1967), going into an institution was associated with failure, becoming a member of a stigmatised category of people, and the possibility of being treated harshly in the company of strangers. By the end of the nineteenth century, the negative image of institutions was reinforced by laws making compulsory admission possible, and (as frightening for patients and residents) making it possible for a voluntary admission to become compulsory and, in the process, for the person to be transferred from a softer to a harsher and more custodial regime.

This history has contributed largely to the impetus behind the growth of community care in the second half of the twentieth century. Yet, despite the closure of many Victorian institutions – those large mental hospitals to be seen in the British countryside, built at a decent distance from respectable communities – residential care continues to co-exist with the collective memories of its history.

The legacy of the nineteenth century meant that people's difficulties and their attendant problems, arising for example from poverty, poor housing, mental illness or unemployment, tended to be blamed on their personal inadequacies. Self-reliance and independence from state welfare agencies were encouraged, and people were penalised for becoming too dependent on them. After World War II, the establishment of the welfare state removed much of the negative connotation attached to receiving welfare. But the traditional attitudes of discouraging dependence on the state remained and, from the late 1980s, resonated with the Conservative government's right wing re-emphasis of the Victorian values of self-reliance, choice and individual responsibility.

The knowledge base, especially of the 'ologies' – sociology, psychology – on which social workers draw in their practice, remains controversial. Some critics argue from a competence-based standpoint, which is itself contested (see the discussion in chapter 3 of Adams, 1997) that qualifying programmes in social work should teach them skills, not so-called irrelevancies about the alleged incidence of poverty and inequality in society. Social work and social services staff are often criticised, and although such criticisms are sometimes based on objective evidence of shortcomings in performance, there are also inevitable divergences of opinion about work done, or not done, based on the different value positions of people involved. The subject matter of the personal social services is people's lives, with all their complications and problems. In such circumstances, it is not surprising that the work of the personal social services offers few clear-cut solutions to most presenting situations. There is much scope for commentators on the personal social services to criticise what social workers do or omit in a particular case. This is because of the inherently problematic nature of the social work task, the diverse values of those involved and the complexities and uncertainties associated with predicting what decisions may best enable people to benefit from services and, in some circumstances, take control of their own lives. The core elements of this role lie in the term 'personal social services', each of the three words of which has significance.

Services

The personal social services provide a service, rather than a product. This distinguishes them from purely materially based, production-oriented activities, notably those in the commercial sector of the economy.

Personal

Services such as education and health have a universal role to play, for the entire population, whereas the personal social services deal with the aspects of people's lives that require additional resources for particular areas of personal need. The tendency for the personal social services to deal with children at risk of harm, problem families, older people who have become infirm, and people with disabilities, leads to these services being viewed as not only specialist, but in some ways bearing the stigma of 'the welfare'. For many older people, this stigma is intensified by what the client feels is a judgement made by a professional about the problem, involving an aspect of personal shortcoming, or deviance, from an assumed norm. Nowadays, the fact that social workers exercise statutory powers to detain people compulsorily under the Mental Health Act 1983, or to remove children from their home when they are considered to be in need of protection, adds to the image of the stigmatising service the visible evidence that some of its tasks involve social control. So, the role of the personal social services spans the continuum between supportive, caring services – residential, and day community care for children, older, disabled or mentally ill adults and families, for example – at one end, and social intervention and supervision – taking children into care and sectioning (compulsorily admitting to hospital) mentally ill people, for instance – at the other.

Social

Alongside, and sometimes in tension with, the personal role of the social services is their social dimension, well illustrated in Rojek *et al.* (1988). To the extent that individuals and groups of people are stigmatised, labelled or treated unequally in society, the role of the personal social services is to redress these inequalities through equality-based practices, i.e. using equal opportunities, anti-discriminatory or anti-oppressive policies and practices.

The fact that the personal social services are concerned not only with meeting the needs of individuals but also with the social dimension of those needs does not mean that staff function overtly as social activists, as may occur in community work. It refers to the way social workers, in particular, address the social implications of the needs or problems presented by a person. For example, a person whose mobility is impaired, and who uses a wheelchair, may feel discriminated against by being regarded as disabled. This may involve stigmatisation in the workplace and exclusion from participation in some activities, as well as denying equal opportunities in staff development and promotion. The personal social services should meet this person's needs in an empowering way, rather than reinforcing the stigma of disability. Thus, work of staff such as social workers in the personal social services is complex and demanding, since it necessitates challenging common perceptions and attitudes and advocating in the interests of people who may be discriminated against by virtue of their gender, age, race, sexuality or disability.

Purposes of the personal social services

The ultimate objectives of the personal social services may be viewed as providing means by which people may be protected and controlled on one hand and their independence and social functioning maximised on the other. The former includes protecting people from themselves as well as from others, for instance, in cases where juvenile offending or child abuse (see chapter 5) puts one or more family members, or society, at risk of harm. The latter involves enabling people to maintain, or achieve, their full potential by ensuring they have access to such services as will empower them and give them the means to sustain the maximum degree of independence (see chapter 7).

Inherently problematic

The relationship between the state and the user of the personal social services is at the heart of debates about the rights and wrongs of what social workers do in any particular circumstances, and the appropriateness or otherwise of support for individuals, families and groups who come into contact with the personal social services. Social workers and probation officers are gatekeepers of societal attitudes towards not just needy and vulnerable people, but also those considered to be out of control. Therefore, there is often a question about whether an individual, perhaps an offender, a person misusing drugs or traveller without a fixed address, should be allowed access to resources; if they should, the next question to address is on what basis resources should be given, in the light of the fact that other members of the community may have to pay for resources, for example, to sustain them as part of community care. In the universalistic welfare state, automatic provision to meet needs is made, but in the 1990s government policies concerning welfare and housing benefits, for example, do not assume that homeless, jobless people are automatically entitled to what are termed state handouts.

Moral and political rather than simply technical

The provision of personal social services in society involves moral and political judgements and is not simply a technical process. The decision about whether to provide aids to enable a disabled older person to continue living in two-storey accommodation they have occupied for many years and do not wish to leave involves wider debates about resourcing, assessing, care planning, implementation, rationing resources and, in some cases, means testing and charging for services. The way the personal social services conduct their work provides an indication of the quality of life in Britain; it demonstrates to a large extent how professionals and the public expect younger, older, disabled and mentally ill people to be dealt with, individually and as client groups. When scandals erupt over the alleged maltreatment of a child, the wish of a white couple to adopt a black child, an old person found dead at home some weeks after the event, it is painful yet ultimately positive that public inquiries, media scandals and controversies raise questions not just about social work, but also about how the state, other professionals, neighbours, relatives and other carers have acted. The half century since the Beveridge Reports of the 1940s has witnessed debates through numerous investigations and inquiries (see, for instance, documents 4 and 6) about the intrinsically problematic responsibilities of the personal social services, questions about whether social work is, or should have full status as, a profession, and uncertainty about the education and training of workers at all levels in the personal social services. Just as social work cannot be depoliticised, deproblematised and made uncontroversial, so the delivery of personal social services transcends techniques and technologies; it is an intrinsically moral and political enterprise, rooted in a value base which involves respecting people's rights and differences and challenging discrimination (see, for instance, the 'O' unit of the N/SVQ occupational standards for caring (Care Sector Consortium, 1992) and the Code of Ethics for Social Work produced by the British Association of Social Workers (BASW, undated). Its practice increasingly addresses such questions as how to work reflectively and anti-oppressively. There are no clear and easy answers to questions such as how to define need and deliver much-needed services where resources are inadequate and how to empower users where they are stigmatised and marginalised and even have their dependence reinforced by relatives and friends who care for them.

Blurred boundaries with criminal justice and health

Some commentators exclude the criminal and juvenile justice systems from the personal social services. It is difficult, for example, to regard a prison as providing a social service for its prisoners. Nevertheless, criminal and youth justice are included in this book. The ideologies of work with offenders may in part be justice-based, controlling – sometimes custodial – and punitive, but in part also in the past they have involved both a rehabilitationist claim on behalf of the offender and also in relation to the victim of the offence and the family of the offender. At the very least, the inclusion of offender work in the personal social services enables the blurred boundaries of these services to be examined. It also takes proper account of the location of probation alongside social services in Scottish social work departments. Also, it enables the similarities in the controlling functions of social workers and probation officers to be examined. Finally, it emphasises the common value base of practice that unites social workers and probation officers. Given this last factor, it is unsurprising that proposals by the Home Secretary Michael Howard in 1995, to detach qualifying training for probation officers from the mainstream of social work training through the Diploma in Social Work (Dip SW) have aroused strong opposition (see chapters 3 and 9).

The boundaries are blurred also between the health and social care functions of the personal social services. While in Northern Ireland joint Health and Social Services Boards co-ordinate services, Scotland, Wales and England rely on collaboration between

purchasers and providers in the complex matrix of health authorities and social work/social services departments as purchasers
and, for example, NHS Trusts and providers of social services
in the voluntary and private sectors. This blurring of boundaries
exists also between housing and social services (see chapters 6 and
11).

Work of the personal social services

The work of the personal social services takes place in a fast-chang-
ing social and demographic context: there are more older, single
people; more people are living alone; there are more lone parent
families; there are large, and probably growing, numbers of carers;
and there are significant numbers of disabled children (for more
details see document 3); as a consequence, the social services
themselves are changing. For example, public expenditure in the
health and social services grew by 2% between 1973/74 and 1978/79
and by 3.4% between 1978/79 and 1990/91 (Hill, 1993, p. 123).
Within the personal social services between 1990/91 and 1994/95,
the total resources available have increased in real terms by 48%,
from £3.6 billion to £6.4 billion (see document 3).

The range of work carried out by staff in the personal social services is illustrated by the chapter headings of parts 2 to 4 of this
book. It extends, for example, from health care assistants in nursing support roles in the health services, work with young children
and their families in playgroups, nurseries and as child minders, to
work as care assistants, managing facilities, care management and
implementing care plans in the social services, as well as various
roles in field social work and the criminal justice system. In some
of these, professional social workers and probation officers prepare
reports for court, assess, plan, intervene, apply the law, evaluate
their practice and take responsibility for their own continuing professional and personal development.

The role of the personal social services involves enabling people
to manage and cope with insoluble difficulties and problems. Some
of the problems are, like life itself, without single identifiable
causes or readily applicable solutions. Some are more expressions
of ongoing circumstances of pain or difficulty in which people find
themselves. Roger Clough captures the quality of work with older
people well in his study of residential homes. He comments: 'It is
staff who are confronted by the depression or loneliness of residents. They have to live with the reality of those feelings, live with
their own uncertainty about the effects of the care they provide,
while at the same time they help the relatives with the guilt and uncertainty *they* feel' (Clough, 1981, pp. 155–56).

Workforce of the personal social services

Nobody really knows how many people are in the statutory, voluntary, private and informal sectors of the workforce of the personal social services in Britain, but the most reliable estimates are that there are about 238,000 workers (see Table 1 in document 2). Women tend to be the main users and providers of personal social services (see document 1). The caring workforce tends to look like a pyramid, with a relatively small number of managers and a growing number of workers at each layer further down the hierarchy. Of employed workers, by far the greatest proportion are direct service, care, domestic and other manual staff. Yet most basic caring work with people is probably carried out by self-carers, relatives, friends, volunteers and untrained workers; there may be as many as 1.5 million informal carers (there were estimated to be 1.25 million carers under the age of 35 in 1985), of whom more than 212,000 may be children and young people, who have had caring responsibilities since before their sixteenth birthday (Becker and Aldridge, 1995, p. 2) (see chapter 6) and a further half million may be self-carers. The numbers involved in such work with people far exceed the employed workforce.

Community care is the most obvious area where the local authority services rely on the effort of other agencies such as health and housing and the voluntary and private sectors. Additionally, some functions of the personal social services are carried out by people working in other human services, notably education, health, housing, criminal and youth justice. In educational work with children, a vast amount of pre-school play group, nursery, infant and junior school provision goes hand in hand with volunteer activity by parents. In the criminal justice system, victim support and prison visiting are two examples of voluntary involvement.

The fragmentation of the personal social services makes the collation of data on the workforce more difficult. Social services departments are more prone to the creation of a network of providers than are health authorities, which tend to be dominated by a smaller number of larger providers. Nevertheless, both are changing shape as the quasi-markets in providing services develop. In future, social services or social work departments will probably provide a small core of direct services to children and families, with the vast majority of services being contracted out to voluntary and private agencies and organisations.

The largely untrained junior ranks of the social services workforce detracts from its status, in contrast with the trend in the health service. The Warner Report (Committee of Inquiry into the Selection, Development and Management of Staff in Children's Homes, 1992) following the alleged abuses against children committed by Frank Beck in Leicestershire children's homes, stated that an unacceptably high 80% of staff in local authority homes were unqualified. Jeffrey Greenwood, chair of the council of the Central Council for Education and Training in Social Work (CCETSW), informed the annual conference of the ADSS in 1995 that three years later 75% remained unqualified, while the proportion of unqualified domiciliary care staff had risen to 93%. In contrast, over 90% of field social workers held a professional qualification. In the health and social care sector, only 24,000 of 134,000 staff registered for training in care awards were from social services and only 8%, as against 20% of the healthcare workers, had so far qualified *(The Guardian,* 22 September 1995).

Personal social services: perspectives and narratives

Narratives of the histories of the personal social services are related to debates about different perspectives on policy and practice. Although social workers may be vilified from time to time in the mass media, often with the implication that without social workers the world – especially for clients – would be a better, happier place, the subject matter of the social services (poverty, old age, mental illness, criminality, disability) cannot be marginalised. Nor can social work be dismissed as an activity of central significance in intrinsically problematic aspects of societal, organisational, familial and individual change and difficulty – empowering, managing, deciding, negotiating, clarifying, reporting and facilitating. The study of the personal social services is a composite of the conflicts and uncertainties in their component aspects; particular services, as Goffman (1967) suggests of institutions, may 'share common internal features, but . . . their roots are to be found in common external social developments and values' (Cohen, 1977, p. 217). Thus, the imagery of helping, controlling, judging, giving charity, treating, enabling, selling services and, more recently, empowering, pervades not only social work and the social services but also the criminal justice system, the hospital, the surgery, the school and the housing department, to say nothing of the building society and industry.

Just as the personal social services can be viewed from different theoretical vantage points, so no single, complete history of them awaits discovery. Their histories have been written in different, competing and conflicting traditions and discourses. The suggestion that narratives of the personal social services history may be typified as liberal, revisionist and counter-revisionist may be criticised for reducing their complexity but enables more complex mapping in particular aspects, such as criminal justice (Adams, 1994, pp. 29–37). One way to interpret these changes in the discourse of the personal social services is to consider how the narratives are voiced, and by whom. Does the analysis rely solely on 'official' published sources? Are the voices of excluded interests, groups and individuals – women and young carers, people with learning disabilities, older people in residential homes – represented in the narrative? Is it assumed that change means better services?

Liberalism: the 'social administration' approach

Before the 1980s, the study of social policy was rooted in what Taylor-Gooby and Dale (1981, p. 9) refer to as the empiricist tradition in social administration, which is by and large a consensual, functionalist, social administration approach (op. cit., p. 15). The five principal features of this are: 'a focus on national policies and problems; a focus on state-provided welfare; on interventionist and prescriptive approach; and finally, empiricism or concern largely with the facts of welfare' (Mishra, 1981, p. 8), a shunning of theory and a tendency to analyse social needs and respond to them from the viewpoint of the contemporary welfare state (Taylor-Gooby and Dale, 1981, p. 11). Taylor-Gooby and Dale (1981, p. 14) quote George and Wilding's remark that the analytic weakness of social administration is increased by the close links between the study of social policy and the government: 'Without realising it, the social administrator, the sociologist or the economist can become a professional advisor paid by governments to find acceptable solutions to prevailing social problems' (George and Wilding, 1971, p. 237). Eileen Younghusband's (1967; 1978) history of social work and Joan Cooper's (1983) history of the personal social services exemplify the dominance of the liberal mainstream of the social administration approach to social policy analysis. This may be inevitable, given their close allegiance with promoting the interests of social work. Younghusband implicitly adopts developmental assumptions about the steady evolution of the personal social services, as an aspect of the onward march of progress towards better health and welfare provision. Korman and Glennerster (1990) is a case study of hospital closure which illustrates features of the social administration tradition: light on theory and heavily reliant on conventional empirical methods of data collection and presentation. Functionalism tends to reduce interpretation of the histories of multiple stakeholders in the human services, with their inherently conflicting interests – such as those of politicians, managers, practitioners, service users and carers – to consensus; it may fail to consider how particular systems originate and what alternatives to them exist; it underplays the influence of human action in the explanation of social change.

In the personal social services, before the 1980s, it was difficult to find texts that adopted critical perspectives. There is still a tension between government-promoted policies and, for instance, initiatives by service users, in the mental health or disability movements, for instance. Hence, the vastly increased quantity of research in the second half of the twentieth century is no guarantee of its increased criticality. Researchers may be funded by government through the Department of Health and Social Services Inspectorate (SSI) and professional bodies such as the Central Council for Education and Training in Social Work (CCETSW) to carry out projects selected from within prevailing policies and practices, rather than independently of the assumptions on which they are based. Consequently, they may hold back from providing full critiques of policy in practice, for fear of losing the next, follow-on grant. Or they may simply stand too close in ideological terms to the topic they are researching to be able to evaluate it independently.

Revisionism: state power and class conflict

Critiques of liberal reformist accounts of the personal social services, notably from within the social administration tradition, are generally couched in terms of a scepticism towards social policy change as the sum total of the humanitarian efforts of individual reformers. From the 1980s, an increasing wealth of more critical analyses is evident, as a scan of issues of the journal *Critical Social Policy* will testify. Beyond this general observation, there is a bewildering array of socialist and radical approaches. Among socialist approaches there are two main traditions – one socialist centralist, which has some Marxist exponents, and the other socialist democratic, which owes much to Fabianism. Chapter 11 considers these in examining possible future scenarios in the personal social services. Peter Squires' (1990) use of Foucault to inform a radical analysis of social policy since Beveridge shows a predilection for examining the key texts – official reports and so on – of social policy, rather than seeking evidence for less formally powerful, but no less significant contributions to history-making 'from below', through the experiences of excluded people – patients, users, carers and oppressed groups.

Counter-revisionism: service users, carers and postmodernism

From the mid-1970s the claims of socialists, whether revisionist or counter-revisionist, intermingled with the voices of advocates of the pluralistic or mixed economy of provision. A healthy, if relatively poorly funded, tradition of critical social policy in Britain is nourished by anti-racist, anti-disablist, anti-ageist, feminist and socialist ideas, as well as from the growing power and influence of the perspectives of service users and carers.

Gladstone's (1979) report from the National Council of Social Service Policy and Planning Unit contrasts the review of the past and present contribution of the voluntary sector in the report of the Wolfenden Committee (Wolfenden Report, 1977) with the more future-directed study (Griffiths *et al.*, 1978) of the potential role of the voluntary sector in Northern Ireland, which argues for 'more localised activity based more on the "mutual aid" principle. This they see as "Tomorrow's Resource" and argue for the encouragement of the trend' (Gladstone, 1979, p. 20). Recognition of the plurality of the contributors to the personal social services advocated by Gladstone could be seen as a foretaste of the fragmentation of the postmodernist world of the personal social services in the 1990s; the monopolistic provision of services by the local authority replaced by dozens of contracts between the local authority social services department and a variety of service providers in the voluntary and private sectors. A further feature, illustrated above by the contrast between the better known and largely anodyne Wolfenden Report and the prophetic study by Griffiths *et al.* (1978) in Northern Ireland, is the dominance of English voices in narratives, as though the distinctive histories of Northern Ireland and Scotland, and to a lesser extent Wales, did not exist. Cooper's (1983) account is a notable exception to this, since it deals specifically with Scotland and Northern Ireland as well as England and Wales. Since the 1980s, the voices of services users have been heard increasingly. In part, this is through the official sanctioning by the NHS and Community Care Act 1990 and the Children Act 1989 of user involvement in community care and children's services; it is also partly through user-led movements in areas such as disability and mental health (Adams, 1997, chapters 7 and 8).

Taylor-Gooby (1994) sees one danger of postmodernism as its use as an ideological smokescreen, obscuring, or turning away from altogether, universalist societal themes such as ideologies and the impact of economic and social policy changes on such aspects as inequalities, market liberalism and the growth of the private sector. However, growing recognition of the contribution of service users and carers to the past, present and future of the personal social services needs to be capitalised on. This does not imply that it is sufficient to bolt surveys of consumers' views on to conventional research designs. It necessitates striving for synthesis, or at any rate dialogue between, narratives and perspectives that stress the impact on the personal social services of economic, social and policy factors and those that take adequate account of the histories and contributions of people on the receiving end of those services.

Changing ideologies: client treatment, consumerism and citizen empowerment

Three distinctive themes run through the history of the personal social services since World War II: treatment, consumerism and empowerment.

Client treatment

Treatment is a term often used simply to describe dealing with people and, in the penal system, for example, contributing to the goals of reform and rehabilitation; however, in this chapter it refers to the quasi-medical approaches that regard people as subjects for treatment, and involve professionals diagnosing and prescribing services to tackle people's problems. It is exemplified in individual or group counselling and individual and family casework, the latter of which dominated social work until the 1970s (see chapter 4).

Consumerism in the managed markets of personal social services

Consumerism refers to the growing importance of political and economic assumptions associated with the purchase and provision of services in health and social care, particularly in the wake of the NHS and Community Care Act 1990 (see chapters 3 and 6). In the 1990s, consumerism has assumed greater importance in aspects of the personal social services such as community care. But it is difficult to reconcile the language of free market economics with the quasi-markets in health and social care, since the government plays a strongly interventionist role in managing them. Further, the assumptions of the free market are based on the notion that the consumer knows what he or she wants and needs and can make rational choices from a range of alternatives, which satisfy wants and meet needs, unobstructed by problems of availability of alternatives, access to services or having sufficient resources to pay.

The rational choice model assumes that people will know what they want and what is best for them and will act rationally – that is, make rational decisions and exercise free choice – to achieve this. The rationality model should be evaluated in the light of how assumptions about the different individual consumers who participate in the market place actually turn out in practice. Scrivens (1992, p. 287) argues that the effective working of internal markets in the health and social care sector is predicated on three groups of participants acting rationally: purchasers of services, service providers and service users. To this list we can add carers.

Theoretical questions apart, the sheer growth of the market place raises the pragmatic limitation on the rationality of the individual, 'derived not from the lack of ability of the individual, but the overloading of the decision system' (op. cit., p. 286). People may become baffled by choice in the increasingly complex market place, and frustrated and therefore dissatisfied because their aspirations grow to exceed their means, as they see the scope and scale of what is on offer.

These restrictions on the working of rationality lead Scrivens (1992, p. 287) to conclude that 'the rational individual will not necessarily seek to act in isolation, convinced that only he or she knows his or her own best interest, but will probably need to share information, have some sense of social co-operation and may well choose to hand over decision making to a suitably trained third party who will be able to act as agent on his or her behalf and make better decisions than those that could be made by the individual.'

Fortunately for proliferating self-advocacy groups and organisations, service users do not have to hand over decision making to third parties, whether professionals, other service users or carers. But the point is well made that the rationality model cannot easily be made to work in practice without recourse beyond the individual to social activity. There is a question as to not only how service users exercise collective power over the supply of services they would prefer, but also whether they can influence collective action by agency purchasers of health and social care services, for example, under the NHS and Community Care Act 1990.

From client treatment to citizen empowerment: a paradigm shift

According to Kuhn (1970, p. 10), a paradigm shift involves innovations that are a step change in that they involve attracting 'an enduring group of adherents away from competing modes of . . . activity.' Kuhn's work draws attention to the fact that rather than change necessarily involving a smooth developmental process, some major changes in theories informing the sciences have involved challenges to existing dominant perspectives from contesting perspectives or paradigms. Initially, new perspectives may be driven by major changes in value positions and ideologies, rather than by empirical research. There are good grounds in the 1990s for regarding the growing predominance of empowerment over treatment approaches in the personal social services as a paradigm shift (Adams, 1996).

While the paradigms that have currency in the work of the personal social services remain part of the essentially contested knowledge and value bases of practice, a shift can be discerned during the post-war years from the dominance of the treatment paradigm. In the mid-1970s, when confidence among professionals in the rehabilitative and improving power of individual treatment was beginning to run low, it was still possible for Pearson (1975, p. 130) to note that 'the wider programmes of "social reform" and "social improvement" of which social work is only one element, have been ignored at the expense of developing technique and specifically psychotherapeutic technique.' In services more explicitly concerned with social work and social care, such as work with children and families and community care, this is expressed in terms of service user empowerment, whereas in criminal and juvenile justice it tends to find expression through advocacy of a number of different approaches to empowerment, based on personal, social or natural justice approaches to work with offenders.

Empowerment is a concept that, in its proper sense, is much more than mere enablement (Adams, 1996, p. 13) and gives people the right to challenge the state- and market-based structures of power (Taylor, 1989, p. 29). The new welfare consumerism begets a consumerist view of user involvement that emphasises choice, quality and participation, the political emphasis being on the supply-led purchase of services. In contrast, genuine self-advocacy is concerned with how people are treated as citizens; it involves their not being devalued or oppressed, and having more control, not just over the services, but over their entire lives (Croft and Beresford, 1989, p. 5).

Some conceptions of citizenship are based on notions of collective rights, whereas others are based on an understanding of individual responsibilities (Squires, 1992, p. 39). In a detailed analysis of the complex relationship between citizenship and informal care of vulnerable people in their own homes, Ungerson (1993, p. 143) records problematic aspects of the concept of citizenship, notably 'whether, for example, it contains a notion of reciprocal rights and duties between the state and citizen; whether citizens' rights are more important than citizen's obligations; whether there are different kinds of citizen's rights – such as civil and social rights – and whether these can be placed in historical sequence, and/or normative hierarchies . . . (and) whether the notion of citizenship is essentially masculine. But [she continues] the one immovable feature of the idea of citizenship is that it is placed in the public domain: it is concerned with how the individual and the state relate to each other across public concerns, and how public institutions, such as the judiciary and the polity, mediate that relationship.' Twine (1992, p. 166) observes that it is necessary to incorporate into the concept of citizenship the notions of social rights as well as opportunities. He argues that social rights are essential for enabling people to develop social inclusion and participation.

It is necessary to develop a radical concept of citizenship that transcends exclusionary practices associated, for example, with nationalism (Taylor, 1989, p. 29). The concept of citizenship all too often offers a gender-blind view, which neglects the private, domestic sphere (Lister, 1991). Domains of empowerment also have a critical dimension, which involves appreciating any demarcations between what is approved and the remainder. This demarcation is relational, i.e. it tends to involve the exercise of power by one person in respect of at least one other. It produces a less than rounded conceptualisation of citizenship, but a limitation that the more powerful person tends not to notice. For example, there is a one-dimensionality to the splitting of public from private citizenship, on which the power of male citizenship rests. It denies the shaping of women's, and children's, rights by social and economic conditions. The artificiality of the public–private divide mirrors other divisions which contribute to the oppression, or even the exclusion, of poor, older, mentally ill or disabled people (Lister, 1991). In this, as in other areas, a feminist dimension is not simply an additional dimension in reflecting on social policy, but is fundamental to all theorising and practice (McIntosh, 1981). Ideas of citizenship usually contain notions of hierarchy, implicitly dividing along the familiar dimensions of inequality – power, social class, gender, ethnicity, age – and so some people being more suitable citizens than others. In this respect the Maastricht Treaty is an advance, since it assumes the concept of the citizen of the European Union (Meehan, 1993).

Empowering the service user: a problematic paradigm

How can the paradigm shift from treating the client to empowering the service user be squared with critical research findings on the shortcomings of the personal social services? There is no simple answer to this question, since there is no consensus among the various stakeholders in the personal social services – politicians, agency managers, purchasers and providers of services, professionals, service users – about the nature and functions of the empowerment paradigm in the sector. The dominance of this empowerment paradigm leaves as problematic the questions of service delivery in social care and social work and justice for offenders. After all, do we hand over responsibility to *all* service users to devise their own care plans? Do convicted criminals deserve empowerment as part of a criminal justice service or simply require punishment? These moral and political questions resurface in the following chapters. The rhetoric of empowerment can be underpinned by either a consumerist or a participative theoretical perspective, for example, in community care (Beresford and Croft, 1993). In criminal and juvenile justice, the justice approach can be informed either by a radical or a right-wing perspective.

From the late 1980s, a broad band of socialist, social democratic, liberal, feminist and anti-oppressive support grew for empowerment as an approach to democratically managing and delivering health and social care services *with*, rather than simply *for*, people in need. The democratic approach attempts to address social inequality and empower the service user.

Empowerment in the personal social services (Adams, 1996) is a term referring to a number of complex ideas associated with practice that liberates service users rather than maintaining or reinforcing their dependency or oppression. Although this empowerment paradigm superficially resembles giving consumers choice, there is a fundamental difference. Enabling service users as stakeholders in the personal social services to participate in shaping, delivering and evaluating their own services in this way implies that they should have the option to become involved in theorising the politicised processes involved. The task of professionals in this situation is to ensure that service users are empowered and that the power of experts, managers and the professionals themselves is not perpetuated.

Clients, consumers or citizens?

Theories and methods of working with people in the personal social services are subject to ongoing debate among educators, trainers and practitioners. Some would say that social work is informed by no single body of theories. Until the 1970s, the dominant paradigm of practice was medico-treatment, which since the late 1980s has been held in some tension between the paradigm of empowerment espoused by many professionals and the ethos of consumerism imposed by government legislation, notably the NHS and Community Care Act 1990. It is doubtful whether empowerment offers a paradigm that transcends both conservative and socialist politics. Claims made by advocates of consumerism for the concept of citizen empowerment are suspect. Certainly, the diverse markets of the personal social services offer a fragmented vision: purchasers of services relating to a proliferation of providers, many of them in small units. It is a postmodern scenario for social work and social care.

Prospects for the personal social services

The economic policies pursued by government directly affect the nature of personal social services that people need. The personal social services did not emerge as a distinct entity until after the Seebohm report of 1968. In 1965, Titmuss' address to the Social Workers' Conference at Eastbourne proposed 'a structural reorganization which places the emphasis on *social service* rather than on biological or sociological criteria – like the family – or on one element in the pattern of needs – like health or rehabilitation. We need departments providing *services*; not departments organized around categories of client or particular fragments of need' (Titmuss, 1979, p. 90). Since Beveridge, the provision of welfare services in Britain has depended on a mixture of public, voluntary and private provision. This was not true of the other elements of the welfare state: health, education, housing and income maintenance. The personal social services were always 'a distinctly mixed bag' (Webb and Wistow, 1987, p. 6). The mixed economy of welfare is not novel, but the voluntary element in it has expanded massively since the 1970s. This is in contrast with the expectations of those members of the Labour Party who anticipated in the 1970s and early 1980s that the voluntary sector would wither away as the welfare state gained power (Mayo, 1994, p. 25). Unfortunately, in Britain since the early 1970s there is little evidence that the profile of needs in the community has been met more effectively by the personal social services, geared as they are increasingly to commercial criteria and to the requirements of managed markets in health and social care. The principle of choice for the consumer is an illusion at one level, while at another it could be said to be irrational and working against the most efficient way of meeting needs. The increased emphasis on community support, self-help and informal and neighbourhood care, in such areas as community care, places unrealistic and ever-growing burdens on communities which, as time passes, are less favourably placed to provide essential community provision. As Mayo (1994, p. 1) puts it: 'neither voluntary effort in general, nor community-based self-help in particular, can be expected to fill the widening gap between social needs and public provision.'

The mention above of managed markets (the term 'quasi-market' is adopted below, as this is more widely used) is a recognition that the devolution of provision to a larger proportion of voluntary and private providers in the mixed economy of care has been accompanied by increasing regulation by the government, particularly by the direct accountability to central government of voluntary agencies through the government grants for which they have to account; the theoretical distinction between voluntary and private sectors in practice is more blurred (Waine, 1992, p. 73). Thus, the market economy in the provision of community care is a market managed by government, to the extent that the limits put by government on available resources do not enable the real demand for services to be met. Tensions between service-led, needs-led and user-led models of practice remain to be worked out in a variety of ways at local level (see the discussion around Figure 3.1 in chapter 3).

Coverage of the rest of this book

An examination of the work of the personal social services (see chapters 4 to 10) shows that in every area, the often divergent perspectives of policymakers, professionals, service users and carers are reflected in practice issues (document 10); the advent of the paradigm of empowerment has heightened the divergence between what services are available and the needs of people. Far from consumerism in the managed markets of the personal social services increasing consumer choice or accountability of the services to empowered service users, the gap between the rhetoric and the reality remains alarmingly wide. Fundamental changes would be necessary to ensure this choice and accountability (see the options for the future of the personal social services examined in chapter 11). Before reviewing each area of the personal social services in detail, chapters 2 and 3 deal respectively with the two great shake-ups since Beveridge and the inauguration of the welfare state – in the 1970s, Seebohm and the establishment of generic social services, and in the 1990s, the creation of quasi-markets for the delivery of community care.

References and further reading

Adams, R. (1994) *Prison Riots in Britain and the USA*, Basingstoke: Macmillan.

Adams, R. (1996) *Social Work and Empowerment*, Basingstoke: BASW/Macmillan.

Adams, R. (1997) *Quality Social Work*, Basingstoke: Macmillan.

Becker, S. (ed.) (1995) *Young Carers in Europe: An Exploratory Cross-national Study in Britain, France, Sweden and Germany*, Loughborough University.

Becker, S. and Aldridge, J. (1995) Young carers in Britain, in Becker (1995), 1–25.

Beresford, P. and Croft, S. (1993) *Citizen Involvement: a Guide for Change*, London: BASW/Macmillan

Beveridge, W.H. (1942) *Social Insurance and Allied Services*, Cmnd 6404, London: HMSO.

Beveridge, W.H. (1943) *The Pillars of Security*, 107–8, quoted in Fraser (1984), 209. *The Evolution of the British Welfare State: A history of Social Policy since the Industrial Revolution*, 2nd Edition, Basingstoke: Macmillan.

Beveridge, W.H. (1944) *Full Employment in a Free Society*, London: Allen and Unwin.

Beveridge, W.H. (1948), *Voluntary Action: a Report of Methods of Social Advance*, London: Allen and Unwin.

Borrie, G. and Atkinson, A.B. (1994) *Social Justice: Strategies for National Renewal*, Report of the Commission on Social Justice (Borrie Report), London: Vintage.

British Association of Social Workers (undated) *Code of Ethics for Social Work*, Birmingham: BASW.

Care Sector Consortium (1992) *National Occupational Standards for Care*, London: HMSO.

Clough, R. (1981) *Old Age Homes*, London: Allen and Unwin.

Clough, R. (1982) *Residential Work*, London: BASW/Macmillan.

Cohen, S. (1977) Prisons and the future of control systems: from concentration to dispersal, in Fitzgerald, M. *et al.* (eds) *Welfare in Action*, Routledge and Kegan Paul, 217–28.

Committee of Inquiry into the Selection, Development and Management of Staff in Children's Homes (1992) *Choosing with Care* (the Warner Report), London: HMSO.

Committee on Local Authority Personal and Allied Social Services (1968) *The Seebohm Report*, Cmnd 3703, London: HMSO.

Cooper, J. (1983) *The Creation of the British Personal Social Services 1962–1974*, London: Heinemann.

Croft, S. and Beresford, P. (1989) User-involvement, citizenship and social policy, *Critical Social Policy*, issue 26, autumn 1989, 5–18.

George, V. and Wilding, P. (1971) Social values, social class and social policy, *Social and Economic Administration*, vol.6, no.3.

Gladstone, F.J. (1979) *Voluntary Action in a Changing World*, London: Bedford Square Press.

Goffman, E. (1967) *Asylums: Essays on the Social Situation of Mental Patients and Other Inmates*, Harmondsworth: Penguin.

Griffiths, H., Nic Giolla Choile, T. and Robinson, J. (1978) *Yesterday's Heritage or Tomorrow's Resource: a Study of Voluntary Organisations in Northern Ireland*, Occasional Papers in Social Administration, Coleraine: New University of Ulster.

Hayek, F.A. von (1960) *The Constitution of Liberty*, London: Routledge and Kegan Paul.

Hill, M. (1993) *The Welfare State in Britain: a Political History since 1945*, Aldershot: Edward Elgar.

Howe, D. (1986) The segregation of women and their work in the personal social services, *Critical Social Policy*, issue 15, spring, 21–35

Jacobs, J. (1992) An introduction to the Beveridge Report, in Jacobs, J. (ed.) *Beveridge 1942–1992*, 5–19, London: Whiting and Birch.

Korman, N. and Glennerster, H. (1990) *Hospital Closure*, Milton Keynes: Open University Press.

Kuhn, T.S. (1970) *The Structure of Scientific Revolutions*, 2nd edn, Chicago: University of Chicago Press.

Le Grand, J. and Bartlett, W. (eds) (1993) *Quasi-Markets and Social Policy*, London: Macmillan.

Lister, R. (1991) Citizenship engendered, *Critical Social Policy*, issue 32, autumn, 65–71.

Local Government Act 1972, London: HMSO.

Marquand, D. (1994), No time for giant-killing, *The Guardian,* 24 October, 20.

Mayo, M. (1994) *Communities and Caring: the Mixed Economy of Welfare*, London: Macmillan.

McIntosh, M. (1981) Feminism and social policy, *Critical Social Policy*, vol.1, no.1, 32–42.

Meehan, E. (1993) *Citizenship and The European Community*, London: Sage.

Mental Health Act 1983, London: HMSO.

Mishra, Ramesh (1981) *Society and Social Policy: Theories and Practice of Welfare*, 2nd edition, London: Macmillan.

Mishra, Ramesh (1990) *The Welfare State in Capitalist Society: Policies of Retrenchment and Maintenance in Europe, North America and Australia*, Hemel Hempstead: Harvester Wheatsheaf.

NHS and Community Care Act 1990, London: HMSO.

NISW (1988b) *Residential Care: the Research Reviewed*, literature surveys commissioned by the Independent Review of Residential Care (Wagner Report Part II), London: HMSO.

Parker, R. (1988) An historical background to residential care in NISW (1988b), 1–38.

Pearson, G. (1975) *The Deviant Imagination*, London: Macmillan.

Poor Law Amendment Act 1934, London: HMSO.

Rojek, C., Peacock, G. and Collins, S. (1988) *Social Work and Received Ideas*, London: Routledge.

Scrivens, E. (1992) Choosing Choice in Social Welfare, in Manning, N. and Page, R., *Social Policy Review 4*, 280–95, London: Social Policy Association.

Social Services Act 1970, London: HMSO.

Squires, P. (1990) *Anti-Social Policy, Welfare, Ideology and the Disciplinary State*, Hemel Hempstead: Harvester Wheatsheaf.

Squires, P. (1992) The People's William and the Citizen's Rights: A critical assessment of the Beveridge Report's contribution to the politics of citizenship in post-war Britain, in Jacobs, John (ed.) *Beveridge 1942–1992: Papers to Mark the 50th Anniversary of the Beveridge Report*, Whiting and Birch, 32–58.

Taylor, D. (1989) Citizenship and social power, *Critical Social Policy*, issue 26, autumn , 19–31.

Taylor-Gooby, P. (1994) Post modernism and social policy, *Journal of Social Policy*, vol.23, no.3, 385–404.

Taylor-Gooby, P. and Dale, J. (1981) *Social Theory and Social Welfare,* London: Edward Arnold,.

Titmuss, R.M. (1979) Social work and social service: a challenge for local government, in Titmuss, R. (ed.) *Commitment to Welfare*, 85–90, London: Allen and Unwin.

Ungerson, C. (1993) Caring and citizenship: a complex relationship, in Bornat, J., Pereira, C., Pilgrim, D. and Williams, F., *Community Care: a Reader*, 143–51, London: Macmillan and Open University.

Twine, F. (1991) Citizenship: opportunities, rights and routes to welfare, *Journal of Social Policy*, vol.21, no.2, 165–75.

Waine, B. (1992) The voluntary sector: the Thatcher years, in Manning, N. and Page, R. (eds) *Social Policy Review 4*, Social Policy Association, 70–88.

Webb, A. and Wistow, G. (1987) *Social Work, Social Care and Social Planning*, London: Longman.

Wolfenden Report, The (1977) *The Future of Voluntary Organisations*, London: Croom Helm.

Younghusband, E. (1967) *Social Work and Social Work Values*, National Institute for Social Work Training, London: Allen and Unwin.

Younghusband, E. (1978) *Social Work in Britain: 1950–1975. A follow-up study* (2 volumes), Allen and Unwin.

CHAPTER 2

Seebohm: family-based treatment in the welfare state

The personal social services have been reshaped radically in the second half of the twentieth century. In the early 1940s, wartime enthusiasm for Beveridge's proposals gave birth to the idea of the personal social services in the welfare state. But it was almost 30 years before legislation formally underpinned social work and social services in newly created departments, in Scotland, England and Wales. In Northern Ireland, the political imperatives imposed by the Troubles contributed to the establishment of a health and social services structure directly accountable to Westminster. By the early 1970s, there was a transition from the universalism of the Beveridge era to the introduction of formal statutory arrangements for managing and delivering personal social services in all parts of Britain. New departments responsible for generic social services were created in the 1970s and social work achieved a distinctive identity, though laying claim to professional status rather than its being taken for granted. This chapter examines the distinctive features of those changes, from World War II to the early 1970s.

Shaping the personal social services

The personal social services were shaped by many factors over the 30 or so years prior to the Seebohm Report (Committee on Local Authority and Allied Personal Social Services, 1968): international trends affecting the UK, the depression of the 1930s and hardships of World War II; the Beveridge Report (Cmnd 6404; see chapter 1) and professional ideology and practice in fields recognised in the 1990s under the labels of social work and social care, but in the 1950s and 1960s led principally by child care, mental health and welfare work.

International trends affecting the UK

From a global standpoint, there is a many faceted connection between economic performance, politics and policies in the UK and in other parts of the world, particularly the USA and other Western countries. Mishra (1990) uses a comparison of social welfare policies in the USA and Britain to argue that the starting point for the two countries in the mid-1970s was different in that there was more institutional support for welfare in Britain. The approach in the USA was residual, and consequently as New Right policies were applied, the welfare state in Britain suffered less contraction than in the USA, where a lesser range of groups and organisations were able to combine to defend services in the welfare field. Propper (1993, p. 36) points out that internal markets based on contracting have operated in many parts of the USA for more than two decades. Le Grand and Bartlett draw attention to a widespread trend in European countries towards the adoption of contracting and quasi-market approaches (Le Grand and Bartlett, 1993, p. 9).

The impact of economic theories promoting capitalism and undermining socialist alternatives has been marked in the USA as well as in Britain, and in Third World countries dependent on the USA economy. For example, New Right thinking has been exported through the activities of international agencies such as the International Monetary Fund (IMF) and through economists applying the ideas of economists such as Friedman and Hayek to countries such as Chile (Mayo, 1994, p. 6). The collapse of one communist government after another in central and eastern Europe after 1989, and the splitting up of the former USSR, has played into the hands of advocates of New Right economic theory, policy and practice. One response to this has been a 'new realism' (illustrated with respect to criminology in chapter 9) which is revisionist in nature. This argues that in the face of the success of the New Right, the best that can be achieved is the more humane management of the market economy, rather than its overthrow by a socialist alternative. Another response has been based on social democratic assumptions. Increasingly, the distance between the social democratic left in Britain and the conservative left has been narrowing. A further response has been socialist democracy as advocated by Miliband (1991, p. 61), who argues that in the longer term a socialist society would need to preserve democracy.

The hardships of World War II

The shift from the selectivity of social policy in the 1930s to widespread support for universalism in the 1940s, as a contribution to the reconstruction of Britain, was brought about partly by World War II; also, from the 1930s there was a growing commitment to Keynesian policies as a means by which Government could use increased public spending as a means of climbing out of economic depression and counteracting the underuse of human resources represented by mass unemployment. The 1939–1945 war substituted shortages of basic food, housing and transport for the problems of unemployment and recession of the 1930s. To address these, during World War II the government increasingly assumed responsibility for developing social policies to meet the needs of all classes of the people. There was a large majority for Labour in the 'khaki election' of 1945 which ejected Winston Churchill from power. But Jones (1991, p. 123) notes that the primary motive of people was not a commitment to collectivism so much as the fact that 'by 1945, most people had had enough of barracks, barbed wire and taking orders, and there was an overwhelming desire for individual freedom and small-scale family life. It was not even a desire for Socialism as such. It was the spirit of "never again".' Titmuss (1950, p. 517) was right to identify a 'revision of ideas and rearrangement of values' which, as a result of people's experiences early in the war, 'allowed and quickly encouraged great extensions and additions to the social services (which) helped many of these services to escape from the traditions of the poor law.' But this mood of enlarging collective responsibility did not extend over the whole extent of people's needs for social services; neither did it last far beyond the Labour government of 1945–1951.

Professional ideology and practice in social work and social care

The history of the personal social services can be written from a developmental perspective, yet the failure of the Poor Law Amendment Act 1834 to obviate large-scale poverty did not prevent its ghosts from lingering on into the 1980s. Stedman Jones (1984) shows how attitudes to poor people and what were viewed as welfare scroungers mirrored the mixture of condescension, philanthropic concern and fear with which respectable middle class people viewed paupers and the 'residuum', now termed the underclass. 'Underclass' theories tend to support negative and uninformed stereotypes, often fuelled by fear, of people who experience a range of consequences of social division and inequality, whether visible in unemployment, poverty, crime, substance misuse or homelessness (Mann, 1994, p. 95). The Charity Organisation Society (COS) regarded the residuum as not worth the investment of time and charity, since apparently they showed no sign of commitment to the Victorian ethic of self-help by pulling themselves up by their own bootstraps (see, for example, the striking analysis by Golding and Middleton (1982)).

The public, professional and political repercussions of the death of Dennis O'Neill contributed to the setting up of a Committee of Inquiry chaired by Myra Curtis to examine how care could be provided for children considered to lack adequate parental care. The Curtis Report (Report of the Care of Children Committee, 1946) was followed by the Children Act 1948, 'the most far-reaching legislation ever made regarding deprived children ... (which) effectively placed ministerial responsibility for the care of deprived children with the Home Secretary' (Bean and Melville, 1989, p. 168). Between the 1940s and the 1970s, the expertise of social workers in mental health, caring for older people and working with children, advanced steadily.

Politics and policies

Public opinion provided much of the impulse behind the wave of legislation that shaped the personal social services and laid the legislative and administrative basis for the welfare state. Three White Papers – *A National Health Service,* February 1944, *Employment Policy*, May 1944, and *Social Insurance,* September 1944 – indicated how far popular feeling, and the increasing association between the Labour Party and its aspirations for power and the public, pushed events along. The White Paper of Butler, *Educational Reconstruction* in 1943, was generally welcomed as the basis for the 1944 Education Act. The Ministry of National Insurance was created in 1944 to take over health insurance. Pensions, unemployment insurance and new family allowances were introduced in 1946, following the Family Allowance Act in 1945. The National Assistance Act 1948 required local authorities to carry out welfare duties for elderly and disabled people and to provide residential care for elderly people who had no other alternative available to them. In July 1948, the National Health Service and the Social Security System became fully operational. From the start, the arrangements for health provision were more controversial than those for social security. The main difficulty faced by the Health Service from the outset was how best to organise the service. There was some logic behind the local authorities running health services in much the same way as they ran the educational services. But there was considerable opposition in the medical professions. The third Beveridge report (Beveridge, 1948) initiated the idea of the personal social services. This report, after those on social insurance and employment, was the weakest of the three Beveridge reports. The assumption of the 1940s and 1950s that the establishment of statutory personal social services would soon make voluntary organisations and charitable endeavour redundant proved to be far from the case. As facilities developed, so more needs emerged. The demand for services outstripped their ever-expanding supply.

The health and social services from 1948 to the 1990s have been structured separately, which has necessitated patients and clients relating to different providers of services for treatment and support. A tripartite structure was set up after the 1948 Act to administer hospitals, medical services and local authority health and welfare services. The local authority health and welfare services included vaccination and immunisation, maternity, child care, domestic help, health visiting, home nursing and ambulance services. The National Assistance Act 1948 made health authorities responsible for providing residential accommodation for poor people and older people. Under this Act, local authorities had to set up children's committees with professional children's officers and took on responsibility for setting up arrangements to provide a more secure family environment for children in care. However, psychologised theories in the 1950s and 1960s gave little encouragement to local authorities to offer clients more than the most basic social work services. The general assumption was that meals on wheels, for example, should be provided through the voluntary sector (Lowe, 1993, p. 265).

The local government context: diversity in the UK

Although the primary impetus for change after World War II came from the government in Westminster, events in Scotland and Northern Ireland played a significant part in shaping policies and practice. Hence, major changes in the personal social services in all four countries of the UK from the mid-1960s led to their rapid expansion in the succeeding decade; they were triggered in Scotland, England and Wales by growing concern about rising juvenile crime. In Northern Ireland, while Cooper (1983, p. 139) may be correct about the level of dissatisfaction with the ability of existing local government to deliver adequate services on an equitable basis, it is undeniable that the reorganisation of welfare services was a product of the pattern of direct political control adopted in the response to IRA terrorism. This led to the setting up of a pattern of regional management that gave ministers in Northern Ireland a greater involvement in the shape and content of health and social services than ministers on the British mainland would probably have felt desirable.

Scotland: social work departments and the treatment paradigm

The Royal Commission on Local Government in Scotland (Redcliffe-Maud, 1969) was published when the major reforms proposed for the social work services by the White Paper *Social Work and the Community* (1966) had already been incorporated into the Social Work (Scotland) Act 1968. Thus, when the Local Government (Scotland) Act 1973 became operational in 1975, it put into practice the two-tier regional and district structure that Wheatley had proposed, following the preference of the Conservative government for two-tier local government. But it did not cut across the organisational arrangements for children's panels and social work services arising from the acceptance of the report of the Kilbrandon Committee in 1964. Scotland was the first country in the UK to adopt a comprehensive approach to providing personal social services. Kilbrandon arose from concern about rising juvenile crime rates, was set up in May 1961 and reported in January 1964. It proposed a new organisational structure within which law-breaking by children would be dealt with by joint education and social measures, as simply one aspect of the problems and issues faced by children and families. After prolonged debate, a distinctly social work (as opposed to social education) perspective, led by practitioners and academics committed to the treatment paradigm, challenged Kilbrandon's notion of a new social education department (Cooper, 1983, p. 37).

The social work profession had a history of advocating a social work approach, in the Cape Committee on Medical Auxiliaries (1951), the Mackintosh Committee on Social Workers in the Mental Health Services (1951), the Younghusband Report (Social Workers in the Local Authority Health and Welfare Services 1959) and the McBoyle Report on the Prevention of Neglect of Children in their Own Homes (1963) (Cooper, 1983, pp. 37–38). Judith Hart, then Joint Parliamentary Under Secretary of State for Scotland, convened an advisory group of three people – Richard Titmuss, Megan Browne, senior lecturer in psychiatric social work at Edinburgh University and Kay Carmichael, lecturer in social work at Glasgow University – who worked with the Association of Psychiatric Social Workers (APSW) and the Institute of Medical Social Workers (IMSW) to develop more far-reaching proposals (Cooper 1983, p. 39). The coalescence of political, civil service and professional interests led to the drafting of the White Paper *Social Work and the Community* (1966), which led to the Children Act (Scotland) 1968. The use of the term 'social work' in this legislation was symbolic of the largely successful struggle by social work interests in Scotland to use the opportunity provided by the initial concern to make effective provision for dealing with delinquency. This was the jumping-off point for a comprehensive social work service enabling social work to achieve parity with education and health departments. It incorporated probation within the treatment paradigm, exemplified in the children's hearings which provided a forum for professionals, children and parents to determine how to respond to children's welfare needs.

Northern Ireland: a centralist approach to joint health and social services

In Northern Ireland, the manner in which local government change impacted on the personal social services reflected the growing social disruption from the late 1960s. The occupation of Northern Ireland by troops from the British mainland was one consequence of the struggles of the republican movement in Ireland. This made more direct government control of the health and social care sector, through four area boards for health and social services, more practicable than it would have been on the British mainland. The one and a half million people of Northern Ireland were heirs to a long history of political and religious struggle between Westminster, republicans and loyalists. Children had torn up cobblestones and thrown them at the police during the unemployment disturbances of the early 1930s. In the late 1960s, the nationalist people of Northern Ireland took to the streets as part of the growing pressure for local government reform. With incidents like that on Sunday, 15 August 1969, when the forces of law and order were brought in and the subsequent rioting led to the killing of ten people, with ten times as many injured, the occupation of Northern Ireland by the British army and a review of local government began. This review body, chaired by Patrick Macrory and established in December 1969, was intended to examine how the functions of local government could be distributed most efficiently under the parliament and government in Northern Ireland. The terms of reference of this review body did not extend to evaluating the principles of local democracy, which was a feature of the Redcliffe-Maud and Wheatley reports (Wilson and Game, 1994, p. 54). The Macrory report recommendations became law in the Local Government (NI) Act 1972. This reduced the number of authorities to 26 district councils from 68 and appointed 9 area boards to decentralise the administration of the centrally provided health and education services.

Although in one sense Northern Ireland lagged behind England in prosperity, in another it had a well-developed community provision, particularly through the tradition of voluntary effort. Since 1950 a single statutory welfare department in each local authority had been responsible for services for elderly and disabled people and children. The Welfare Services Act 1947 had set up local authority education, public health and children's and elderly people's services, and the Mental Health Act (Northern Ireland) 1948 had made hospital authorities responsible for services for mentally ill people.

The Health and Social Services (Northern Ireland) order 1972 set up four area boards, co-ordinating the local delivery of services in 17 districts. Each service retained its own identity, membership of the Boards being by ministerial appointment (Cooper, 1983, p. 143). The existence of this relatively unified structure for the health and personal social services gave Northern Ireland an advantage over the rest of the UK. But service development was hampered by two factors: the lack of an appropriate administrative structure and the lack of an academic and professional infrastructure, to enable workers in the personal social services to become professionally qualified and acquire a critical grasp of contemporary research and theories concerning practice. The core of qualified social workers remained relatively small, until the personal social services began to expand from the late 1960s. In 1966, there were 250 social workers; by 1974 there were more than 500 (Darby and Williamson, 1978). This expansion was encouraged by the development of Certificate in Social Work (CSW) courses, the employers' policy of seconding staff for training and the importance attached to inservice training (Cooper, 1983, p. 138). There was a tradition of voluntary and private agency involvement, not least through the Churches and organisations such as the Belfast Charity Organisation Society, founded in 1906.

England and Wales: three-tier structure

The Local Government Act of 1963 replaced the London County Council with an enlarged Greater London Council, in circumstances of some acrimony. In 1966 a Royal Commission was established for England and a similar one for Scotland, the former chaired by Lord Redcliffe-Maud and the latter by Lord Wheatley. Both reported in 1969. A White Paper from the Secretary of State for Wales was held to be sufficient to deal with the circumstances of Wales. The Labour government was committed to unitary authorities but in June 1970, when the Conservative government was elected, this proposal was overturned and two- and three-tier systems of local government was retained in the Local Government Act 1972, implemented in 1974.

Improving social work training: 1950s and 1960s

During the 1950s and 1960s there was growing recognition of the need to provide services that reached beyond the five major social services, to people whose needs were still not met. Welfare legislation mainly seemed to have benefited the middle classes. There was a need for what Kathleen Jones (1991, p. 162) has called 'a sixth service which could act on behalf of those who lacked the knowledge, initiative and energy to act for themselves.' At that time, the dominance of the treatment paradigm led to little questioning of this conceptualisation of social workers as advocates *for* clients.

The growing recognition of the need for social work raised the profile of debates about education and training for social workers. For much of the second half of the twentieth century, social work education and training have been insufficient in quantity (Walton, 1975, p. 209) and quality to match the increasing demands on the profession. One source of pressure was the growing bulk of legislation that social workers needed to use in their work. The treatment ideology and casework were mutually reinforcing features of the foreground of practice throughout the two decades after World War II.

The Younghusband Reports: towards a unified social work profession

Eileen Younghusband produced two reports in the years immediately following World War II, on the nature of social work and the training of social workers (Younghusband, 1947, 1951). These recommended changes in the structure and content of social work training courses. Pressure for change built up as a result of the increasing reputation of the 'generic' applied social studies training course for social workers introduced by the London School of Economics from 1954, making available a common core of knowledge on which individual specialisms could be developed (Younghusband, 1978, vol. 1, p. 99). Younghusband chaired a working party set up in 1955 to address the training and employment of social workers in local authority health and welfare services, which reported in 1959 (Report on Social Workers in the Local Authority Health and Welfare Services, 1959). Younghusband recommended a great expansion of social work employment in local authorities, the setting up of a National Institute of Social Work Training and a new two-year qualification, the Certificate in Social Work, to run in Colleges of Further Education alongside the more advanced university courses. The Health Visitors' and Social Workers' Training Act of 1962 implemented Younghusband's main proposals, and 'social work entered on a new phase of unification and professional development' (Jones, 1991, p. 164). In 1963, the formation of a Standing Conference of Organisations of Social Workers both illustrated and contributed to a greater sense of coherence and common purpose among the social work profession, which, however, remained staffed by a relatively low-paid and largely unqualified workforce.

Rediscovery of poverty and maternal deprivation: triumph of social democracy

In the 1960s, two influences on the ideology of the personal social services, as reflected in the Children and Young Persons Act 1969 and in the Seebohm Committee in the late 1960s, were research into poverty and maternal deprivation. Poverty was 'rediscovered' in the research of Abel-Smith and Townsend (1965) in the early 1960s, but its implications took four or five years to filter into social work practice, and then struggled for two further decades against the legacy of the COS, enshrined in the Family Welfare Association (FWA).

The growing emphasis on preserving nurturing contact between very young children and their mothers was a result of the work of Bowlby, originally published in 1951 in a report for the World Health Organisation (see preface to first edition, reprinted in Bowlby, 1965) and subsequently published as a Pelican book in 1953 and then, in response to controversy over its content, in a second edition with additional material but substantially the same conclusion (Bowlby, 1965). Bowlby's research highlighted the negative impact on children of separation from their mothers. The concept of maternal deprivation was used to justify community-based, casework-based, preventive work – fostering and adoption-based child care rather than residential work (see Packman, 1975).

Ingleby and the Children and Young Persons Act 1963

The children's departments established by the Children Act 1948 in each local authority had the purpose of meeting the best interests of each child. But this Act did not provide for the prevention of neglect or child abuse, and forbade the giving of material help to people in the form of cash or housing: it was the early 1960s before this happened, following the Ingleby Committee Report (Report of the Committee on Children and Young Persons, 1960). The recommendations of Ingleby were reflected in the Children and Young Persons Act 1963. Fostering and adoption gradually replaced much residential child care as the desirable ideal for treating children in need, although a decade or more later around a hundred thousand children and young people remained in residential care (document 7).

Organisational and professional shortcomings were apparent in the 1960s, in the somewhat piecemeal, under-trained and ill-resourced personal social services. The staff tended to adopt the judgemental attitudes of their Victorian antecedents in the COS. The presumption was that the institution was the first resort for problems of mental health, 'handicap' or child care and for people with problems whose main feature was their chronicity and visibility rather than their seriousness. In the community, social work with families was provided largely on the assumption that self-help, voluntary effort and help within the family should be sufficient. The channelling of public resources into such areas as the building of new housing and schools contrasted with the lack of residential and day care facilities to assess and support children and their families, older and disabled people. Thus, services for children did not even fulfil the requirement of the Children Act 1948 that such residential facilities should be provided, to ensure professional decisions could be made about whether to place them in foster care or small children's homes built on the Curtis Report's (Report of the Care of Children Committee, 1946) principle of providing substitute families. In the absence of such provision, large numbers of children continued to be warehoused in large residential institutions. Meanwhile, more than 37,000 older people in 1960 were still living in former work houses and other accommodation inherited from the Poor Law, rather than sheltered accommodation or nursing homes.

Contradictory trends: the 1960s

The 1960s were contradictory. On one hand, on 7 February 1967, the National Front was formed out of a merger of several fascist and racist groups. In April the Conservatives gained many seats in local elections and Labour lost control of London for the first time since 1934. On the other hand, a mood of growing radicalism and political activism was displayed in widespread student protests in Britain, the rest of Western Europe and the USA and, on 15–19 July 1967, the conference 'The Dialectics of Liberation' at the Roundhouse in London, addressed by the psychiatrist R.D. Laing, Stokely Carmichael and Herbert Marcuse. The origins of user empowerment movements lay in the political and social activism of the 1960s.

The peak of the treatment paradigm was the widespread 'magical' thinking among social workers (see chapter 4) that with casework they could change the world. The 1960s saw the rapid expansion of child care and mental health departments (particularly the former), and the 1970s their incorporation into reformed social services departments, as their leading staff took up management roles in these new, enlarged, corporate bases for generic social work practice. In the 1960s, social democratic ideals of community and treatment reached their high point in the Children and Young Persons Act 1969 and a year later signalled the meeting of the hitherto unacknowledged needs of disabled people (Chronically Sick and Disabled Persons Act 1970).

The Children and Young Persons Act 1969 was the most significant legislation for children and families before the Children Act 1989. It attempted measures to divert offenders from the juvenile justice system, introduced Intermediate Treatment as a largely community-based alternative to custody, and integrated approved schools and remand homes into a new community homes system.

But, as chapter 5 indicates, this Act marked a peak rather than ushering in a new era. The 1970s brought a change of government and enabled latent opposition to the welfare and treatment assumptions of the Act to become manifest. Moves towards reasserting law and order by the Conservative government were supported by many police and magistrates, who felt that the welfare needs of problem children and young people were being attended to at the expense of the interests of justice. These moves were fed by moral panics about skinheads (Cohen, 1987) and muggings – in many cases a code word for street crime involving young black people (Hall *et al.*, 1978).

On 20 April 1968, Enoch Powell made a speech in Birmingham forecasting 'a river of blood' unless the government encouraged voluntary repatriation to reduce the number of black and Asian ethnic minorities in inner cities. In that year, *Cathy Come Home* was shown on BBC television and had a great impact on the viewing public as well as promoting debates about the plight of homeless people and people with drink problems, as well as the treatment of service users by professionals.

Social workers' struggles to achieve professional status were given added momentum by: enhanced public expectations of what social services could deliver; greater prosperity leaving local authority with increased resources; real expenditure on the personal social services, static during the 1950s, doubling between 1960 and 1968; an increasing public demand for services, through a rise in the proportion of older and infirm people in the population and rising recorded juvenile crime; changing attitudes toward people with problems; a reduced tendency for social workers to make moral judgements about their clients' behaviour; the growing popularity of community-based services, with scientific progress, for example, in the development of drugs enabling mentally ill people to live safely in the community; and improved care for children with Down's syndrome and children with cerebral palsy, leading to an increase demand for education and social services for them (Lowe, 1993, p. 266).

The Seebohm Reforms: 1965 to 1970

Producing the Seebohm Report: 1965–1968

The origins and establishment of the Seebohm committee in 1965 have been dealt with by Phoebe Hall (1976). The scope and limitations of this committee, as well as its ideological assumptions, are evident in its move from its terms of reference, 'to review the organisation and the responsibilities of the local authority personal social services in England and Wales' to its key recommendation:

'a new local authority department, providing community-based and family oriented service.' (1968, p. 11). Significantly, there was opposition to the terms of reference of the Seebohm committee, not least from Richard Titmuss, who believed that it would perpetuate divisions within social work. Perhaps inevitably, but in any case to general advantage, the committee extended its brief: 'we decided very early in our discussions that it would be impossible to restrict our work solely to the restrictions of two or even three generation families. We could only make sense of our task by considering also childless couples and individuals without any close relatives; in other words, everybody' (Lowe, 1993, p. 266).

Significance of Seebohm

The Seebohm *Report of the Committee on Local Authority and Allied Social Services* was published in 1968. In 1971, the local government services in areas such as mental health and child care were reorganised and combined, as the report had recommended. The aim was to provide a more powerful 'social services' department, commanding more resources, and therefore providing a more comprehensive, less stigmatising and more accessible service for the whole community. Yet the report reflected contemporary preoccupation's with corporate efficiency as a basis for family focused social work (Hall, 1976). Momentum was created and the number of social workers climbed: it was as though the new social services departments were self-generating, self-elaborating and mutually competitive (Adams *et al.*, 1981, p. 11).

From the outset, therefore, the personal social services, like the welfare state, represented as much a consensus of the British people about previous provision as a distinctive innovation motivated by universalism. The personal social services were not created – they evolved from an existing widespread view about the value of focusing the energies of the state on keeping families together.

Seebohm marked a new era of higher profile social work. Yet it remained controversial, primarily for having promoted generic social work at the expense of traditional specialisms and therefore, critics claimed, the quality of child care and mental health practice in particular. It was criticised also for failing to make a convincing case for social work as a profession, for failing to specify criteria on which priorities could be based and for not indicating where decision-making power should lie (Lowe, 1993, p. 267). The local government reorganisations of 1971 and 1974 interrupted the implementation of Seebohm. Nevertheless, partly due to the impact of the Children and Young Persons Act 1969, child care in the community received increased attention in the wake of Seebohm. Welfare services still largely carried out by unqualified staff, such as domiciliary care – meals on wheels and home helps – for older and infirm people, benefited only indirectly through the creation of an enhanced infrastructure as the organisational base for social services. Further, the emphasis of many services, such as disability, remained at the level of physical help, while as resources became more constrained after the economic crisis sparked by rising oil prices in late 1973, services in areas such as mental health became increasingly crisis-oriented rather than continuing to provide specialist psycho-social and therapeutic support.

Generic social work: Local Authorities Social Services Act 1970 and BASW

The formation of a generic organisation for social workers coincided with Seebohm's combining different specialist activities in one generic social work task. In the same year as the Conservatives gained a surprise election victory on 18 June 1970, the Local Authorities Social Services Act became law. The Act introduced a duty to employ adequate staff to help the director of social services carry out personal social services functions. It introduced in each local authority an enlarged social services department uniting specialisms such as child care and mental health and creating the rationale for a generically trained and organised social work profession.

The British Association of Social Workers (BASW) was formed on 24 April 1970, amalgamating the Association of Social Workers, Association of Child Care Officers, Association of Family Case Workers, Association of Psychiatric Social Workers, Institute of Medical Social Workers, Moral Welfare Workers' Assocation and Society of Mental Welfare Workers. But such incorporation, in parallel with the creation of the generic social work task under Seebohm, did not end debate over whether social work was a profession. Indeed, the very claim of social work to unified professional status in the 1970s intensified criticism of its alleged lack of professionalism when scandals erupted. This, and the compromised professional autonomy of social workers through their lack of an undisputed knowledge and practice base, as well as their divided accountability to both employers and clients, has contributed to the failure of BASW to establish itself by the 1990s as the equivalent of other professional bodies, such as the Law Society or the Royal College of Nursing.

The death of Maria Colwell in 1973 caused tremors in medical as well as social work quarters. Consultants and doctors were increasingly willing to co-operate in new arrangements for inter-agency liaison to monitor children suspected of being abused, now put onto newly created registers. Thus the Colwell scandal led to strengthened inter-agency procedures for monitoring existing and suspected child abuse and created a climate of increased willingness of police, doctors and social workers to work together. Despite these traumas, this period saw the establishment of generic social work in social services departments in England and Wales and social work departments in Scotland, and a growing influence of community-based casework and groupwork in child care and mental health. But as late as the 1970s, many workers were still all too ready to consign their clients to residential institutions, as the numbers of children in residential care showed (see document 6).

Given the aim of Seebohm that all aspects of a person's needs should be dealt with through one professionally based social work service, and if possible by one social worker, the failure to address the areas of learning disability as opposed to physical impairment, and mental health was striking. The DHSS published *Better Services for the Mentally Handicapped* in 1971 and *Better Services for the Mentally Ill* in 1975. These groups of people, however, remained marginal in terms of the supply of resources to meet their needs in the community. The Chronically Sick and Disabled Persons Act 1970 made it a duty of local authority social services departments to provide services and facilities for disabled people. This Act required local authorities to register disabled people and publicise to them the services they had a right to expect. However, one of the frustrations of the implementation of this Act for disabled people and carers was the failure to make available sufficient funds to resource it properly, with the result that, as social services departments ran into resource constraints, demand outstripped the supply of various services.

Local government reorganisation

The Local Government Act 1972 was operational from April 1974. It abolished county boroughs and reduced the number of county councils in England and Wales. It replaced municipal boroughs, urban and rural districts within these counties (there were 1250 of these) by 333 districts councils. It established six metropolitan counties (Greater Manchester, Merseyside, West Midlands, Tyne and Wear, South Yorkshire and West Yorkshire), containing 36 metropolitan districts. It retained a third tier of government outside the major cities, in the form of the parish. In Wales, parishes were replaced by communities. These either had community councils or held community meetings rather like those held in parishes in England.

The reorganisation of local government in 1974 coincided with further expansion in social services staffing, stimulated partly by the increasing demand for better publicised and more accessible welfare services. Partly also, the Children and Young Persons Act 1969 brought more children and young people within the ambit of social workers (Kahan, 1970, p. 63).

Before 1971, child care workers were responsible in the children's departments for child care, including work with foster parents of children boarded out and supervising adoptions. Mental welfare officers were often based in the health departments of the local authorities. Their work was mainly social work with mentally ill people and people with learning difficulties. Other specialist staff in the welfare departments worked with people with physical impairments, such as blindness and hearing loss.

The situation of some professionals, such as hospital social workers, remained uncertain. Hospital social workers, known as lady almoners, later became hospital almoners and were subsequently retitled medical social workers (MSWs). Some worked in chest clinics, others in special clinics for venereal diseases, but most worked in hospitals (Willmott, 1978, p. 41). After the National Health Service Re-organisation Act 1973, the National Health Service was reorganised in 1974. Until then, health services were partly run by local authorities and the NHS more or less formed three parts: hospitals, general practitioners and local health services. Afterwards, these services came together (op. cit., p. 149). After the reorganisation of the NHS, medical social workers stayed in the hospitals, but as employees of the local authority social services departments, and were simply known as social workers (op. cit., p. 42).

Subsequent to the Seebohm reorganisation of 1971 and local government reorganisation of 1974, there were undoubted gains in the organisation, particularly the coherence, planning and delivery, of social services. A managerial and professional framework now existed, an infrastructure of financial arrangements, to support the new generic social work departments. There were more social workers and more managers. The growth of professionalisation and managerialism in the personal social services went hand in hand. There was a massive influx, or rise, of men to management positions in the more administrative and organisational roles which increasingly replaced the practice-based posts formerly occupied by women. Some child care staff went to work for specialist voluntary organisations, such as National Children's Homes or Barnardo's, so as to stay in practice. In 1950, 96 out of 144 children's officers, for example, were women, whereas by the end of 1970 the majority of heads of children's, welfare and mental welfare departments were men (Walton, 1975, p. 235). Social work, in common with other human services such as education, healthcare and teaching, has tended to provide occupations for more women at the practice level than the 'traditional' professions such as medicine, law and engineering.

Training was expanding, and in the medium to long term this was to have an impact on fieldwork in particular. Group care – a term increasingly used to describe residential and day care services (see chapter 8) – remained a Cinderella area, largely operated by unqualified care staff. Growing size and managerialism bring self-evident gains, but size does not necessarily guarantee standards. It is doubtful whether the quality of personal social services as a whole had improved. Some centres of expertise, in areas such as child care and psychiatric services in mental health, had become dissipated; the needs of disabled people were still scarcely addressed; clients were subjected to a preponderance of treatment; services in areas such as child care and work with older people were geared excessively to residential rather than community and home-based services; people with physical impairments were too often incarcerated in hospitals and stigmatised with labels such as 'subnormal'; too many delinquents were in custody; resources to supply social work and social services were running out. So was the period in power of the Labour government,which would expire in the general election of May 1979, marking the formal birth of Thatcherism. By that date, most of the United Kingdom had a tiered system of local government 'with all the attendant tensions inherent in such divisions: competing mandates, the blurring of lines of responsibility and accountability for service provision, (and) resource jealousies' (Wilson and Game, 1994 p. 55).

The social as well as the personal dimensions of the role of the social worker contributed to the functions of the personal social services. Halmos (1978) examines the tension between the personal and political aspects of this role. The last quarter of the twentieth century has witnessed a shift towards anti-discriminatory concerns in social work which express a view of the social functions of the profession: these concern the extent to which the problems of the individual are shaped by structural – demographic, economic, social, organisational – divisions and oppressive features of society. The value base of social work, in the revised occupational standards published by CCETSW (1995), sets out the dual responsibilities of social workers in working to meet people's individual needs while taking due account of the impact on them of discrimination and oppression. This echoes Halmos's (1965) view 30 years earlier of social work as a profession with a moral basis, increasingly occupying the former territory of religion in society. It also goes some way to explaining why the practice of social work raises so much controversy, since its anti-oppressive response to people's problems confronted Thatcherite consumerism increasingly explicitly. This conflict was particularly apparent in community care, as the next chapter shows.

References and further reading

Adams, R., Allard,S., Baldwin, J. and Thomas, J. (1981) *A Measure of Diversion? Case Studies in Intermediate Treatment*, Leicester: National Youth Bureau.

Abel-Smith, B. and Townsend, P. (1965) *The Poor and the Poorest: a new analysis of the Ministry of Labour's Family expenditure surveys of 1953–54 and 1960*, London: G. Bell.

Beveridge, W.H. (1948) *Voluntary Action: a Report of Methods of Social Advance*. London: Allen and Unwin.

Bowlby, J. (1965) *Child Care and the Growth of Love*, 2nd edn, Harmondsworth: Pelican.

Bean, P. and Melville, J. (1989) *Lost Children of the Empire: The Untold Story of Britain's Child Migrants*, London: Unwin Hyman.

Brewer, C. and Lait, J. (1980) *Can Social Work Survive?* London: Temple Smith.

CCETSW (1995) *Rules and Requirements for the Diploma in Social Work*, CCETSW Paper 30, Rev. edn., London: CCETSW.

Chelf , C.P. (1992) *Controversial Issues in Social Welfare Policy,* London: Sage.

Children and Young Persons Act 1963, London: HMSO.

Children and Young Persons Act 1969, London: HMSO.

Chronically Sick and Disabled Persons Act 1970, London: HMSO.

Cochrane, A. and Clarke, J. (eds) (1993) *Comparing Welfare States, Britain in International Context,* London: Open University, Sage.

Cohen, S. (1987) *Folk Devils and Moral Panics: the Creation of the Mods and Rockers*, Oxford: Blackwell.

Committee on Local Authority and Allied Personal Social Services (1968) *The Seebohm Report*, Cmd 3703, London: HMSO.

Committee on Medical Auxiliaries (1951) (Cape Committee), Edinburgh: HMSO.

Committee on Social Workers in the Mental Health Services (1951) (Mackintosh Committee), Edinburgh: HMSO.

Cooper, J. (1983) *The Creation of the British Personal Social Services 1962–1974*, London: Heinemann Educational.

Culpitt, I. (1992) *Welfare and Citizenship, Beyond the Crisis of the Welfare State?* London: Sage.

Darby, J. and Williamson, A. (1978) *Violence and the Social Services in Northern Ireland*, London: Heinemann.

DHSS (1971) *Better Services for the Mentally Handicapped*, London: HMSO.

DHSS (1975) *Better Services for the Mentally Ill*, London: HMSO.

Frost, N. and Stein, M. (1989) *The Politics of Child Welfare*, Hemel Hempstead: Harvester Wheatsheaf.

Golding, P. and Middleton, S. (1982) *Images of Welfare: Press and Public Attitudes to Poverty*, Oxford: Martin Robertson.

Hall, S. *et. al.* (1978) *Policing the Crisis: Mugging, the State and Law and Order*, London: Macmillan.

Hall, P. (1976) *Reforming the Welfare: the Politics of Change in the Personal Social Services*, London: Heinemann.

Halmos, P. (1965) *The Faith of the Counsellors*, London: Constable.

Halmos, P. (1978) *The Personal and the Political: Social Work and Political Action*, London: Hutchinson.

Health and Social Services (Northern Ireland) Order 1972, Belfast: HMSO.

Health Visitors' and Social Workers' Training Act 1962, London: HMSO.

Jackson, T. and Marks, N. (1994) *Measuring Sustainable Economic Welfare – a Pilot Index 1950–1990*, London: NEFC.

46   The Personal Social Services

Jones, K. (1991) *The Making of Social Policy in Britain 1830–1990*, London: Athlone.

Kahan, B. (1970) The child care service, in Townsend, P. *et al.*, *The Fifth Social Service: A Critical Analysis of the Seebohm Proposals*, London: Fabian Society.

Labour Party Study Group (1964) *Crime – A Challenge to Us All* (The Longford Report), London: The Labour Party.

Lee, P. and Raban, C. (1988) *Welfare Theory and Social Policy, Reform or Revolution?* London: Sage.

Le Grand, J. and Bartlett, W. (eds) (1993), *Quasi-Markets and Social Policy*, London: Macmillan.

Local Authorities Social Services Act 1970, London: HMSO.

Local Government Act 1963, London: HMSO.

Local Government Act 1972, London: HMSO.

Local Government (N.I.) Act 1972, Belfast: HMSO.

Local Government (Scotland) Act 1973, Ednburgh: HMSO.

Lowe, R. (1993), *The Welfare State in Britain since 1945*, London: Macmillan.

Macrory, P. (1970) *Review Body on Local Government in Northern Ireland*, Cmnd 540 (NI) (Macrory Report), Belfast: HMSO.

Maidment, R. and Thompson, G. (eds) (1993) *Managing the United Kingdom, an Introduction to its Political Economy and Public Policy,* London: Open University, Sage.

Mann, K. (1994) Watching the defectives: observers of the underclass in the USA, Britain and Australia, *Critical Social Policy*, issue 41, autumn 79–99.

Marshall, T.H. (1967) *Social Policy*, revised edn, London: Hutchinson.

Mayo, M. (1994) *Communities and Caring: the Mixed Economy of Welfare*, Basingstoke: Macmillan.

Mental Health Act (Northern Ireland) 1948, Belfast: HMSO.

Miliband, R. (1991) Reflections on the crisis of Communist regimes, in Blackburn R. (ed.) *After the Fall,* p. 16, London: Verso.

Mishra, R. (1990) *The Welfare State in Capitalist Society: Policies of Retrenchment and Maintenance in Europe, North America and Australia*, Hemel Hempstead: Harvester Wheatsheaf.

National Assistance Act 1948, London: HMSO.

National Health Service Reorganisation Act 1973, London: HMSO.

Packman, J. (1975) *The Child's Generation: Childcare Policy from Curtis to Houghton*, Oxford: Blackwell,.

Poor Law Amendment Act 1834.

Propper, C. (1993) Quasi-markets, contracts and quality in health and social care: the US experience, in Le Grand, J. and Bartlett, W. (eds) (1993) *Quasi-Markets and Social Policy*, 35–67, London: Macmillan.

Redcliffe-Maud, Lord (Chairman) (1969) Royal Commission on Local Government in England 1966–1969, vol. 1 Report, Cmnd 4040, London: HMSO.

Report by Sir Walter Monckton on the Circumstances which Led to the Boarding Out of Dennis and Terence O'Neill at Bank Farm, Miserley and the Steps Taken to Supervise Their Welfare (1945), Cmnd 6636, London: HMSO.

Report of the Care of Children Committee (1946) (Curtis Report), Cmnd 6922, London: HMSO.

Report of the Committee of Inquiry into the Care and Supervision Provided in Relation to Maria Colwell (1974), London: HMSO.

Report of the Committee on Children and Young Persons (1960) (Ingleby Report), Cmnd 1191, London: HMSO.

Report on Social Workers in the Local Authority Health and Welfare Services (1959) (Younghusband Report), London: HMSO.

Report on the Prevention of Neglect of Children in their Own Homes (1963) (McBoyle Report), Edinburgh: HMSO.

Rodgers, B. and Stevenson, J. (1973) *A New Portrait of Social Work*, London: Heinemann.

Scottish Home and Health Department/Scottish Education Department (1964) *Children and Young Persons, Scotland, Report* (Kilbrandon Report), Edinburgh: HMSO.

Social Work (Scotland) Act 1968, Edinburgh: HMSO.

Stedman Jones, G. (1984) *Outcast London, a Study in the Relationship between Classes in Victorian Society*, Harmondsworth: Penguin.

Titmuss, R.M. (1950) *Problems of Social Policy,* Official History of the Second World War, United Kingdom Civil Series, London: HMSO.

Walton, R.G. (1975) *Women in Social Work*, London: Routledge and Kegan Paul.

Ware, A. and Goodin, R.E. (eds) (1990) *Needs and Welfare*, London: Sage.

Webb, A.L. and Wistow, G. (1987) *Social Work, Social Care and Social Planning*, London: Longman.

Welfare Services Act 1947, London: HMSO.

Wheatley, Lord, Chairman (1969) *Royal Commission on Local Government in Scotland* (Wheatley Report), Cmnd 4150, Edinburgh: HMSO.

White Paper (1966) *Social Work and the Community*, Edinburgh : HMSO.

White Paper (1970) *Reform of Local Government in England,* Cmnd 4276, London: HMSO.

White Paper (1943) *Educational Reconstruction,* London: HMSO.

White Paper (1944) *Employment Policy*, London: HMSO.

White Paper: (1944) *A National Health Service*, London: HMSO.

White Paper: (1944) *Social Insurance,* London: HMSO.

Willmott, P. (1978) *Consumer's Guide to the British Social Services*, 4th edn, Harmondsworth: Penguin.

Wilson, D. and Game, C. (1994) *Local Government in the United Kingdom*, London: Macmillan.

Wootton, B. Seal, V.G. and Chambers, R. (1959) *Social Science and Social Pathology*, London: Allen and Unwin.

Younghusband, E. (1947) *Report on the Employment and Training of Social Workers*, Dunfermline: Carnegie United Kingdom Trust.

Younghusband, E. (1951) *Second Report on the Employment and Training of Social Workers*, Dunfermline: Carnegie United Kingdom Trust

Younghusband, E. (1978) *Social Work in Britain 1950–1975: a Follow-up Study*, two volumes, London: Allen and Unwin.

CHAPTER 3

Consumerism versus empowerment: the quasi-markets of social care

This chapter examines the period from the 1970s to the early 1990s, in the early years of which the personal social services expanded rapidly, before undergoing a dramatic period of reconstruction. It would be tempting, but mistaken, to locate the origins of the shift towards the creation of internal markets in health and social services in the late 1980s; likewise, the development of the new managerialism that sustains these markets in the 1990s derives not from the New Right, or Thatcherism, but from the much older inheritance of rationalism, expressed in a belief in the virtues of scientific management; this gained ground in the public sector from the 1960s and was nourished in the quasi-markets of the 1990s.

Conflicting interests and approaches

Some of the signs of the complex interplay between different interests are evident in the legislation produced by the Thatcher government after 1979. The 1970s began with the previous Conservative government leading a backlash to re-establish law and order, in reaction to the treatment philosophy of the Children and Young Persons Act 1969. But once Labour took power in 1974, reforms continued. In the face of Conservative-led campaigns to re-assert law and order, the Labour government brought in the Race Relations Act 1976, which made racial discrimination in such areas as employment and training unlawful and set up the Commission for Racial Equality. Yet, after nearly four years of growth, the oil crisis in the Middle East and the growing economic problems of the 1970s set the context for the atmosphere of budget cutting and uncertainty which was increasingly evident over the work of the personal social services. A degree of bureaucratisation had overtaken the generic social services departments, and now there was pressure to cut back on office-based managers. In the professional arena, no sooner had generic social work been established in the new social services departments than it was under attack, not least from critics claiming that generic social workers could not compete in expertise with their predecessors who specialised in child care and mental health. Thus, a constellation of factors – economic pressures, constraints on public expenditure, the growth of a strong professional culture in social work at the same time as, and possibly stimulated by, controversies over notorious scandals – fostered the conditions for managerialist control by managements.

The atmosphere of conflict in which the personal social services evolved during the 1970s, and controversies over the establishment of quasi-markets from the late 1980s, indicate the widely differing perspectives of stakeholders in policy and practice: politicians of all parties; agency managers and professionals in the statutory, voluntary, private and informal sectors; service users and carers.

Between the early 1970s and the mid-1990s, the treatment paradigm was displaced from its previously dominant position in the professional literature and practice of social work, and the paradigm of empowerment attained a high profile in the professional literature. Despite this, Department of Health guidance on community care, for example, tended to reflect rather than to resolve tensions between a needs-led approach and the resource-led approach implicit in the ideology of the quasi-marketplace. Meanwhile, the commitment of many professionals and users to user-led approaches cut across both treatment and consumerism. This potentially created further confusion. The needs-led approach required by the NHS and Community Care Act 1990, involving negotiating by the care manager or assessor, is in tension with the user-led approach which some self-advocates among service users may demand; it also may be undermined by the managerially-dominated and resource-constrained, or service-led approach prevalent in the marketplace (see Fig. 3.1). The espousal of consumerism across the human services by members of the Conservative government that took office in May 1979 was expressed not only in ministerial support for charters for service users in different sectors, but also in a willingness to adopt the rhetoric of what might be called an equality-based approach. Nevertheless, during the first half of the 1990s there was continual attrition, much of it informal, between the perspectives of ministers, senior civil servants in the Home Office and Department of Health and the Social Services Inspectorate, and staff in professional bodies such as CCETSW and key educational interests such as the Standing Conference of Heads of Probation Courses and the Joint Universities Council Social Work Education Committee (JUC/SWEC).

In the 1980s, the phrase 'return to Victorian values' was commonly used to convey the ideology of Thatcherism. While historically inaccurate, this phrase usefully captures the trajectory of

treatment	needs-led
empowerment	user-led
consumerism	service-led

Figure 3.1 Approaches to Community care

government policy under Margaret Thatcher, Conservative Prime Minister from 1979 to 1991. In the personal social services, the impact of this particular blend of New Right thinking was evident in the emphasis on provision through self-help and the voluntary sector, which Gladstone had described towards the end of the previous Labour government as though it were a new kind of radical pluralism (Gladstone, 1979). However, voluntary and private care were still viewed as an adjunct to statutory services rather than as their principal source of provision, in contrast with a decade later when, in community care for example, they would constitute more than three-quarters of all social services provision. Other Thatcherite policies that impacted on practice included a re-emphasis of so-called family values and law and order in the context of economic policies that put low inflation before the maintenance of jobs, drawing a positive correlation between full employment and rising inflation.

Managerialism and the new quasi-markets: 1970s to the late 1980s

New Right ideology may not have been the midwife to managerialism, but it proved an effective cradle of a process of much longer standing. Between the late 1970s and the early 1990s, the wind of change blew consistently and with growing strength through the public sector, bringing with it the values, culture, language and practice of the management of commercial organisations in the private sector. Farnham and Horton have catalogued these (1993a, pp. 237–238): the rational approach emphasising strategic management in objective setting; the separation of policy from administration and delegating responsibility for service delivery to executive units, truncated hierarchies with devolved responsibilities and middle managers held responsible for meeting targets; performance indicators; a style of human resource management that encourages individualism and discourages collectivism among staff. Farnham and Horton's argument is that the development of a 'public service orientation' towards service users as consumers meshes with the development of quasi-markets; it shifts from supply-led to demand-led services not dominated by professional providers but impelled by the needs of users (op. cit., p. 238).

It would be a mistake to view the changes since the 1970s in the way that the social services were structured and delivered as largely the outcome of thinking by the New Right in the UK. Nevertheless, attitudes and policies of the New Right expressed by the Conservative government since 1979 nurtured the shift towards managerialism. It would be an overstatement also to describe the early years of the New Right as though they were exclusively led by Margaret Thatcher, who was Prime Minister for a dozen years.

The influence of the New Right internationally, notably from the USA, cannot be overestimated. The New Right in the USA in that period in many ways provides a template for developments in Britain, in that it follows neo-liberals such as Hayek and Friedman, assuming the benefits, and even the inevitability, of unequal social status and unequal access to goods and services (Samson, 1990).

Two particularly contrasting appraisals of the impact of the New Right on the welfare state in this period are possible: the first, that Thatcherism has destroyed it; the second, that the changes have made no difference. Between these extremes, a balanced view may be that economic and policy changes have cut deep into the welfare state and changed it, but it has not been destroyed; in some aspects, gains have actually been made. For instance, the growth of self-advocacy and user-led movements have contributed to resistance to the consumerist ideology of the marketplace. At the same time, another consequence of New Right policies has been to extend the roles of private and voluntary providers of welfare services in the so-called 'mixed economy of care'. In the mid-1990s, it remains to be seen whether the existing level of services can be maintained and whether the monopoly of state provision via the local authority will simply be replaced by new monopolies in the high profit areas, as in healthcare, where a few large providers may push alternatives to the margins, leaving little choice and restricted access to services for the less mobile, poorer and disabled people.

From another perspective, Mayo observes that the more significant impact of the New Right has been 'not by dismantling public welfare provision but by restructuring it, particularly through the introduction of internal markets or quasi-markets' (Mayo, 1994, p. 4). Since the New Right did not exclusively control ideas about political and social policies between the 1970s and the 1990s, it is doubtful how far the New Right has directly changed the provision of welfare in Britain in this period. Glennerster and Midgely (1991, p. 11) suggest that while there is evidence of New Right policies having 'negative consequences for the welfare state ideal ... the extent to which they have significantly altered institutionalised approaches to government welfare provision is debatable.' It is vital not to caricature the state and the market as polar positions in relation to universalism and individualism, and thereby risk neglecting the interlinking of elements of both in much contemporary social policy (Taylor, 1989, pp. 21–22). The Government's commitment to privatisation was expressed only indirectly in the health and social care sector, through the compromise policy of introducing quasi-markets in community care. Survey data confirm that during Margaret Thatcher's three Conservative governments, most public opinion accepted that privatisation was a policy stemming from government, with little popular demand to support it

(McAllister and Studlar, 1989). Be that as it may, this policy effectively maintained central government control of the mixed economy of welfare, while ensuring a radical change in the balance away from public and towards voluntary and private provision. The financial constraints of the late 1970s coincided with an enhanced role for the voluntary sector. Councils of Voluntary Service (CVSs), for example, played an expanded role as co-ordinators and sponsors of smaller local voluntary groups, while large, UK-wide voluntary organisations such as the NSPCC, Barnado's and the Children's Society provided contract-based specialist services in child care and social work with families.

Nature and development of quasi-markets

As Le Grand and Bartlett (1993, p. 3) argue, the government took broad social policy initiatives in 1988 and 1989 which retained state financing of key services, but made major changes in the way they were provided. State provision was replaced by a significant level of independent provision, through the voluntary and private sectors. Independent providers would compete with each other in a number of quasi-markets; centrally regulated agencies – in community care, health authorities and local authorities – acted as purchasers of services by allocating resources to selected providers. The quasi-markets in community care resulted more from political pressures than from an intrinsic desire to compromise an essential enthusiasm for free market values. All the same, as Mayo points out, the apparent lack of consistent and coherent impact of New Right policies is not altogether surprising, given the internal inconsistencies within New Right thinking, and its blend of economic individualism, cultural traditionalism and authoritarian populism (Mayo, 1994, p. 3).

Increased accountability: quality as a means of central control

A paradoxical feature of the claimed 'hands-off' local services approach of the Thatcher government was the introduction, even before quasi-markets were introduced, of means by which central government could monitor and regulate the personal social services (Adams, 1997). First, the Audit Commission in England and Wales was set up, under the Local Government Finance Act 1982. Then, from its inception in 1985, the Social Services Inspectorate took a proactive role in monitoring, or rather controlling, the quality of personal social services. In this, the publication by the SSI on inspecting home care services (Department of Health, Social Services Inspectorate, 1990) was significant, because it set out the framework and the method to be adopted. This involved the systematic collection of statistical and qualitative data on 'policy, management structures, staff and financial resources available, service management and delivery processes, and the nature of the services being provided' (op. cit., 1990, p. 2). The style and trajectory of such activities were products of a quasi-commercial version of managerialism.

Restructuring education and training in social care and social work

There was an increasing question mark over education and training for the workforce of the personal social services. This focused on the view of employers that the heavy concentration on qualifications of social workers was not justified by the quality of training many received and their growing recognition of the need for training the much larger numbers of care workers, who by and large were least qualified and had the most day-to-day contact with service users. During the 1980s, employers were gaining in power to voice their criticisms of university- and college-based training courses. They exerted pressure on government departments and professional bodies such as CCETSW to develop workplace-based training that built on the experience of the Certificate in Social Service – an employment-based programme below undergraduate level largely intended for staff in residential and day care. In 1994, the Government response to widespread criticisms, especially from employers, of the shortcomings of qualifying social work training was to institute a review of the Diploma in Social Work, in parallel with a Home Office review of qualifying training for probation officers. The review of the Dip SW led to a more competence-based programme based on a statement of occupational standards. The review of probation training led to the publication of the Dews Report (Dews and Watts, 1994) and, on 29 September 1995, Michael Howard announced his agreement with the recommendations of the Dews Report, and his intention to distance probation qualifying training from the Diploma in Social Work and to encourage the recruitment of personnel who had formerly worked in the police and the armed services. Opposition was fierce, notably from the National Association of Probation Officers (NAPO), the Association of Chief Probation Officers (ACPO), JUC/SWEC and probation qualifying programmes in universities. A well-orchestrated campaign began with a debate in the House of Lords on 14 April 1995, during which no fewer than three former Home Secretaries spoke against the proposals, coming to a head in the autumn of 1995, when NAPO announced it was seeking a judicial review to challenge the Home Secretary's intentions.

Professionals within social work and social care in the UK campaigned with some success to establish anti-discriminatory practice at the core of the value base of the standards for caring work at N/SVQ levels 2 and 3 and the Diploma in Social Work which replaced the CQSW and CSS in the early 1990s. Continuing controversy over the role of social work within the personal social services focused on the view of key politicians in the ruling Conservative government that CCETSW's commitment to anti-discriminatory practice, and the place of the 'ologies' – notably sociology – in the professional qualifying curriculum of universities, were problems to be rectified. Central government in the 1990s was at odds with social work interests over what some ministers perceived as unwarranted activism by some social work educators and practitioners in promoting social change and anti-oppressive practice, especially that concerned with promoting the interests of particular discriminated-against groups, rather than adopting a broadly-based commitment to equality. The review of the occupational standards for the Diploma in Social Work ordered by Virginia Bottomley, secretary of state at the Department of Health, in 1993, became a battleground over these issues. One key question of the 1990s was whether managers and practitioners would ration personal social services to people as consumers of health and social care, or assert anti-oppressive values and negotiate to work with them as empowered service users, to assess, design, resource and deliver the services they needed.

Restructuring human services provision

In its first few years in power, the Thatcher government continued to process legislation in education, criminal justice and mental health. Quite apart from its content, one cumulative effect of this legislation was to increase dramatically the scope and intensity of powers, duties and responsibilities exercised by local authority providers of personal social services. The Education Act 1981 required local authorities to integrate children with special needs into ordinary schools where possible. It introduced new measures for assessing children with special needs and placing them in appropriate settings, using a 'statement' of their needs. The Criminal Justice Act 1982 reflected the trend towards law and order by introducing more sanctions than had been contained in the Children and Young Persons Act 1969. The Mental Health Act 1983 provided for the compulsory and informal admission to hospital of people with mental health problems. It defined 'mental disorder' for the purpose of the law. It set up Mental Health Tribunals to protect the interests and rights of mental health patients. The Registered Homes Act 1984 required residential care homes to be registered and inspected. The Police and Criminal Evidence Act 1984 extended police powers to stop and search suspects. On the other hand, it introduced measures to regulate the detention, questioning and treatment of suspects by police. The Disabled Persons (Services, Consultations and Representation) Act 1986 provided for an authorised representative of a disabled person, or person with a mental or physical impairment, and for an assessment or a statement of needs similar to that introduced in the Education Act 1981. The Data Protection Act 1984 introduced measures to regulate agencies keeping computerised personal details of people on records. The Access to Personal Files Act 1987 allowed people access to records, for example, medical and employment records, held on them. This was long overdue since, as emerges in chapter 4, for about 20 years the aspirations of professional social workers towards such principles as confidentiality had tended to be contradicted by the bureaucratic realities of the local authority context in which they worked (Pearson, 1975, p. 34). The argument that social workers could claim only semi-professional status was based largely on the grounds that their professionalism was compromised by their dual accountability – to values and practices in meeting client needs on one hand, and to the employing agency and the state on the other (Etzioni, 1969). Satyamurti (1981) has provided a detailed insight into the factors at work in the period when Seebohm was being implemented and field social workers were attempting to manage these tensions, in their generic roles in the new social services departments. Simpkin (1979) has charted the struggles of social workers in the 1970s to seek 'solutions' to contradictory, and probably insoluble, problems of their working context through aspirations such as managerialism and professionalism.

The above debates overlay changes of great significance for the personal social services. These involved: local government reorganisation in the wake of the report of the Redcliffe-Maud Commission in 1969; new legislation, in some ways, ironically, making tensions manageable between different stakeholders in the personal social services – politicians, managers, professionals, services users and carers; also, in a two-year period at the end of the 1980s, the introduction of legislation creating quasi-markets, which had revolutionary implications for the structure, finance, control and delivery of human services.

Creation of quasi-markets in health and social care

Two mutually contradictory themes were evident between 1988 and 1993: first, the concept of empowerment arrived (Adams, 1996, chapter 1); second, the creation of quasi-markets produced a consumer–provider relationship between the worker and the person receiving services. The former aspect was introduced in chapter 1 and its implications are worked through in chapters 4 onwards; the rest of this chapter deals with the implications of the latter for community care.

Le Grand and Bartlett (1993, p. 10) comment that quasi-markets in the field of welfare differ in one or more of three ways from conventional markets. They may be 'non-profit organisations competing for public contracts, sometimes in competition with for-profit organisations; consumer purchasing power either centralised in a single purchasing agency or allocated to users in the form of vouchers rather than cash; and, in some cases, the consumers represented in the market by agents instead of operating by themselves.'

The establishment of quasi-markets in health and social care services took place in the years between the Local Government Act 1988 and the implementation in 1993 of the NHS and Community Care Act of 1990. Two main kinds of changes paved the way: generic and service-specific. The former included the introduction of contracting out and compulsory competitive tendering in local authorities in the broader privatisation strategy of the Conservative government; the latter involved legislation to change specific services such as the financing and management of schools and the purchase and provision of services in health and social care.

Generic changes

Privatisation, contracting out and competitive tendering

The privatisation strategy of the Conservative government, contracting out, competitive tendering and compulsory competitive tendering (CCT) were features of New Right moves to undermine the public sector, each with different implications for the operation of public services. Contracting out involves a specific public sector function such as dustbin collection being put out to tender, the public sector provision terminated and the staff redeployed, retired or made redundant. Competitive tendering involves the introduction of a system of tendering in which the public sector body itself can bid, alongside private providers, and the functions of planning and financing the service are retained by the public sector body. CCT regulates the process through the Local Government Act 1988, which extended compulsory competitive tendering to many services in local authorities and other bodies such as development corporations and urban development corporations, and through the Local Authorities (Goods and Services) Act 1970. The supporters of CCT argued that it improved the cost-effectiveness of the public sector by enabling services to be bought in from the most competitive bid from an external contractor, rather than being provided directly by the authority. In contrast with a privatised organisation, competitive tendering procedures in local government involve the local authority retaining responsibility for deciding what level of service it requires, and how it will be supplied. Because the local authority is permitted to tender itself through its direct labour organisation, and continues to pay for the service from public funds, it is possible that its own tender will succeed and the service will be supplied, as before, by the public sector. Cutler and Waine (1994, pp. 86–104) point out that no simple conclusions can be drawn about the impact of compulsory competitive tendering on the move towards privatisation through the awarding of contracts to direct labour organisations in authorities controlled by different political parties, savings to local authorities through competition between contractors, the quality of services, and whether such efficiency gains as take place are at the expense of the pay and conditions of employed staff. Although there is evidence that the operation of compulsory competitive tendering tends to lead to de-unionisation of labour and downgrading of the importance attached to the application of regulatory frameworks to employment protection, the judgement as to whether it should be introduced is based on political rather than economic arguments (op. cit., p. 104). In the 1980s, CCT largely covered support services supplied by manual staff; in the 1990s, government strategy was to extend it to such professional services as accounting, legal architectural, housing management and personnel services (op. cit., 1994, p. 78). In the 1990s, privatisation in areas such as railways, gas and water supply and telecommunications has involved a significant level of government control before, during and after privatisation, through a regulatory framework involving contracting out and CCT. This ensures that the companies concerned are not free to operate as they wish.

Service-specific changes

Schooling: At the level of specific services, the Education Reform Act 1988 provided a model for the impending changes in health and social care. It introduced four novel principles to primary and secondary education: local management of schools meant that parents and other local representatives on the management committee could exercise significant influence over how their school was run, as a semi-independent education provider; schools could opt out and be funded directly by central government, independently of local authorities; formula funding meant that the level of resources allocated to a school depended on the 'formula', one element of which was the number of pupils it attracted; open enrolment involved parents having a larger degree of choice than before as to where they sent their children to school.

Housing: The Housing Act 1988 allowed local authority tenants to choose non-local authority landlords, and local authorities were encouraged to sell off their housing stock to housing associations. Le Grand and Bartlett (1993, p. 6) note the significant expansion of the housing association movement 'to supplant local authorities as the main new providers of social housing; while the role of the state as a funder is shifting from general "bricks and mortar" subsidies to individual means-tested subsidy in the form of Housing Benefit.'

Health and social care: The White Paper *Working for Patients* (Department of Health, 1989a) was implemented in the NHS and Community Care Act 1990. It divided the functions of purchase of services from their provision, and introduced GP fundholders who purchased. There were two kinds of purchaser organisations: directly managed units still under health authority control, and trusts that operated largely independently of the health authority. In parallel with these changes, some key recommendations of the Griffiths Report (Department of Health and Social Security, 1988) were incorporated in the White Paper (Department of Health, 1989b) and appeared in the NHS and Community Care Act 1990. These shifted the role of social services departments in community care from direct service provision to being enabling authorities, purchasing services from independent provider units, through budgets allocated to care managers who would manage each package of care for a particular service user.

Such changes involved three shifts. (1) The centre of gravity of local political and economic power shifted from the state to the new triangle of relationships between the purchasers, providers and users of services. (2) The state shifted from direct power to control the service user, through decisions about whether to allocate services, to making available services that the service user might or might not choose to receive. (3) There was a shift from lifelong, comprehensive services being available as of right to particular services being purchased for, or by, a service user, in a time-limited contract. This last feature is predicated on the assumption that the consumer in the market economy of health and social care is a rational individual, able to obtain adequate services. This contradicts many service users' lack of real choice of, and access to, services, which exists for two reasons: because the lack of an adequate range of available services limits, or even eliminates, real choice on the part of service users; and because service users' lack of personal resources prevents them from having access to the services they need. So while quasi-markets in education, housing and health and social care display features of a voucher system, the individual being allocated a given resource to claim a service, this depends on having access to suitable services to meet personal needs. Nevertheless, criticisms of the principles of vouchers should not be levelled solely at the Conservative government introducing them. As Le Grand and Bartlett (1993, pp. 7–8) note, from a Left-wing viewpoint Michael Young and Patricia Hewitt have proposed voucher schemes for GPs and children under five respectively.

Paradoxically, the period of Conservative government which saw the greatest inroads into public services for 40 years also witnessed unprecedented advocacy by central government on behalf of the citizen as consumer of social services; linked with this was a widespread promulgation by user groups in this sector, supported in the main by workers in face-to-face contact with them, of service user and carer empowerment.

Decentralisation of provision: centralisation of power

The introduction of quasi-markets in health and social care has undermined the position of organisations such as trade unions and local authorities committed to policies in conflict with government policy. Whitfield (1992) argues that the promotion of more commercial activity in the public sector has been a function of 'the enabling state'; it has led to less opportunity for local authorities to pursue policies based on social rather than market values, and to more fragmented and poorer quality services (Mayo, 1994, p. 5).

Other legislation

The late 1980s and early 1990s saw a spate of significant legislation in social services work with children, community care and criminal justice. The Children Act 1989 was the most comprehensive legislation for children ever passed by Parliament. Section 17 of the Act typified its promotion of the interests of the child as paramount; this required local authorities to safeguard and promote the welfare of children in their area who were in need, by providing a range and level of services to meet those needs (see chapter 4 for more details of the Act). The Criminal Justice Act 1991 introduced many measures, mainly affecting adult offenders. Part III of this Act made provisions affecting young offenders, social work in general and child protection work in particular. The NHS and Community Care Act 1990 was implemented by April 1993, and changed quite dramatically the way in which health and social services are organised.

Community care

Although the concept of community care could be said to be as old as social work, mutual aid and self-help in communities, in the late 1980s there was increasing pressure from a number of directions, for legislation in this area (see chapter 6). Most notably, there was a convergence between the government's commitment to cost-cutting through closing large residential institutions and devolving direct responsibility for provision to the voluntary and private sector and the findings of research. The weight of support for community care, as in the criminal justice and mental health areas, was generated by an unlikely alliance between libertarians and conservative monetarists. The great weight of research casting doubt on the effectiveness, in terms of benefit to the resident, of most forms of large institutional provision for mentally ill, learning disabled, older people and children was brought together in the Wagner Report (NISW, 1988). Wagner also drew attention to the costs of residential care, rather than the quality or effectiveness of care, as the key to arguments against it (op. cit., Appendix) (pp. 41–55) as well as highlighting a number of difficult practice issues.

The NHS and Community Care Act 1990 was the central pivot influencing other aspects of the personal social services during the closing decade of the twentieth century. The creation of quasi-markets in community care represented the government's response to the somewhat anarchic growth of provision and the rapidly increasing costs of, for example, private residential care, met in many cases by social security payments. The management of the process of care planning and implementation, spelt out in the Griffiths Report (1988), the White Paper *Caring for People* (Department of Health, 1989b) and subsequent guidance (see, e.g. Department of Health, 1991a, 1991b), was intended to bring the sector under control by creating a market mechanism for the purchase of services by the social work or social services department from a range of statutory, voluntary and private providers.

Policy statements about consumerism and the development of market models of care provision claimed that the Act would bring increased choice to the consumer, and made reference to the importance of users of services having a say in the services they receive. The Act requires greater collaboration than hitherto between different departments, notably health and the personal social services. This is linked with the development of services across the statutory, voluntary, private and independent sectors, and a shift away from the principle of state provision. State provision has been replaced by the market model of service providers competing for contracts with authorities and agencies.

The term 'mixed economy' is used to distinguish the complex pattern of statutory, voluntary, private and informal provision from the simple pattern of state and local authority services which was a widespread principle of the welfare state after 1945. However, 'mixed' implies a richer mixture and range of provision than formerly, without any guarantee that this will occur. Government rhetoric represented the creation of markets to deliver community care as involving a shift to a mixed economy of welfare in a free market for supplying services as and when demanded by customers, as though the development of informal, private and voluntary provision alongside state provision would of itself make enhanced services more accessible to more people. But, largely because of government measures to cap resources, these new markets were not free to deliver on demand, according to people's needs. The benefits of quasi-markets lay with their central government managers and not necessarily with service users.

Impact of the New Right

In the face of New Right policies, one response by its opponents is to argue for decentralisation and democratisation, which improve the quality of welfare services and the fit between services and people's needs. These approaches rely on self-care and self-advocacy, for example. Some strategies of decentralisation have been criticised for not necessarily resulting in improved quality of services. Some have been linked with consumer involvement, and again have been criticised for not enhancing participation in local democracy. Further, both these examples can be criticised for emphasising self-help and in effect increasing the reliance on individuals, families and communities caring for each other on an informal basis. The arguments against user participation are understandable, since democracy gives permission and power to criticise and, paradoxically, to undermine it.

Another response has been to allow organisations and groups representing particular interests in the community to come forward and represent their own needs. Thus, women's organisations and black and ethnic minority groups have made their wishes known in the consultations over the construction of community care plans in many local authorities in Britain. Some of these organisations have set out to provide services for themselves. Some groups for disabled people, for example, believe that this is the only way to avoid their continued oppression. But, having examined examples of the initiatives in detail, Mayo (1994, pp. 17–18) observes that:

> Neither equal opportunities specifically, nor community participation, community development and self-help more generally, can simply be left to the operations of the free market ... but ... there is no reason to suppose that, left to themselves, such organisations will be able to continue to operate at their present

level, let alone to play a more significant role in the direct provision of services. On the contrary, there is evidence from the experiences of organisations in the USA to suggest that contracting services out to the voluntary sector, in the current context of the mixed economy of welfare, may strengthen the largest and best established organisations but at the potential cost of pressurising them into adopting increasingly commercial and/or bureaucratised ways of operating. Meanwhile the smaller more directly-community based organisations may be far less able to participate in the mixed economy of welfare.

Quasi-markets in health and social care: 1990 to 1993

In 1991, the Thatcher era ended when the Prime Minister was forced out of office. However, the 1992 general election left the Conservative government, led by John Major, still in power. Despite the change of Prime Minister, the reshaping of the institutions of government continued in the early 1990s, through the process of contracting out the core responsibilities of the state to new government agencies. This happened in the replacement of the civil service institutions with Next Steps agencies, such as the Benefits Agency, the Child Support Agency and Prison Service. The distinguishing features of these agencies were that they resembled private and voluntary organisations in their autonomy from the civil service and in their responsibility for running their own budgets. They resembled quangos in their semi-autonomous management and organisation. They tended to be accountable to their own hierarchies rather than to local or central government. The controversy in the autumn of 1995 when Michael Howard, then Home Secretary, dismissed Derek Lewis, Director of the Prison Service, revolved around which of them should have carried responsibility for various shortcomings of the service, notably evident in security breaches at Whitemoor and Parkhurst prisons. Gray (1995) describes the new agencies as an ironic re-creation in the market economy of Thatcherism, of a corporate style of institution that Thatcherism set out to destroy from the late 1970s, and the 'triangular coalition of government, employers and trade unions' that exemplifies the pre-Thatcherite era. He adds that the 1990s were witnessing

'... a species of market corporatism, in which a growing proportion of the Nation's economic resources is pre-empted by an expanding managerial class charged with the task of overseeing internal markets. This managerial new class disposes of vast resources and exercises immense powers over individual lives, without being subject to the disciplines of real markets, and even when made up, as often it is, of decent people struggling to do an impossible job – without the guidance of any established professional ethos.'

The quasi-markets in health and social care offered a fragmented map of contractual relationships, which were essentially cost-driven. The impact of this in the long term remained to be seen. In the short run, the additional complexities of co-ordinating the management and delivery of services presented new challenges. In a rural area, for example, a part-time home care assistant might work to a line manager in social services in one nearby town and liaise with staff in a community health trust run from another town. Thus, the problems of working together could be left to be managed by the least qualified and experienced member of a providing organisation.

Impact of NHS and Community Care Act 1990

The wide-ranging changes in policy and practice ushered in by the NHS and Community Care Act 1990 were not matched by comparable changes in the law, to ensure that fair and adequate services were delivered (Bynoe, 1995, p. 18). Media reporting of the denial of services to individuals contributed to public concern about the failure of community care in the face of the need to run services commercially. Such examples indicate a trend towards health authorities concentrating resources on acute rather than chronic services, and raise the question of the political, as opposed to the clinical, reasons for decision-making in health and social care. Rationing of services increasingly took place, and was sometimes furthered by putting a price on them, curtailing certain services held to be ineffective or unnecessary and prioritising them according to their impact on people's quality of life. There was a particular impact on the personal social services in areas such as nursing home provision for older people. Demarcation disputes between health and social services occurred over who should pay for the continuing care, for example, of older people requiring residential nursing provision for their chronic conditions.

By 1993, questions were already being asked about changes required in the arrangements for structuring and managing the delivery of community care. Notably, David Knowles, president of the Institute of Health Services Management, proposed in his inaugural address that the NHS should give up its purchasing role (see pp. 131–32 below). Subsequently, the idea was taken up by both major sides of the political spectrum. Conservative-led Wandsworth took over the function of health provision; Labour-run Birmingham announced detailed consideration of the idea and, in late May 1994, the Labour-controlled Association of Metropolitan Authorities (AMA) discussed a paper proposing 10 to 15 pilot schemes to test the principle (Brindle, 1994, pp. 12–13).

The policy changes at the turn of the 1980s and 1990s have been complex and difficult for local authorities to manage (Challis,

1990). During 1993–1994, the Department of Health expected local authorities to improve collaboration with housing departments, increase the use of non-residential care, raise the level of involvement of users and carers, develop more joint planning and commissioning to include GP fundholders and develop positive relationships between purchasers and providers of services. At the same time, the Department of Health wished to see change of a 'steady state' kind (Lewis *et al.*, 1995). The implementation of community care involves local authorities in the demanding task of managing change simultaneously on several fronts: the establishment of needs-led assessment and care management systems; becoming enabling authorities and separating purchase from provision of services; establishing joint planning to achieve what is termed a 'seamless service'. All this means that change in itself is difficult, but 'change without noise may be impossible' (op. cit., p. 92).

The increased participation of voluntary organisations in the mixed economy has implications for how the contract culture develops. Certain areas of practice may lend themselves to provision by voluntary organisations, such as advocacy and campaigning (Lewis, 1993, p. 189). But participating voluntary organisations have to acclimatise to an increasing rate of change (op. cit., p. 191). There is a need also to develop bases for incorporating service users, carers and voluntary organisations into the new planning and managing environment (Lewis *et al.*, 1995, p. 96). The corollary is to ask how formal systems in the local authority 'mirror and embrace the properties of informal support systems' (McGrath and Grant, 1992, p. 96).

Current trends indicate that in the future a larger number of dependent people will be reliant on a smaller proportion of active earners. In what has been referred to as the 'sandwich generation', working adults have responsibilities for not only caring for their elderly relatives but also providing for the increasing educational demands of their children (*The Guardian*, 8 August 1994).

Norman Warner (1994), former director of Kent County Council and adviser to the Association of District Councils, comments that the changes in social services as a result of the Local Government Review will cause some problems, through the lack of experience of staff and the transition from being relatively large departments to relatively small purchasers of services, and also some positive opportunities. Warner comments that the size of a social services department is not a guarantee that it will be well managed and cost-effective. 'The recent inquiry following the death of the toddler Leanne White in Nottinghamshire showed that a big county department serving over a million people can get things wrong with disastrous consequences' (Warner, 1994).

Implementing quasi-markets: from 1993

Economic welfare was reported in a study published in 1994 to have fallen markedly since the mid-1970s (Jackson and Marks, 1994). According to the authors, economic welfare needs to be adjusted for environmental damage, income inequality and the quality of life. They argue that conventional estimates of economic growth do not indicate the impact on people's quality of life of the depletion of natural resources, health, individual well-being, environmental quality, personal and collective security and the widening gap between rich and poor people from the mid-1970s to the mid-1990s.

This difficult economic climate did not prevent the Conservative government from embarking on a further review of local authority services. The reorganisation of local government due to take effect from April 1996 is the biggest shake-up of local services for 20 years. The new unitary authorities are smaller and their role is to enable rather than directly manage service provision.

Between 1981 and 1991, for example, the number of older people in local authority homes fell by about 20% while the numbers in private and voluntary homes rose by about 300%. By the early 1990s, the majority of children being looked after by local authorities were in the foster care of self-employed foster parents, who were being paid fees and expenses. One in three children in residential care were likely to be in voluntary or private provision (Warner, 1994). One claimed advantage of the shift to unitary authorities was the bringing together of housing and social services departments, although it will not be possible to evaluate the outcomes of this for some time. In some London boroughs, community care assessment and planning activities were already combined in the same local authority and even in the same department.

Additionally, Warner (1994) argues that

smaller social services authorities will find it easier to build effective local relationships with NHS Trusts on issues such as hospital discharges and provision of community health services. This is certainly likely to be the case with GPs. Up to 40% of the population will soon be served by GP fund holders controlling their own budgets and making their own purchasing decisions. It is difficult to see how large social services departments are any particular help in fostering the essentially local linkages with GPs and NHS Trusts.

The then President of the Association of Directors of Social Services (ADSS), Denise Platt, disagreed with Warner's comment that the size of the new unitary social services departments would not be significant, for several reasons. First, without special funding arrangements, at present not in prospect, authorities serving populations below a certain level would probably not be able to generate sufficient income to purchase the necessary services. Second, joint board arrangements between departments would become increasingly necessary but there was no certainty that they would be more economic, efficient and effective. Third, child protection systems would become more complex, with a need to co-ordinate over a wider range and a larger number of authorities and agencies. Platt quotes Sir William Utting, former Chief Inspector, Social Services Inspectorate, writing in the journal *ADSS News:* 'Structural change which fragments current responsibilities for PSS [personal social services] will harm the vulnerable people who need and use them.... partnership with parents and participation by users and carers will not simply take a back seat – they are unlikely to get into the auditorium' (Platt, Letter to *The Guardian*, 30 July 1994, p. 26).

The struggle between consumerist assumptions underlying policy and practice in the health and social care sector and the commitment of professionals in social work to an empowered practice is not likely to be resolved by the creation of unitary authorities in the local government reorganisation of the mid 1990s. As this book is being written, in the autumn of 1995, it is increasingly unlikely that even in the event of a change of political control in the general election of 1996 or 1997 these changes will be reversed. There are two major reasons for this: first, the restructuring of the relationship between the individual and the state, capital and labour, exemplified through the spread of share-holding in de-nationalised telephones and power utilities, is well-nigh irreversible; second, the centre of gravity of politics has shifted away from confrontation between the Conservative Party and a left-wing Labour Party, in the light of the drift of the latter towards policies that sit more squarely with social democracy. So, even in the event of a change of government, in the forseeable future the current infrastructure for, and direction of, community care policies and practices will probably be maintained rather than dismantled. Chapter 11 speculates on future political and policy options. Chapters 4 to 10 consider specific aspects of the personal social services, including in chapter 6 a more detailed examination of aspects of community care.

References and further reading

Access to Personal Files Act 1987, London: HMSO.
Adams, R. (1996) *Social Work and Empowerment*, London: BASW/Macmillan.
Adams, R. (1997) *Quality Social Work*, London: Macmillan.
Adler, R. and Dearling, A. (1986) Children's rights: a Scottish perspective, in Franklin, B. (ed.) *The Rights of Children*, 205–229, London: Blackwell.
Arnold, E. (1987) *Whose Child? Report of the Public Inquiry into the Death of Tyra Henry*, London: Borough of Lambeth.

Audit Commission (1986) *Making a Reality of Community Care,* London: HMSO.

Audit Commission (1989) *The Probation Service: Promoting Value for Money,* London: HMSO.

Beresford, P. and Croft, S. (1993) *Citizen Involvement: a Practical Guide for Change,* London: Macmillan.

Brindle, D. (1994) The purse-snatchers, *The Guardian,* 25 May.

Bynoe, I. (1995) Radical outlook, *Community Care,* no.1086, 14–20 September, 18.

Campbell, B. (1984) *Wigan Pier Revisited: Poverty and Politics in the 80s,* London: Virago.

Care Sector Consortium (1991) *National Occupational Standards for Working with Young Children and Their Families,* London; HMSO.

Care Sector Consortium (1992) *National Occupational Standards for Care,* London: HMSO.

Challis, L. (1990) *Organising Public Social Services,* London: Longman.

Children and Young Persons Act 1969, London: HMSO.

Clarke, J. (ed.) (1993) *A Crisis in Care? Challenges to Social Work,* London: Sage and Open University.

Clough, R. (1981) *Old Age Homes,* NISW Social Services Library no.42, London: Allen and Unwin.

Coulshed, V. (1990) *Management in Social Work,* London: Macmillan.

Criminal Justice Act 1982, London: HMSO.

Criminal Justice Act 1991, London: HMSO.

Cutler, T. and Waine, B. (1994) *Managing the Welfare State: the Politics of Public Sector Management,* Oxford; BERG.

Darvill, G. and Smale, G. (eds) (1990) *Partners in Empowerment: Networks of Innovation in Social Work,* London: NISW

Data Protection Act 1984, London: HMSO.

Department of Health (1991) *Implementing Community Care: Purchaser, Commissioner and Provider Roles,* London: HMSO.

Department of Health (1989a) *Working for Patients,* White Paper Cmnd 855, London: HMSO.

Department of Health (1989b) *Caring for People: Community Care in the Next Decade and Beyond,* Cmnd 849, London: HMSO.

Department of Health, Social Services Inspectorate (1991a) *Care Management and Assessment,* practitioners' guide, London: HMSO.

Department of Health, Social Services Inspectorate, Scottish Office Social Work Service Group (1991b) *Care Management and Assessment,* managers' guide, London: HMSO.

Department of Health and Social Security (1988) *Community Care: an Agenda for Action* (Griffiths Report), London: HMSO.

Dews, V. and Watts, J. (1994) *Review of Probation Officer Recruitment and Qualifying Training* (Dews Report) (unbound; Consultant's report), London.

Disabled Persons (Services, Consultation and Representation) Act 1986, London: HMSO.

Douglas, R. and Payne, C. (1991) *Learning About Caring: an Introductory Package for Staff Development in Residential and Day Care Work,* section B, Practice Guides 1–4, London, National Institute for Social Work.

Education Act 1981, London: HMSO.

Elcock, H. (1993) Local government, in Farnham D. and Horton S. (eds), *Managing the New Public Services,* 150–171, London: Macmillan.

Etzioni, A. (ed.) (1969) *The Semi Professions and their Organisation: Teachers, Nurses, Social Workers*, New York: Free Press.

Farnham, D. and Horton, S. (1993a) The new public service managerialism: an assessment, in Farnham, D. and Horton, S. (eds), *Managing the New Public Services*, 237–254, London: Macmillan.

Farnham, D. and Horton, S. (eds) (1993b) *Managing the New Public Services*, London: Macmillan.

Gladstone, F.J. (1979) *Voluntary Action in a Changing World*, London: Bedford Square Press.

Glennerster, H. and Midgely, J. (eds) (1991) *The Radical Right and the Welfare State*, Hemel Hempstead: Harvester Wheatsheaf.

Gray, J. (1995) The re-inventing of the NHS, *The Guardian*, 3 January.

Grimwood, C. and Popplestone, R. (1993) *Women, Management and Care*, London: Macmillan.

Harrison, S. and Hunter, D., (1994) *Rationing Health Care*, London: IPPR.

Hockey, J. and James, A. (1993) *Growing Up and Growing Old – Ageing and Dependency in the Life Course*, London: Sage.

Home Office (1988) *Punishment, Custody and the Community*, Cmnd 424, London: HMSO.

Jackson, T. and Marks, N. (1994) *Measuring Sustainable Economic Welfare – a Pilot Index 1950–1990,* London: NEFC.

Kanter, R.M. (1984) *The Change Masters,* London: Unwin.

King, R.D. and Morgan, R. (1976) *A Taste of Prison: Custodial Conditions for Trial and Remand Prisoners*, London: Routledge.

Kubler-Ross, E. (1981) *Living with Death and Dying*, Souvenir, London.

Le Grand, J. and Bartlett, W. (eds) (1993) *Quasi-Markets and Social Policy*, 1–12, London: Macmillan.

Levy, A. and Kahan, B. (1991) *The Pindown Experience and the Protection of Children: the Report of the Staffordshire Child Care Inquiry 1990*, Stafford: Staffordshire County Council.

Lewis, J. (1993) Developing the mixed economy of care: emerging issues for voluntary organisations, *Journal of Social Policy,* vol.22, no.2, 173–192.

Lewis, J., Bernstock, P. and Bovell, V. (1995), The Community Care Changes: Unresolved tensions in policy and issues in implementation, *Journal of Social Policy,* vol.24, no.1, 73–94.

Littlewood, J. (1992) *Aspects of Grief: Bereavement in Adult Life*, London: Routledge.

Local Authorities (Goods and Services) Act 1970, London: HMSO.

Local Government Act 1988, London: HMSO.

Local Government Finance Act 1982, London: HMSO.

McAllister, I. and Studlar, D.T. (1989) Popular versus elite views of privatization: the case of Britain, *Journal of Public Policy,* vol.9, no.2, 157–78.

McGrath, M. and Grant, G. (1992) Supporting 'Needs-led' services: Implications for planning and management systems (A case study in mental handicap services) *Journal of Social Policy*, vol. 21, Part 1, 71–97.

Mayo, M. (1994) *Communities and Caring: the Mixed Economy of Welfare*, Macmillan, London.

Mental Health Act 1983, London: HMSO.

Miliband, R. (1991) Reflections on the crisis of communist regimes, in Blackburn, R., 1991, *After the Fall,* London: Verso.

Mishra, R. (1990) *The Welfare State in Capitalist Society: Policies of Retrenchment and Maintenance in Europe, North America and Australia*, Hemel Hempstead: Harvester Wheatsheaf.

NHS and Community Care Act 1990, London: HMSO.

NHSTD (1993) *Developing Managers for Health and Social Care: Building Strategies for Shared Management Development using HSSM*, managers' and trainers' guide, Bristol: NHSTD.

NISW (1988b) *Residential Care: the Research Reviewed*, literature surveys commissioned by the Independent Review of Residential Care (Wagner Report Part II), London: HMSO.

Pearson, G. (1975) Making Social Workers: Bad promises and good omens, in Bailey, R. and Brake, M. (eds) *Radical Social Work*, London: Edward Arnold, 13–45.

Police and Criminal Evidence Act 1984, London: HMSO.

Prime Minister's Office (1991) *The Citizen's Charter: Raising the Standard*, Cmnd 1599, London: HMSO.

Race Equality Unit (1989) *Community Care: Race Dimension,* Duff, R. (ed.), REU/NISW, London.

Race Relations Act 1976, London: HMSO.

Redcliffe-Maud, Lord (chairman) (1969) *Royal Commission on Local Government in England 1966–69*, vol.1 (Report), Cmnd 4040, London: HMSO.

Registered Homes Act 1984, London: HMSO.

Report of the Inquiry into Child Abuse in Cleveland (1988), Cmnd 412, London: HMSO.

Samson, C. (1990) Inequality, the New Right and mental health care delivery in the United States in the Reagan era, *Critical Social Policy*, issue 29, autumn, 40–70

Satyamurti, C. (1981) *Occupational Survival: the Case of the Local Authority Social Worker*, Oxford: Blackwell.

Simpkin, M. (1979) *Trapped within Welfare*, Basingstoke: Macmillan

Smale, G. and Tuson, G. (1993) *Empowerment, Assessment, Care Management and the Skilled Worker*, London; HMSO.

Social Services Inspectorate (SSI) (1987) *From Home Help to Home Care: an Analysis of Policy, Resourcing and Service Management*, London: HMSO.

SSI (1988) *Managing Policy Change in Home Help Services*, London: HMSO.

SSI (1989) *Managing Home Care in Metropolitan Districts*, London: HMSO.

SSI (1990) *Inspecting Home Care Services: a Guide to the SSI Method*, London: HMSO.

SSI (1991) *Women in Social Services: a Neglected Resource*, London: HMSO.

Harrison , S. and Hunter, D. (1994) *Rationing Health Care* London: IPPR.

Taylor, D. (1989) Citizenship and social power, *Critical Social Policy,* issue 26, autumn, 19–31

Tomlinson, D.F. (1993) *No Longer Afraid: the Safeguard of Older People in Domestic Settings*, London: HMSO.

Ungerson, C. (1993) Caring and citizenship: a complex relationship, in Bornat, J., Pereira, C., Pilgrim, D. and Williams, F., *Community Care: a Reader*, 143–151, London: Macmillan and Open University.

United Nations Children's Fund (undated) *New Dimensions, Fair Conditions*, London: UNICEF.

User-centred Services Group (1993) *Building Bridges Between People Who Use and People Who Provide Services*, London: NISW.

Utting, W. (1992) *Children in the Public Care: a Review of Residential Child Care*, London: HMSO.

Waine, B. (1992) The voluntary sector: the Thatcher years, in Manning, N. and Page, R. (eds) *Social Policy Review 4,* 70–88, London: Social Policy Association.

Warner, N. (1994) Size doesn't matter, *The Guardian*, 27 July, 12–13.

Webb, R. and Tossell, D. (1991) *Social Issues for Carers: a Community Care Perspective,* London: Edward Arnold.

Webb, A.L., and Wistow, G. (1987) *Social Work, Social Care and Social Planning,* London: Longman.

Wertheimer, A. (ed.) *A Chance to Speak Out: Consulting Service Users and Carers about Community Care,* London: King's Fund Centre.

White Paper on *Caring for People* (1989), London: HMSO.

Whitfield, D. (1992) *The Welfare State,* London: Pluto Press.

Wilmott, P. (1978) *Consumers' Guide to the British Social Services,* 4th edn, Harmondsworth: Penguin.

Wilson, D. and Game, C. (1994) *Local Government in the United Kingdom,* Basingstoke: Macmillan.

PART TWO

Services for children and families

CHAPTER 4

Families

Efforts to prevent family break-up, the promotion of the unity of the family as a desirable goal, and consequently a focus on the family as the primary site for intervention by the state have been at the heart of government ideology for the personal social services since the 1960s. This chapter examines the aspects of the personal social services that focus on social work with the family as a whole (rather than on working separately with family members, whether children, young people or adults, as they move in or out of the family or contribute to the creation of a new one), as families form and reform.

Context of services for families

Many marriages break down and the number of divorces is increasing, the latter rising from 2.8 per 1000 in 1981 to 3.1 per 1000 in 1993, the highest rates in the European Union (Social Trends, 1996, p. 57). The rate of remarriage is also significant, and by 1992 the number of births outside marriage was almost a third (OPCS, 1995). As a consequence, some social work approaches focus on the family as a group and some on work with family members. Over the years, many adults come into contact with the personal social services as a consequence of separation or divorce, or because they are involved in fostering or adoption. The issue of family stability and the question of how far the personal social services should buttress so-called traditional family values remains as controversial in the 1990s as it was when the Seebohm Committee met in the 1960s.

Aspects of such measures to give social work support to families in the community are reminiscent of the efforts of the family caseworkers of the Charity Organisation Society (COS), who from its foundation in 1869 attempted to distinguish between families deemed incapable of helping themselves, and so not meriting charity, and those judged capable of self-help, for whom support should be provided. More than a century later, Patricia Morgan of the right-wing Institute of Economic Affairs argued that lone-parent benefits should be abolished, and financial incentives given for couples to stay together to bring up children (The ethnic time-bomb, *Sunday Express*, 13 August 1995, 1–2). This was in the wake of her report commenting that the government was actively discriminating against married couples and working fathers in favour of single parents (Morgan, 1995).

Psychologising people's problems

There was a consensus about the basis of social policy from the nineteenth century which supported the functions of the family and which, in the second half of the twentieth century, spans the major political parties (Rustin, 1979, p. 149). These policies accorded with the prevalence in social work of medico-treatment-based family casework. Woodroofe (1962, p. 119) describes how what she calls 'the psychiatric deluge' swept over social work in the USA from the 1920s, influenced by Mary Richmond's (1917) classic text emphasising a model of social casework in which diagnosis and treatment fused, and thence to Britain. Woodroofe notes, however, that British social work, in a society where the welfare state provided people with a measure of insurance against the grossest want and deprivation, was not as psychotherapeutically oriented as social work in the USA (Woodroofe, 1962, p. 147). This underpinned the treatment paradigm and provided explanations for the failure of the welfare state to eradicate poverty by suggesting that people's difficulties were caused by individual personality problems, were quasi-hereditary through the culture or poverty or the cycle of deprivation, rather than being products of societal, environmental or social policy factors. For much of the twentieth century, family-based social work theory and practice colluded, though probably not deliberately, with the economic and political and social policy justifications for keeping families intact.

The omnipotence of casework

Even practitioners who did not follow the reductionist tendency of psychologically based theories to reconcile explanations with a psychiatric world view, and in a different sense social workers, used social casework as the basis for making ever grander and more excessive claims. Barbara Wootton and her colleagues commented in the 1950s that 'modern definitions of "social casework" if taken at their face value, involve claims to powers which verge upon omniscience and omnipotence' (Wootton *et. al.*, 1959, p. 271). These claims were for the ability of professionals not just to change people, but also to improve their environments. Florence Hollis, in one of the standard textbooks on social casework at the time, defines the activity of the caseworker as to assist 'families and individuals in developing the capacity and the opportunity to lead personally satisfying and socially useful lives' (Hollis, 1948, p. 5). Wootton describes as the peak of pretentiousness Swift's assertion of casework as enabling a person 'to deal with the problems which he faces in his social environment' (quoted by Wootton from Kasius, 1954, p. 103).

The treatment paradigm

Attachment theories – emphasising the importance of the affectionate and emotional bond between two individuals – and their converse, theories of separation, formed a central strand informing approaches to all areas of social work and gathered momentum in the early 1960s. In the 1990s, the work of Vera Fahlberg (1981) has become accepted as authoritative, but a generation earlier it was research by Dr John Bowlby (1965) on the correlation between maternal deprivation and problem behaviour that reinforced the development of the treatment paradigm and, by stressing the importance of early socialisation and of the mother–child relationship within the family, justified a move towards community-based social work with children and their families. While Bowlby was criticised by subsequent researchers (Rutter, 1972), feminists and the Left, there was no significant breaching of his proposition of a positive correlation between the development of infants and early caring (Rustin, 1979, p. 151). The thrust of the treatment paradigm differs in minor ways in different areas of practice, but its basic ideology is unchanged. Here it is illustrated first in the area of delinquency and then as applied to work with problem families. As is summarised below, referred to again in chapter 5, and analysed in detail by Bottoms (1974, pp. 319–345), a complex process of interaction between political, social policy and professional interests led to arguments for family-based and community-based child care which were embodied in the Children and Young Persons Act 1969. The consensus among these advocates of this Act was not shared by critics of the treatment paradigm, whether inspired from a radical direction or from the political Right. David May (1971, pp. 361–362) has summarised the main assumptions of the treatment model, as it stood at that time, viewing it from the standpoint of criminology:

1. 'that explanations for delinquency are to be found in the behavioural and motivational systems of delinquents, and not in the law or its administration
2. that in some identifiable way delinquents are different from non-delinquents.' These differences are usually located 'in systems of norms and values, socialisation experiences or psychological disorders
3. that the delinquent is constrained and cannot ultimately be held responsible for his actions. The constraints might be physiological, psychological or sociological' and ... 'lead, almost inevitably, to delinquent conduct
4. that delinquent behaviour *per se* is not the real problem. It possesses significance only as a pointer to the need for intervention. It is the presenting symptom that draws attention to the more intractable disease.'

The pressure group Justice for Children criticised the social welfare approach of the juvenile courts, arguing that since judicial impartiality and fairness, particularly in sentencing, were severely hindered by the welfare approach, such 'treatment' could affect a child and his family negatively (Geach, 1978, p. 11).

The general hypothesis of the treatment paradigm was that delinquency could be attributed either to personality failure or to family circumstances, or to some combination of these factors. The tendency no longer to distinguish between so-called deprived and depraved children and young people was evident in the Report of the Advisory Council on the Treatment of Offenders (1962) and the Longford Report (Labour Party Study Group, 1964). The treatment paradigm framed delinquency as just one sign of the disease of poor upbringing. As Stott (1952) put it: since 'if delinquency is seen as part of the evil of unhappy childhood (and) if we prevent the latter, delinquency will also be prevented, as with the removal of the cause of a disease the symptoms disappear.'

The problem family: social democracy and social work

In the 1960s, social work focused on the 'problem family', a notion developed by the Ingleby Committee in 1960 (Report of the Committee on Children and Young Persons, 1960) and later by David Donnison, Peggy Jay and Margaret Stewart (1962), whose Fabian-inspired essays influenced the Longford Committee towards proposing a new family service; this aimed to provide social work for those maladjusted people who fell through the net of universalistic welfare. Delinquency, apparently, was simply a special form of deprivation (Labour Party Study Group, 1964, p. 17). In England and Wales the 1965 White Paper, *The Child, the Family and the Young Offender* (Home Office, 1965), and in Scotland the Kilbrandon Report (1964) followed this train of thought. The former was abortive, leading in England and Wales to fresh proposals in the 1968 White Paper *Children in Trouble* (Home Office, 1968) and a year later to the Children and Young Persons Act 1969, but Kilbrandon became the basis for the Social Work (Scotland) Act 1968.

Widespread assumptions about the character of the so-called 'normal' family in society shape the responses of policymakers, service-providing agencies and professionals in the personal social services. The family may be regarded as any primary living arrangement that caters for the development, education, upbringing and other needs of child and adult family members. A popular view is that a typical family consists of a married, white, heterosexual couple living with their two natural children. The reality is that a variety of family forms exists; many children are conceived, born and brought up by only one of their natural parents; many families break up and reform as adults and children enter and leave the household, once, twice or three times in a generation. In many communities, the reconstituted 'second' or 'third' family is the norm. The number of people who identify themselves as family members, but who live alone, almost doubled between 1961 and 1994–5 (Social Trends 1996, p. 50). At the same time, increased proportions of people cohabit without marrying, more women than ever work outside the family home, more households consist of adults from more than one ethnic background and more children are brought together in households with other previously un-related children.

The unequal distribution of wealth, income and power in society affects family members. Poverty, due to factors such as chronic un-employment and the high cost of housing, has a major impact on families, particularly where there are more dependants, such as children or older people. Women within households where there is an adult male may experience financial inequalities, masked by the total amount of income to the household. Whereas all families, whatever their composition and differences in terms of family members, should be treated equally and have equal rights to ser-vices, the reality is that many family members experience discrimi-nation and oppression. There has been growing awareness since the 1960s of longstanding problems associated with what is often termed domestic violence but is, in effect, criminal violence in the home. The origins of the Women's Aid movement, and the conse-quent creation of women's refuges in many parts of Britain, exem-plify self-help responses to this problem in recognition that in most violence in the home, men are the aggressors. Increased public awareness of criminal violence in the home has lent support to feminist arguments concerning the family as a locus of gender-based oppression.

Social policies tend to reflect the assumed rather than the actual nature of the family and the roles of family members, emphasising the largely gender-based divisions between domestic and paid work. Additionally, policies tend to push people who are not able-bodied working adults to the margins and to penalise older people, non-heterosexual couples, black and disabled people. The Social Security Act 1986 defines households as single-earner units. Housing legislation and provision is geared largely to meeting the needs of family groups in households, rather than single persons and lone parents with children. The NHS and Community Care Act 1990 operates on the assumption that relatives and friends, the bulk of whom are women, will act as informal carers and thereby fill gaps in state provision. The Major government has reinforced in the 1990s the Thatcherite insistence on the traditional role of the mother in the home, looking after the children while the father works to support them. Thus, government policy is reliant on the family as the major provider of community and child care services. The assertion by Tony Blair, leader of the Labour Party, that children brought up in a two-parent, stable family were likely to develop better than children brought up by a single parent indicates a convergence in this area between the ideologies of the two main political parties (*The Guardian*, 30 March, 1995).

Growing incidence of family break-up

The changing demography of the family could be regarded simply as evidence of other changes in society. However, given the commitment of the major political parties in Britain to various aspects of family policy as ways of addressing what are perceived as the benefits of keeping families together at all costs, it is unsurprising that law-making in this area has concentrated on promoting the family as the focus for the preventive and interventive work of the personal social services. For example, the Children Act 1989 is directed largely towards reinforcing parental responsibility as a contribution towards safeguarding the interests of the child. Much policy and practice in work with families focuses on the impact on family members, and children in particular, of rising rates of separation and divorce. Subsequently, the Child Support Act 1991 was a political response to the great increase in the numbers of single parent families living on income support, which increased from 330,000 in 1980 to 780,000 in 1989, and the decreasing proportion of these receiving maintenance from the other parent, from 50% in 1981–1982 to 23% in 1988–1989 (Hoggett, 1993, p. 86). The Child Support Agency (CSA) was set up to enforce payments in the light of the fact that court orders had been found to be ineffective in many cases. The CSA has reinforced the stigmatising of partnerships that are not permanent, in some cases increasing the financial hardship of couples who separate and divorce. It proved to be a well-nigh indefensible measure for the government, in view of its harsh impact on adults and, indirectly, children already experiencing the hardships and traumas of separation and divorce.

Legal basis for services for families

The Children Act 1989 provides the legal basis for the bulk of social work with children and families, and is the most comprehensive legislation affecting children and families in the second half of the twentieth century. The legal antecedents to the Children Act 1989 consisted of more than 20 items of legislation between the Children and Young Persons Act 1969 and the Children Act 1989. They fall into two categories: public law, which covers interventions by public authorities, and private law, which covers aspects not involving public authorities. Allen (1992, p. 3) categorises them thus:

Public law	Private law
Children and Young Persons Act 1969	Family Law Reform Act 1969
Children Act 1975	Guardianship of Minors Act 1971
Child Care Act 1980	Guardianship Act 1973
Foster Children Act 1980	Matrimonial Causes Act 1973
Children's Homes Act 1982	Children Act 1975
Criminal Justice Act 1982	Legitimacy Act 1976
Health and Social Services and	Domestic Proceedings and Magistrates'
Social Security Adjudications Act 1983	Courts Act 1978
Children and Young Persons	Child Abduction Act 1984
(Amendment) Act 1986	Child Abduction and Custody Act 1985
	Family Law Act 1986
	Family Law Reform Act 1987

In the 1980s, pressure for reform came from different sources and the distinction between public and private law became clear. The Report to the House of Commons Social Services Committee (1984), arising from the work of the Committee since 1982 in enquiring into children in care, recommended a review of the law regarding children and also the rationalisation of the legal framework of child care. The Review of Child Care Law (1985), the response of the Department of Health to the above proposals, was the basis for subsequent reforms. It led to the White Paper *The Law on Child Care and Family Services* (Home Office, 1987), which proposed a major overhaul of child care law. In parallel, the Law Commission 1984–1988 undertook a review of private law, involving four publications and a subsequent report, Review of Child Care Law: Guardianship and Custody (Law Commission, 1988). This recommended a similar overhaul of the law.

At the same time as the Children Act was being framed and implemented, concern about the quality of professional and family-based care for children came to a head with a number of scandals and inquiries, receiving wide coverage in the mass media. Chief among these was the crisis in 1987 in child protection work associated with events in Brent, which produced the inquiry report of 1985 (see document 4.), and in Cleveland, which led to the Report of the Inquiry into Child Abuse in Cleveland (1988).Within a few years there was a scandal over residential child care methods, which came to light in the inquiry into the Pindown regime (Levy and Kahan, 1991) (see document 6).

The Children Act 1989 embodies the principle that the welfare of the child, including child protection, should come before every other consideration in all work, decisions and court proceedings; where possible children should be looked after in the family; parents should have the fullest possible responsibility for their children; legal proceedings should be avoided wherever possible; all services for children purchased or provided by the authorities should be planned and delivered in partnership with adults holding parental responsibility.

The Children Act contains 108 sections and 15 schedules, organised in 12 parts. It brings together in one legal framework many aspects of public (involving public agencies) and private law (involving individuals and families) affecting parents and children. Apart from promoting the welfare of the child, it legislates in other important areas. Parents should share responsibility for their children until they reach 18 years of age and should be left to exercise this either until things go wrong or until they need help. Parental responsibility is the general term used to describe the philosophical and the practical basis for the relationship between parents, their children and the rest of society. It includes 'the collection of tasks, activities and choices which are part and parcel of looking after and bringing up a child' (Hoggett, 1993, p. 11). Parents who have parental responsibility can only lose this altogether if the child dies, or leaves the family through adoption or being freed for adoption, although an unmarried father may revert from being a parent with parental responsibility to simply being a parent (Hoggett, 1993, p. 9). In the event of problems, for example, if parents separate or divorce, most children still need meaningful contact with both their parents. Disputes between parents should be determined on the sole basis of what is in the best interests of the child. The wider family may have a significant role to play in contributing to the welfare of the child, and the state, through local authorities, should support parents rather than undermining them. Children at risk of suffering harm should be looked after by the local authority, where possible in partnership with parents and the family, and in any case until and unless children have found a new family. Where possible, children should exercise rights to take part in these processes and take as many decisions as possible for themselves.

The welfare checklist

The checklist of factors that the court and professionals must take into account when considering the welfare of the child includes the following: the ascertainable wishes and feelings of the child concerned (judged according to the child's age and understanding); the child's physical, emotional and educational needs; the likely effect on the child of any change in his or her circumstances; any harm that the child has suffered or is at risk of suffering; and the range of powers available to the court under this Act (Hoggett, 1993, pp. 75–79).

The British Nationality Act 1981 may be relevant where issues concerning the rights of a spouse to stay in Britain are concerned (Brayne and Martin, 1993, p. 286); divorce may affect the rights of a non-naturalised person to stay in Britain. A married person may seek a protection order from a court under the Domestic Proceedings and Magistrates' Courts Act 1978 (Brayne and Martin, 1993, p. 288).

Differences between England, Wales and Scotland

The responsibilities of parents are complicated by many different practices in different parts of the UK. In general, the law in England, Wales and Scotland has moved towards abolishing differences between formal and informal arrangements, whether or not people are married.

The notion of parenthood

Developments in genetic engineering, surrogate parenting and artificial insemination have affected the notion of what it is to be a parent, a mother, or a father. A woman may give birth to a child produced from an embryo from another woman. From the standpoint of the child and the women involved, it is important to ascertain who is the 'real' mother. It may also be difficult to determine who the father is, for example, when the mother has been artificially inseminated, depending on who is living with her at the time, and whether it is known from whom the sperm was donated. These two issues are different, since the mother who conceives, carries and bears the child is physically bound to the baby, regardless of the genetic origins of the child (Hoggett, 1993, p. 48). Some of these issues are addressed in the Human Fertilisation and Embryology Act 1990, which makes the concepts of mothering and fathering more flexible to take account of progress in the technology of fertilisation and transplant.

Approaches to work with families

Four main types of approach exist: protection, care, therapy and advocacy (Fig. 4.1). Protection entails aspects in which the prevention or minimisation of harm to the family, or family member, is uppermost; care consists of nurturing or supportive activities; therapy involves approaches directed towards bringing about change in one or more aspects of the experience and functioning of family members and/or the family; advocacy refers to a range of activities

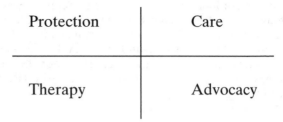

Protection	Care
Therapy	Advocacy

Figure 4.1 The four main types of approach to work with families

in which another person, another group or the family member concerned takes action on behalf of the person, problem or situation.

Protective work

Protective work may be undertaken with families whose members experience loss or abuse. Aspects of protection from abuse are considered in relation to children in chapter 5. This section examines work with families experiencing and responding to losses, including separation and divorce.

Working with families undergoing losses and transitions

People undergoing losses and changes tend to deal with them as they would deal with any disruptive life experience, in a number of ways, through the following stages: immobilisation, in which the person feels paralysed; minimisation, which involves the person making light of the event; depression, which may affect adolescents and older people in particular; letting go, which involves accepting the situation for its reality; testing, in which the person begins to try out the new situation; search for meaning, which involves the person reaching for an understanding of how things are different now; internalisation, which involves the person incorporating into her or his psyche and behaviour the changes that have occurred (Herbert, 1988, pp. 109–110).

People tend to pass through these general stages in different ways. The traumas of loss and bereavement, perhaps of a child, a partner or another close relative, will induce a variety of responses depending on the circumstances and mental states of those involved. Accidents involving loss of mobility, or a loss due to the separation of the parents or divorce, may produce similar traumas, which will require working through. Research suggests that children in families undergoing separation or divorce can experience immediate as well as longer term problems (Parkinson, 1987, pp. 48–52).

The formation of new families as new relationships develop can involve the traumas associated with change, as families are reconstituted. Sometimes, a single parent will continue to take on the tasks of running the household. A diversity of patterns of family care, such as a gay couple bringing up children, amplifies the need for professional services – not because such differences are inherently a problem, but because sometimes poverty, the nurture of children or the maintenance of gender and behaviour boundaries would benefit from agency support. Substitute care such as nurseries, playgroups or child minders, in the statutory, voluntary or private sectors, may be necessary if parents work full-time and the children are young.

Work with separating and divorcing parents

Social workers have a role to play in dealing with the impact of separation and divorce, particularly on children. Where parents are agreed about arrangements for themselves and for the children, cases of separation and divorce are not contested through the courts. The Children Act 1989 requires that arrangements for the upbringing and welfare of the children should be examined and the powers of the Act used where the circumstances require it, in order to meet the best interests of the child. The private law orders of the Children Act 1989 (Section 8 orders), which are different from the public law order used by authorities to protect children from harm, can be used as part of family proceedings. These are proceedings under High Court jurisdiction regarding children. Probation officers provide court welfare services, involving reporting to the Courts on how the interests of the child can best be met, in situations where separating or divorcing parents cannot agree (James and Wilson, 1986; James and Hay, 1993). In addition, informal mediation between couples may be carried out by voluntary mediation or conciliation services. Mediation is the process by which couples who cannot agree meet on neutral territory and, with the help of a third party, work out their own arrangements, retaining their own authority and responsibility for reaching and making their own decisions (Roberts, 1988, p. 3).

Care approaches: work in family centres

Voluntary agencies and self-help groups and organisations have contributed to residential and community-based child care provision. This trend increased in the 1960s following Seebohm and in the 1970s after the Children and Young Persons Act 1969. Family centres and family resource centres catered for younger children, and intermediate treatment facilities (after 1974 when the relevant sections of the 1969 Act were implemented) catered for young people, in huge, largely irrelevant lists. In the Yorkshire Region, 'of 1038 registered facilities in the initial Scheme at its publication in July 1973, there were 326 civic and 288 voluntary youth clubs, 228 uniformed groups including 111 scout and 55 guide groups, 68 activity groups including 24 sports clubs, 55 educational facilities including 15 FE centres, and no less than 15 residential adventure and sea voyage facilities. Only 11 of the remaining facilities were identifiable as mainstream social work, being provided by community homes. There was not a single facility run by a field social worker in the entire scheme!' (Adams, 1988, p. 179). Bob Holman (1988, pp. 188–189) compared a sample of voluntary and local authority centres with prevention as their objective. The local authority family centres typically were large, well equipped and well staffed, providing facilities for a larger area and catering for users referred by statutory agencies, and providing a service for a major client group, such as an attendance unit for poor school attendance, or intermediate treatment for offenders, or day attendance for mothers with young children on the abuse register, or who were diagnosed as experiencing mental health problems. The centres were an integral part of social services provision. Consequently, there was relatively little space for unqualified volunteers and local community involvement in the running of the centres, or with power to change them. Two of the statutory family centres were based in council houses and had more scope for neighbourhood involvement. This did not lessen their role in catering for people who were referred, but it indicated that their role overlapped with facilities in the voluntary sector.

Holman argues that the existence of voluntary projects should not free statutory authorities from their duty to provide preventive services (op. cit., p. 191). But Holman identifies three distinctive ways in which projects in the voluntary sector can contribute: through skills in using local resources, often having to manage on relatively slender budgets; through providing help without stigmatising people; through being strategically placed to promote the work of prevention, by providing activities that relieve people's stress without acting as though there was a crisis. At one extreme, voluntary projects that Holman studied provided services which helped to improve the coping skills of families without making people feel they were failing, while at the other they enabled people to take part collectively in small-scale community action. Also, voluntary projects often acted as allies of people already involved with statutory agencies (op. cit., pp. 191–193).

Therapeutic approaches: working with the family as a system

Much work with the family as a group is informed by systems theories. A strong tradition of family therapy growing largely from systems theories has developed in Britain and the USA since the 1960s, represented by such practitioners as John Burnham (1986) and Sue Walrond-Skinner (1976, 1981). Systemic work with the family regards the family as a system and family members as its subsystems, elements or sub-units. The system is open, in the sense that family members relate to other individuals and family systems. A change, loss or problem arising that affects one person is regarded in terms of its effect on the whole system. The strengths of this approach are that it focuses attention on the whole rather than attributing blame to one person, such as blaming the parents for the problems of the children. It also helps to examine the context in which the family operates, i.e. the connection with other family systems and also the wider social systems within which the family is located. For example, problems of poverty, housing and unemployment may impact on the family and affect the behaviour of one or more of its members, as well as how he or she feels. A further dynamic concerns the need to go beyond identifying specific behaviour by the parents as the cause of subsequent behaviour by the children. Research evidence indicates that the general family climate in the system as a whole is a more predictive factor than, for example, behaviour of one of the parents at a specific time. Finally, it helps if the systems approach can be used to direct the attention of family members, and therefore focus the work, on the present and planning for the future, rather than examining the past in great detail. The Milan school – often described as systemic – structural therapy (Minuchin, 1974) and the strategic approach (Haley, 1976) are among other approaches.

From the early 1970s in Britain, critical sociologists influenced the trend of therapeutic work with families (Pearson, 1974). Some therapists have worked to redress imbalances in power between therapist and client. Also, while there is a balance to be struck between identifying significant features of the context in which problems arise, including the past, and ways forward from the present, it is also important to enable family members to address their present circumstances and gain control for the future over the factors affecting them. An approach that has been found helpful in this respect is brief therapy (Berg, 1993). This goes further than simply maintaining a balance between a view of the past and a view of the present. It refuses to allow examination of the past and simply directs questions towards what family members would like to happen, and then focuses on how plans may be made to enable them to achieve that hope or expectation.

Systems theory must be viewed sceptically since it has not lived up to the three claims that might have been made for it: to provide a unified profession of social work with a basis for practice, to provide a general theory to underpin social work practice, and to enable a variety of approaches to social work to be integrated (Payne, 1994, p. 9). Payne argues that part of the retreat from grand claims made for systems theory as a solution to problems of social work is because first, one response to criticisms of generic social work has been a return to specialisation in terms of client groups, and second, 'the scenario of the 1990s is one of mainstream social work becoming, if anything, more conservative, procedural and managerial, in effect returning to its historical role of helping individuals as opposed to achieving radical social change through systemic action' (op. cit., p. 10). Payne instances *The Essential Social Worker* by Martin Davies (1981).

On the positive side, Payne draws attention to the fact that a systems approach is not a unitary approach; a unitary approach may or may not be based on systems theory. Further, 'thinking systematically means thinking creatively, laterally, in patterns and looking for alternative ways of reaching common goals ... hopefully a systems perspective will result in more strategic changes being made to social work practice, such as less reliance on individual case work, more attention to team, group and community based ways of working, and the creative use of residential care not just as residual or optional approaches, but as valid strategies' (Payne, 1994, p. 20).

Advocacy approaches

Professional advocacy, peer advocacy or self-advocacy by family members may be appropriate as a means of countering the problems of discrimination that some, such as lone parent families, families with black members or migrants, travellers or refugees may encounter. Travellers, migrants and refugees minority groups possess distinctive cultures and traditions. The difficulties they experience in obtaining education, health and social services are made worse by their mobility. Refugees often occupy substandard housing when they arrive in Britain. Social workers have been involved with the arrival in Britain and the resettlement of many refugees, notably Ugandan Asian and Vietnamese people. Language and cultural differences may make it difficult to ascertain, for example, what mental health problems exist among them. Subsequently, work with them needs to address their individual needs and take up issues of discrimination and oppression on their behalf. Travellers often live on sites that lack basic facilities and are dirty and unsafe. The more mobile they are, the greater the health and social problems they experience (Pahl and Vaile, 1988, pp.

211–212). The vulnerability of travellers to eviction or housing in substandard sites by local authorities, with antagonism towards travellers in general fanned by mass media coverage of new age travellers, has been increased by the Criminal Justice and Public Order Act 1994. This measure gave the police enhanced powers to deal with new age travellers, but it may be used also to oppress other travellers.

Addressing criminal violence against women

Increasing attention has been paid to growing violence against women, especially under 30 (Social Trends 1996, p. 164) – known euphemistically as domestic violence – since the 1960s, stimulated by the women's movement and by the growth of women's organisations and groups, such as rape crisis centres, women's aid and survivors of sexual abuse. A continuum of oppression exists, from sexual harassment and obscene phone calls to attempted rape, rape, father–daughter incest, sexual assaults at work or at home, threatened and actual physical violence (Bart and Moran, 1993). Many aspects of women's experiences have been gathered through mutual aid and self-help activity, and passed on to different agencies – police, lawyers, social workers – for their implications for the ways services are organised and delivered to be taken up (see chapter 5 for a discussion of responses to child abuse). There is much scope for agencies to extend understanding of the impact on the individual of threatened and actual violence and improve their responses to violence and attempted violence against women. The police are increasingly willing to become involved in criminal violence in the home, since they gained powers to compel the spouse of a defendant to give evidence, under the Police and Criminal Evidence Act 1984.

Work with families with black members

A common, and valid, criticism of many texts on social work, social care and social policy is that they are ethnocentric, in that they give weight to the views and experiences of a dominant ethnic group at the expense of others. An authoritative guide to education and training materials designed to combat racism identifies three kinds of Eurocentrism (a focus on white European people): exclusion, or ignoring the existence of black families; tokenism, or adding black families as though with an afterthought; pathology, which involves describing and interpreting them 'as inherently disintegrating and problematic. Many texts indulge in crude cultural stereotypes in which black families are seen as strange, different and inferior

... based on a frozen view of black cultures. The "norm" against which black families are, implicitly or explicitly, judged is white. Indeed, the "norm" presents a myth of the good or ideal family which is white, nuclear, middle-class, heterosexual, male-dominated and able-bodied' (Gambe *et al.*, 1992, p. 22).

Bandana Ahmad (1989) identifies two major ways in which responses to black children and their families may be structured by racism: the punitive and cohesive approach and the liberal or safe approach. Although Ahmad implies rather than uses the terms punitive and cohesive, she refers to social workers who 'do not hesitate to remove black children from their families, who, according to them, are not suitable parents, or whose child care practices are seen as sub-standard'. In the liberal approach, she identifies social workers who are so keen not to be labelled as racist 'that they tend to shy away from their duties of protecting the black child from abuse'.

While the general legislative framework of the Children Act 1989 provides a progressive welfarist approach, Jack and Stepney (1995, p. 27) suggest that it cannot resolve a number of longstanding conflicts, between the state, the family, the individual parent and the child. In the face of complex problems, it is not surprising that examples of good partnership and service user involvement are quite scarce (op. cit., p. 36). They instance Family Group Conferences in Gwynedd, in which the extended family is given responsibility for planning a child's care. Again, they point to respite care for disabled children, in which the most successful schemes provide good quality, local child care, on demand – within certain limits – with professionals *not* acting as gatekeepers of the service (op. cit., p. 36).

Issues in work with families

The knowledge base informing work with families remains problematic. This is due in part to conflicts in ideology about what constitutes an adequate, effective family and partly to unresolved debates about the values that should inform services for families. Although much government policy is alleged to be directed towards preserving the family, the incidence of family change, breakup and re-making is higher nowadays than it has been. At the same time, relatively little attention is given to the theories about the nature and lives of families (Herbert, 1988, p. 37) and also to critical research into family life, which is sensitive to issues of class, gender and ethnicity, to mention some among many dimensions of division and oppression.

The achievements of legislative changes such as the Children Act are undermined by the trajectory of Government social policies. In Parton's (1994) view, the Audit Commission's (1994) review of services for children and families identifies the shortcomings of poor planning, co-ordination and wastage of health and social services resources in the wake of the Children Act 1989, but fails to respond to them adequately. First, it does not address the fact that children's services are experiencing difficulties not because needs simply are not being met, but because, given social workers' multiple accountabilities for their decisions – to children, to other family members including parents, to colleagues in other agencies such as the police, and increasingly to the courts – there are increasing tensions in the work between these different interests. Second, the report assumes that risk assessment can be made precise and quantifiable, by supplying guidance to social services on risk management and criteria for child protection investigations; but Parton notes that 'all forms of risk assessment contain imponderables and are highly contested'. Third, the dimensions of need are also contested. Fourth, no amount of strategic planning of health and social services can compensate for the worsening material conditions of many of the poorest families. Parton draws on the DSS statistics which demonstrate that whereas the average family's real income increased by 36% between 1979 and 1990, that of the poorest families declined by 14% (DSS, 1992). While the principle of redirecting resources from child protection is laudable, without major changes in social and economic policies neither families nor professionals can solve the problems that remain (Parton, 1994, p. 18).

Practitioners may seek solutions to these problems by developing further expertise. But the risk is that thereby they accumulate professional power at the expense of the client. There is a danger of therapeutic teams 'becoming so obsessed with their own processes that the interventions with families only represent the latest strategy in internal team rivalry. The team may enjoy power and influence, become "hooked" on this, and simply seek more at the expense of the humanity of their therapy' (Dale *et al.*, 1986, p. 209).

References and further reading

Adams, R. (1988) Finding a way in: youth workers and juvenile justice, in Jeffs, T. and Smith, M. (eds), *Welfare and Youth Work Practice*, 171–86, Basingstoke: Macmillan.

Advisory Council on the Treatment of Offenders (1962), *Non-Residential Treatment of Offenders Under 21*, London: HMSO.

Ahmad, B. (1989) Protecting black children from abuse, *Social Work Today*, 8 June.

Allen, N. (1992) *Making Sense of the Children Act: a Guide for the Social and Welfare Services*, London: Longman.

Audit Commission (1994) *Seen but Not Heard: Coordinating Community Child Health and Social Services for Children in Need*, London: HMSO.

Bart, P.B. and Moran, E.G. (1993) *Violence Against Women: the Bloody Footprints*, London: Sage.

Berg, I.K. (1993) *Family Preservation: a Brief Therapy Workbook*, London: BT Press.

Bottoms, A.E. (1974) On the decriminalisation of English juvenile courts, in Hood, R. (ed.), *Crime, Criminology and Public Policy: Essays in Honour of Sir Leon Radzinowicz*, 319–345, London: Heinemann.

Bowlby, J. (1965) *Child Care and the Growth of Love*, Harmondsworth: Pelican.

Brayne, H. and Martin, G. (1993) *Law for Social Workers*, 3rd edn, London: Blackstone Press.

Burnham, J. (1986) *Family Therapy*, London: Routledge.

Central Statistical Office (1982), *Social Trends 13,* London: HMSO.

Child Abduction Act 1984, London: HMSO.

Child Abduction and Custody Act 1985, London: HMSO.

Child Care Act 1980, London: HMSO.

Child Support Act 1991, London: HMSO.

Children Act 1975, London: HMSO.

Children Act 1989, London: HMSO.

Children and Young Persons (Amendment) Act 1986, London: HMSO.

Children and Young Persons Act 1969, London: HMSO.

Children's Homes Act 1982, London: HMSO.

Criminal Justice Act 1982, London: HMSO.

Criminal Justice and Public Order Act 1994, London: HMSO.

Dale, P., Davies, M., Morrison T. and Waters, J. (1986), *Dangerous Families: Assessment and Treatment of Child Abuse*, London: Tavistock.

Davies, M. (1981) *The Essential Social Worker*, London: Heinemann/Community Care.

Department of Health (1987) *The Law on Child Care and Family Services*, London: HMSO.

DHSS (1985) *Review of Child Care Law*, London: HMSO.

Domestic Proceedings and Magistrates' Courts Act 1978, London: HMSO.

Donnison, D., Jay, P. and Stewart, M. (1962) *The Ingleby Report: Three Critical Essays* (Fabian Research Series 231), London: Fabian Society.

DSS (1992) *Households Below Average Income 1979–1990/94*, London: HMSO.

Fahlberg, V. (1981) *Attachment and Separation*, London: British Association of Adoption and Fostering.

Family Law Act 1986, London: HMSO.

Family Law Reform Act 1969, London: HMSO.

Family Law Reform Act 1987, London: HMSO.

Foster Children Act 1980, London: HMSO.

Gambe, D., Gomes, J., Bijaykapur, B.J., Rangel, M. and Stubbs, P. (1992) *Improving Practice for Children and Families: a Training Manual*, Leeds: CCETSW.

Geach, H. (1978) Justice or Welfare? *Youth in Society*, no.31, 11.

Guardianship Act 1973, London: HMSO.

Guardianship of Minors Act 1971, London: HMSO.

Haley, J. (1976) *Problem Solving Therapy*, New York and London: Harper Colophon.

Hanvey, C. and Philpot, T. (eds) (1994) *Practising Social Work*, London: Routledge.

Herbert, M. (1988, reprinted 1992) *Working with Children and their Families*, Exeter: BPCC, Wheatons.

Hoggett, B. (1993) *Parents and Children: the Law of Parental Responsibility*, 4th edn, London: Sweet and Maxwell.

Hollis, F. (1948) *Social Casework in Practice*, New York: Family Service Association of America.

Holman, B. (1988) *Putting Children First: Prevention and Child Care*, Basingstoke: Macmillan.

Home Office (1965) *The Child, the Family and the Young Offender*, White Paper, Cmnd 2742, London: HMSO.

Home Office (1968) *Children in Trouble*, White Paper, Cmnd. 3601, London: HMSO.

Home Office (1987) *The Law on Child Care and Family Services*, White Paper, London: HMSO.

Hood R. (ed.) (1974) *Crime, Criminology and Public Policy: Essays in Honour of Sir Leon Radzinowicz*, London: Heinemann.

Human Fertilisation and Embryology Act 1990, London: HMSO.

Jack, G. and Stepney, P. (1995) The Children Act 1989 – protection or persecution? Family support and child protection in the 1990s, *Critical Social Policy,* issue 43, summer, 26–39.

James, A.L. and Hay, W. (1993) *Court Welfare in Action*, Hemel Hempstead: Harvester Wheatsheaf.

James, A.L. and Wilson, K. (1986) *Couples, Conflict and Change: Social Work with Marital Relationships*, London: Tavistock.

Jeffs, T. and Smith. M. (eds) *Welfare and Youth Work Practice*, Basingstoke: Macmillan.

Kasius, C. (ed.) (1954) *New Directions in Social Work*, New York: Harper.

Kilbrandon Report (1964) *Children and Young Persons: Scotland,* Cmnd 2306, Edinburgh: HMSO.

Labour Party Study Group (1964) *Crime – a Challenge to Us All* (Longford Report), London: Labour Party.

Law Commission (1988) *Review of Child Care Law: Guardianship and Custody,* London: Law Commission.

Legitimacy Act 1976, London: HMSO.

Levy, A. and Kahan, B. (1991) *The Pindown Experience and the Protection of Children: the Report of the Staffordshire Child Care Inquiry, 1990*, Stafford: Staffordshire County Council

Matrimonial Causes Act 1973, London: HMSO.

May, D. (1971) Delinquency control and the treatment model: some implications of recent legislation, *British Journal of Criminology*, vol.11, no.4, 359–370.

Minuchin, S. (1974) *Families and Family Therapy*, London: Tavistock.

Morgan, P. (1995) Farewell to the Family? London: Institute of Economic Affairs.

NHS and Community Care Act 1990, London: HMSO.

OPCS (1995) *Conceptions in England and Wales*, London: OPCS.

Pahl, J. and Vaile, M. (1988) Health and health care among travellers, *Journal of Social Policy*, vol.17, no.2, 195–213.

Parkinson, L. (1987) *Separation, Divorce and Families*, London: BASW/Macmillan.

Parry, N., Rustin, M. and Satyamurti, C. (eds) (1979) *Social Work, Welfare and the State*, London: Edward Arnold.

Parton, N. (1994) A lost opportunity, *Community Care*, 21–27 July, no.1026, 18.

Payne, C. (1994) The Systems Approach in Hanvey, C. and Philpot, T., *Practising Social Work,* London: Routledge.

Pearson, G. (1974) Prisons of Love: the reification of the family in family therapy, in Armistead, N. (ed.), *Reconstructing Social Psychology*, Harmondsworth: Penguin.

Police and Criminal Evidence Act 1984, London: HMSO.

Report of the Advisory Council on the Treatment of Offenders (1962) *Non-Residential Treatment of Offenders under 21*, London: HMSO.

Report of the Committee on Children and Young Persons (1960) (Ingleby Report), Cmnd 1191, London: HMSO.

Report of the Committee on One Parent Families (1974), Cmnd 5629 (Finer Report), London: HMSO.

Report of the Inquiry into Child Abuse in Cleveland (1988), Cmnd 412, London: HMSO.

Report to the House of Commons Social Services Committee (1984), enquiring into children in care, London: HMSO.

Richmond, M. (1917, reprinted 1925) *Social Diagnosis*, New York: Russell Sage Foundation.

Roberts, M. (1988) *Mediation in Family Disputes*, Aldershot: Wildwood House.

Rustin, M. (1979) Social work and the family, in Parry, N., Rustin, M. and Satyamurti, C. (eds) *Social Work, Welfare and the State*, 140–160, London: Edward Arnold.

Rutter, M. (1972) *Maternal Deprivation Reassessed*, 8–21, Harmondsworth: Penguin.

Sibley, D. (1981) *Outsiders in Urban Societies,* Oxford: Basil Blackwell.

Social Security Act 1986, London: HMSO.

Social Security Adjudications Act 1983, London: HMSO.

Social Trends 26 (1996), London: HMSO.

Social Work (Scotland) Act 1968, Edinburgh: HMSO.

Stott, D.H. (1952) *Saving Children From Delinquency*, London: London University Press.

Walrond-Skinner, S. (1976) *Family Therapy: the Treatment of Natural Systems*, London: Routledge and Kegan Paul.

Walrond-Skinner, S. (ed.) (1981) *Developments in Family Therapy: Theories and Applications since 1948*, London: Routledge.

Woodroofe, K. (1962) *From Charity to Social Work in England and the United States*, London: Routledge and Kegan Paul.

Wootton, B., Seal, V.G. and Chambers, R. (1959) *Social Science and Social Pathology*, London: Allen and Unwin.

CHAPTER 5

Children and young people

This chapter focuses on aspects of community-based work with children and young people; it deals with child abuse and child protection, some of the main approaches to work with children, and some key issues that arise. Group care of children and youth justice are dealt with in chapters 8 and 10 respectively.

Context of services for children and young people

The child care service was established formally by the Children Act 1948, following the Curtis Report (Report of the Care of Children Committee, 1946). But the status of childhood, like the maintenance of a balance between acting on behalf of children to protect them and promoting their rights to an autonomous position (see the introduction to Franklin (1986) for a discussion of this), has always been somewhat precarious.

A critical appreciation of the history of childhood necessitates locating childhood, and responses to children, in their economic and political context (Gillis, 1974). Aries (1962) and Plumb (1973) have located changing conceptions of childhood, particularly as a so-called inferior and immature status, and 'adolescence' as inherently problematic, in Western Europe and Britain in particular, in the context of wider shifts occurring in society. Linda Pollock (1987) has called this into question. Pollock contributes to a body of evidence casting doubt on the sweeping generalisation of Aries that childhood did not exist as a concept prior to the seventeenth century, in that as soon as children were able to leave the nursery they entered the adult world, including the world of work. Pollock emphasises the continuity between previous and present approaches to parenting. She points to the need for the analysis of the complex relationship between themes of change and those of continuity in studying the history of childhood and parenting. Hoyles (1979) also shows how the views and experiences of children themselves add insights to such research.

These wider debates apart, successive laws over the past 150 years have undeniably given children a place in society as dependants legally entitled to nurturing and schooling up to adulthood; they have extended children's rights to protection from the grossest forms of abuse and exploitation, such as through child labour and prostitution; and they have encouraged, initially through the voluntary sector, the development of preventive as well as interventive work to 'save' children. From the mid-nineteenth century, some children were 'rescued' from poverty and deprivation by philanthropists such as Dr Barnardo, founder of what is now Barnardo's, and Reverend Stephenson, founder of National Children's Homes. The religious and reformative connotations of terms such as 'save' and 'rescue' were relevant to these philanthropic endeavours, which bore fruit in organisations that have changed much, but in the 1990s still provide specialist child care services, many of which are now purchased by many local authorities. Mary Carpenter (1851) campaigned successfully for the creation of explicitly child-focused residential institutions for the nurturing and disciplining of children through the Reformatory Schools (Youthful Offenders) Act 1854 and Industrial Schools and Reformatory Schools Act 1857 (Heywood, 1959, p. 47). Such efforts in the 1850s to separate children from adult prisoners by housing them in reformatories contributed to the establishment of special courts for juveniles in 1908. Efforts to raise the age of criminal responsibility bore fruit in the Children and Young Persons Act 1969.

However, the customising of institutions to the needs of children and young people has its down side; the impetus towards controlling children and young people is evident in measures in 1994 to create tough custodial measures specifically designed to deal with persistent young offenders (see chapter 10). Unfortunately for children, perhaps, measures to care for them in the early nineteenth century were not ideal. More often than not, they embodied workhouse-style regimes in large warehouse-like residential institutions, often mirroring the arrangements for life and labour made by mill owners or manufacturers. More than 150 years later, the low priority given to meeting the distinctive needs of children and young people is evident in the fact that fifteen-year-old children are still being locked up alongside adults in prisons, such as Hull prison (*Hull Daily Mail,* 28 July 1995).

In the nineteenth century, child rescue was seen as a means of countering the effects of urban degeneration. Rescue could involve holidays in the country, or the more drastic step of compulsory emigration. In the succeeding century, more than 130,000 children were sent to Canada, Australia, Africa and New Zealand, an upheaval often involving great personal trauma, as a means of relieving those in Britain of the cost of keeping them and providing those in the colonies with cheap labour. The policy of 'emigration' – offenders were transported for crimes in previous generations – persisted until the late 1960s. The widespread exploitation and abuse of these children has only recently begun to be extensively documented (Bean and Melville, 1990).

The emergent institutions for socialising children – orphanages, schools, reformatories – required staffing, and this development was furthered by educated women of the late nineteenth century seeking emancipated yet socially acceptable roles as teachers and social workers (Platt, 1969). Philanthropists like Mrs Pardiggle in Dickens' *Bleak House*, who harangued poor families with the scriptures in one hand, set out to inculcate the spirit of self-help in parents whose children could be viewed as able to be saved from the neglect and corruption of family and neighbourhood and from urban degeneration, preferably by removal to the cleansing atmosphere of the countryside (Carlebach, 1970, pp. 24, 60–3; Stedman Jones, p. 286). Economic pressures forced many women into domestic and caring jobs in orphanages and child care establishments. Social changes in the roles and expectations of women heightened their motivation to seek outlets from the household and independence through such work (Hobsbawm, 1995, pp. 215–216). A massive expansion in employment opportunities for women occurred with the growth of bureaucracies supporting services for people. In Britain, the numbers of women employed in national and local government increased from 7,000 in 1881 to 76,000 in 1911 (op. cit., p. 201). The Edwardian era witnessed the growth of boys' clubs as part of the movement to divert children and young people from trouble by keeping them off the streets, as well as the enormously popular birth of the scout movement, in a period when nationalism, imperialism and the aspiration to build a strong, healthy young generation at home were factors that converged in the arms race with Germany which led up to the outbreak of war in 1914. In a review of Cooter (1992), Pringle (1993) asserts the need to acknowledge the significant academic and popular influence of 'national efficiency', with its racist assumptions, on the development of child care policy and practice. He notes the need to consider the contribution to this of the requirements of capitalism.

Child abuse

The second half of the twentieth century has seen debates about the protection of children given two new twists: by research on the damaging consequences for children of parental separation and divorce (see chapter 4) and by the growing attention paid to incidents of child abuse whether emotional, physical or sexual.

Although in most Western Countries, including Britain and the USA, there is a general prohibition on sexual activities between adults and children, there is not universal abhorrence of this, as is demonstrated by evidence of paedophilia through the British Paedophile Exchange, and through cases of child abuse coming to light through professional agencies, inquiries and the courts. Sexual abuse of children is not specified in British criminal law of sexual offences, although a number of different Acts apply, the most serious of which is that forbidding sexual acts of intercourse with a minor, i.e. a child less than the age of informed consent (for girls this is 16 and for boys there is no lower age limit for heterosexual intercourse, save that in law a boy under 14 is held to be incapable of it: for homosexuals it is an offence when one partner is under 21, since he is not considered to be legally capably of consenting before that age to such a relationship) (La Fontaine, 1990, pp. 22–23).

Child sexual abuse involves the misuse of power by one person over another. It refers mainly to 'the activities of adults who use children for their sexual gratification' (op. cit., p. 41). Sexual abuse includes bodily contact of all kinds, such as fondling, genital stimulation, oral and/or anal intercourse, and may also include suggestive behaviour such as exhibitionism or sexual innuendo (op. cit., p. 41). Reference to the people living in a household as a family cloaks the uneven and unequal distribution of power between individual members of the household. This applies not only between children and adults but also between younger and older, male and female children. Abuse between related children is termed incest. The criminal law distinguishes between incest and other criminal offences. Debate occurs over the common assertion that people living with an abuser, typically women living with an abusing man, may not know of his abuse of the children. Feminists may respond to the charge that the woman must have known by asserting that such a woman may never know and, in any case, because of her relative powerlessness, should not be held responsible.

Responses to child abuse

Parton (1985) argued that it became 'news' that child abuse was much more pervasive than was at that time reflected in official statistics or in what many professionals were prepared to admit. Successive child abuse scandals hit the headlines in the mass media, inquiries were carried out and remedial action was proposed and undertaken. Parton argues also that policy and practice should be informed by an understanding of child abuse based on structural inequality, an argument not previously fully recognised. (op. cit., p. 198). Parton's argument is that the understanding of how and why certain forms of parental activity are defined as appropriate or inappropriate, abusive or non-abusive, is a function not only of individual behaviour but also of the changing role of the state and its relationship with the economy and the family. He suggests the need for a more broadly based approach focusing on how major institutional structures systematically adopt or reject particular policies. He suggests that the definition of child abuse and the nature of policy responses to it are outcomes both of the demands made by moral entrepreneurs who promote the issue, and of the responses of different sections of the state apparatus (op. cit., p. 12). King (1995) questions the proposition that child protection policy and practice are determined by prevailing political ideologies, as argued by Parton (1985, 1991) and Frost and Stein (1989). Undoubtedly, there are close connections between politics and policies in this area. This chapter and the preceding one have referred to the undeniable longstanding association between the ideology of preserving family life, which has crossed party lines with ease in British politics since the 1950s, and the treatment paradigm which has informed social work with families for most of the twentieth century.

Since the death of Denis O'Neill in the 1940s, the murder of Maria Colwell marked the most significant progress towards the co-ordination of multi-disciplinary, multi-professional and multi-agency responses to child abuse. The Colwell inquiry (1974) was not the first. The Houghton Committee (Departmental Committee on the Adoption of Children, 1972) recommendations considerably improved adoption and fostering practice, in terms of the rights of foster parents, providing continuity for the child and limiting the influence that natural parents could exercise in longer term care (Parton, 1985, p. 90). Significantly, the mass media showed little interest in the Colwell case from when it first surfaced in May 1973, when the inquiry was set up, until the inquiry opened on 10 October. Between 10 October and 7 December it received enormous press coverage (op. cit., p. 91) and led to increased pressure on doctors and other healthcare professionals to improve their collaboration with police and social workers.

During the 1980s, partly prompted by publicity arising from the handling of cases where women had alleged rape, the police overhauled and greatly improved their approaches to investigating such situations. The Cleveland (1988) and Orkney (1992) inquiries were salutary reminders of the need for professionals to maintain a balance between protection and over-zealous intervention. By the late 1980s, public and professional concern about child murders by their carers prompted the DHSS publication *Working Together* (Department of Health and Social Security, 1988, later expanded into Department of Health, 1991), which addressed child abuse, protection and rescue for the first time. But these inquiries generated controversy over the demands put on children by the requirements of the criminal courts for evidence to be assembled and presented in ways that contradicted the rights of children to protection from the trauma of investigation, and their giving evidence and being cross-examined by a defence lawyer. Beatrix Campbell (1995, p. 19) writing in the wake of subsequent research suggesting that the child protection system has been swamped by too many investigations not leading to prosecutions (Department of Health, 1995a), maintains that new arrangements made after Cleveland shifted the balance too far towards protecting the accused person. Her point is that government guidance that professionals should redirect their energies, therefore, into family support and prevention takes no account of the number of investigations that may have led to protective work before prosecution became necessary.

Since the 1980s, from one point of view child protection services have become largely medicalised and crisis-based. Parton (1985) argues that child abuse was conceived in the 1970s as a medico-social problem which required treatment by doctors, particularly paediatricians and social workers. In the 1980s and 1990s, debates about sexual abuse and parental rights suggest that social work can contribute both to reforms in child protection practices and to discussions about the nature of the family (Parton, 1991, p. 214). According to the second annual review of the Children Act 1989, some local authorities had not allocated more than 10% of child protection cases to social workers, Hereford and Worcester being at the top of this league with 20%. Child protection work tended to squeeze out preventive work with children and families under Section 17 of the Children Act 1989 (Department of Health, 1994). The number of children on child protection registers peaked, at 45,300 in 1991, falling to 34,900 by March 1994 (Department of Health 1995b, Table 5.44, p. 71). A record 28,500 children were placed on child protection registers in England during the year to March 1994. The proportion of children placed on registers as a result of discussion at initial child protection conferences rose from 58% in 1992–3 to 62% in 1993–4 (*The Guardian*, 3 February 1995).

Brian Waller, director of social services in Leicestershire, argues the rationalist view that, informed by such research, the best practice will emerge and cost-effective services will be developed that provide an appropriate balance between prevention and protection (Waller, 1995). A critical view of child protection policies and practices is that the quasi-markets for health and social work and social care increasingly resemble a supermarket, where goods and services for children in need of protection are purchased and supplied (Thorpe, 1994). In other words, the market model tends towards commercial activity rather than exemplary child care practice.

The Department of Health used the publication of research into child protection in mid-1995 as the opportunity to advise local authorities that they should shift their emphasis from the investigation of child abuse, towards supportive work with families in crisis (*The Guardian*, 22 June 1995). This shift was based on the finding that approximately 120,000 out of 160,000 child protection cases are not progressed, 96% of investigated children staying home and three-quarters of the remaining 4% being at home within six months. Some critics argued that the solution was a firmer approach, setting up one agency to manage the investigation of suspected abuse, by regarding it as an alleged criminal assault (Hawker, 1995, p. 4). Gray *et al.* (1995) have critically assessed this policy in the light of research suggesting that a preventive policy all too often protects the abuser rather than the abused child.

Legal basis for services for children and young people

The legislation regarding work with families (see chapter 4) equally covers work with children and young people. Until the Children Act 1989, many previous laws applied: for example, child protection came under the Children and Young Persons Act 1969. The local authority has statutory responsibility for protecting children under section 47 of the Children Act 1989, whereas other involved agencies and organisations do not. Child Protection Conferences, while not required in this Act, are the accepted means by which involved professionals make decisions about the immediate protection of, and sometimes further work with, a child considered at risk of harm, or already harmed. Such measures may include emergency protection, care, supervision orders through the court, or arrangements for the child to be looked after by the local authority. These are all technical terms with legal force under the Children Act 1989. Some additional points are made below, with specific reference to children.

Balancing the interests of children against other interests

The Social Work (Scotland) Act 1968 contains a number of procedural checks which attempt to balance the interests of the children, the parents and the state in making decisions about children in need. Sometimes, as in the case of children abusing other children (National Children's Homes, 1992), there may be a conflict between meeting the interests of the abusing child – who may have been abused in the past – and the child she or he abuses. The children hearing involves a panel of people with an interest in or knowledge of social work or child care. These tend to be lay people who reflect the views of society in general. It is not a court and its proceedings are not formal. The child and the parents tend to be present without legal representation. A child considered to be in need of compulsory measures of care must meet one of a dozen grounds of the 1968 Act, such as that the child is beyond the control of the parents, is subject to moral danger, has been a victim of a Schedule 1 offence, or has committed an offence. Schedule 1 offences are serious offences involving the physical or sexual abuse of children.

The situation of children of unmarried parents

By 1994, 32% of children were born to unmarried parents; many of these children were born into relationships as long-term as many marriages (Social Trends, 1996, p. 61). Despite some changes in the law to recognise the social reality and implications of this, the Family Law Reform Act 1987 removed some of the differences affecting the legal position of the child, improving the situation of the father, but not giving the father automatic responsibility for the upbringing of the child. The Children Act 1989 continued this trend, there being no requirement to include in discussions over parental responsibility the children of unmarried parents, or relationships traced through unmarried parents in legal documents (op. cit., p. 23). Section 8 of the Children Act 1989 provides for a number of orders aimed at resolving issues arising in the care and upbringing of a child: a residence order, a contact order, a specific issue order, a prohibited steps order, and orders varying or discharging any of these. Normally these orders are used between private individuals, and especially parents.

Approaches to services for children and young people

The four main types of approach identified in Fig. 4.1 (chapter 4) are protection, care, therapy and advocacy. These express tensions between providing *for* and working *with* children, and thereby dilemmas in the relationship between the transitional status of, and responses to, children, and the treatment and empowerment paradigms. Should children be protected or liberated? There is not, nor perhaps should there be, a simple answer to this question. Protection entails the prevention of harm or abuse to the child; care involves nurturing the child; therapy takes the form of activities intended to bring about change in the child; advocacy refers to action on behalf of or by the child, such as protest (Adams, 1991), directed to meeting personal needs.

Protective approaches

Whenever there is a scandal, or a report of abuse, much attention tends to be focused on the investigation of allegations of child abuse; there is a consequent neglect of the further work, which often should continue for years, with victims and perpetrators. There are many associated issues, such as the future access of the perpetrator, if related to and formerly living with the victim, to the household. Some professionals believe that perpetrators of abuse, particularly sexual abusers, can never be trusted not to reoffend.

There are issues also concerning the difficulty of bringing success-ful prosecutions in court following allegations of abuse where chil-dren's accounts cannot be corroborated from other sources of evidence. Outside such centres as Gracewell in Birmingham and Grendon Underwood prison near Aylesbury, resources to treat perpetrators of abuse are thinly spread. Social workers may, for example, have to weigh the potential stress to a child of partici-pation in prosecution as a witness against the chances of conviction of, and treatment for, the perpetrator, if sent to prison.

Child protection: preventive and long-term work

A report by Save the Children Fund (1994) proposes that centres providing flexible day care, benefits advice, education for parents, and women's training sessions will help to prevent distress and family breakdown, thereby saving on later intervention services. A study of six local authorities' child protection services carried out by the Social Services Inspectorate (SSI) revealed that none of the inspected authorities had a policy or guidance on record-keeping and 'in all the authorities, inspectors considered recording was below standard' (Social Services Inspectorate, 1994). The avail-ability of specialist resources counterbalances weaknesses in the statutory sector. Agencies such as Barnardo's and the NSPCC have tended in many areas to take on responsibility for carrying out more long-term work with children and families. Doyle (1990) has written authoritatively on how work with abused children and their families goes beyond the immediate action regarding child protec-tion and involves dealing with the long-term impact of abuse and carrying out further work with survivors of abuse.

Working with children needing protection

The promotion of the welfare of children is a prime purpose of the Children Act 1989, but this positive goal may not be the sole con-cern of many professionals concerned with investigating suspected child abuse. Social workers spend much time in intervention and assessment in such cases, rather than in long-term work with chil-dren who are the victims of abuse, or preventive work. Thus, many of the resources of the personal social services are allocated to child protection work, especially work with children who have been physically or sexually abused. But this is only the most pub-licly discussed aspect of the work, which also includes children sub-ject to emotional abuse and neglect, whose impact on a child's development may be just as serious although it may not seem at the time to have caused major traumas. The consequences of emotional abuse or neglect may be more difficult to address, since the actual problem may not be evident in the form of a particular incident or symptom.

Care approaches

Working with children and young people in the care system

Local authorities have a duty to provide services for children in need, whether they are living with their parents or are being looked after by the local authority – in residential care, fostered or adopted. Such caring services may include domiciliary care for disabled children, nurseries, pre-school facilities, family centres, or counselling.

Working with pre-school children and their parents

A well-established momentum exists for research and practice reinforcing the benefits of partnership with parents and pre-school work with young children. Pugh argues for a general framework enabling the flexible development of local services for children under five. Pugh and Holman have argued that this should take up factors that seem particularly likely to affect adversely the development of young children, such as taxation and benefits policies designed to address poverty and financial hardship (Pugh, 1988, p. 81; Holman, 1988, pp. 123–124).

The London-based project Parents, Teachers and Children (PACT) evaluation demonstrated that the regular involvement of parents, sisters, brothers and grandparents to help children to read at home on a one-to-one basis led to an improvement in the reading of children, related to increased skills and motivation (Griffiths and Hamilton, 1984). This is typical of a great body of similar research. The campaign in Britain among advocates of pre-school support for children draws on research from the USA, notably from the Head Start programme which aimed to break the cycle of disadvantage as it was then understood: poverty, poor parenting and poor performance – including delinquency – by children. In the USA, the Perry Pre-School project is an example of the kinds of initiative that have led to increased support for pre-school intervention with children, including those from disadvantaged backgrounds (Schweinhart and Weikart, 1980). High Scope is an approach to working with young children that originated in 1962 in the Perry Pre-School project in Michigan, one of the Head Start programmes. The High Scope initiative involved research of a longitudinal kind, providing accumulating data suggesting that children with whom early work was done tended later to do better at school and to avoid many problems contributing to delinquency. It is based on the theories of Piaget (1948), and specifically the assumption that children learn most effectively from activities that they plan and carry out themselves, in other words by key components of active learning: materials, manipulation, choice, language and support. The conceptual framework for this lies closer to the empowerment paradigm than to medico-treatment.

It is a moot point whether adoption and fostering work have more in common with caring or therapeutic work. For the purposes of this chapter, they are included here.

Adoption work

Adoption law was changed fundamentally in 1975 following the Houghton Committee Report (Departmental Committee on the Adoption of Children, 1972), implemented in the Adoption Act 1976. Social workers play a key role in processing adoption applications and procedures. Adopted children and young people increasingly exercise their rights to ascertain the identity of their birth parents. The adoption process is lengthy and complex, involving assessing, approving and preparing potential adoptive parents for their role and ensuring that the best interests of the child are met. Adoption procedures are governed by the regulations (Adoption Agencies Regulations 1983; Adoption Agencies Regulations (NI) 1989) and involve examinations and screenings, as well as reports on the full health history of birth, parents and the child's health. Some mothers state before the birth that they wish their baby to be adopted and this intention needs checking carefully.

Foster care

Social workers are concerned also with working with foster care situations. They normally place the child and approve, train and support foster parents throughout the fostering process. Foster parents have to accept that older children placed with them may be experiencing difficulties that will require patience and understanding. In some parts of the country, notably Lothian, there is an increased likelihood in comparison with other parts of the UK, that fostered children will subsequently be found to be infected with HIV (O'Hara, 1993, p. 56).

Therapeutic approaches

Therapeutic work, whether short- or long-term, may involve drama, music or art therapy with children who have been abused (Cattanach, 1993, 1994). It is not always the case that therapeutic services are beneficial. When parents separate, therapy can actually be counterproductive, accentuating a child's feelings of loss and strangeness (Randall, 1990, p. 16).

Advocacy work with children

Professional advocacy, peer advocacy and self-advocacy involving children individually and collectively have progressed in the last quarter of the twentieth century. Self-help and user-led groups involving children who have been in care have been well-established since the late 1970s.

Children may be abused by an individual, by an institution or by a system. In the case of children undergoing the Pindown regime, it is easy to identify the nature of the abuse and the source of it, in the regime of residential child care adopted. However, abuse by the system may be less easy to identify, more insidious, and its impact less easy to discern. In such circumstances, advocacy, self-advocacy and peer advocacy – through self-help groups or organisations – are particularly important approaches to work with children. The National Association for Young People in Care (NAYPIC) is the best known, and well-established, self-help organisation for young people being looked after by local authorities. It fulfils a collective advocacy role as well as enabling young people to relate to it, and to each other in its various activities, on an individual basis.

Issues in services for children and young people

Partnership between agencies

Partnership is a principle that operates at the level of work with parents and children, and between agencies. Section 27 of the Children Act 1989 authorises local authorities to ask for help from other local authorities and health authorities to fulfil their responsibilities under Part III. The Children Act deals only with the responsibilities of the social services department, but the government acknowledged the need, during debates on its passing through parliament, for it to mesh with social security and housing legislation (Allen, 1992, p. 56). Wider action to combat the impact of poverty and inequality, homelessness and joblessness on a broader front would be necessary to address the problems that lead to children being in need and at risk of significant harm (Holman, 1988, p. 93). This remains a problematic goal.

Children's rights: protection versus liberation

The rights of the developing child to various freedoms are in tension with the needs of the child for protection. The proposal that a 'national' commissioner be appointed to contribute to safeguarding children's rights (see document 5a), points to the fragility of legislation and local complaints procedures within children's social services as the main vehicle for promoting their interests. The Children Act 1989 has progressed the recognition of the status of the child as a person. The Act states that the wishes and feelings of the child should be ascertained, as far as is possible given the age and understanding of the child, and contribute to informed decisions being made about the child's future. Under the Act, a child may make an application for an order about his or her own upbringing, provided he or she has sufficient understanding to make the application, and may ask for an order regarding the place of living, whom to visit or stay with or have contact with, or regarding a particular aspect of upbringing (Hoggett, 1993, pp. 24–25). The court must take account of the wishes and feelings of the child that can be ascertained, bearing in mind the age and level of understanding of the child, and must regard the welfare of the child as paramount (op. cit., p. 25). Thus older children can exercise more influence, since in general their wishes will be considered more powerful arguments by professionals and by the court.

In 1994, a report endorsed by 183 children's organisations in the UK drew attention to the contrast between the government's ratification of the UN convention on the Rights of the Child and the fact that about a third of children in Britain still lived in poverty, many of whom did not have access to adequate housing and health care, and suffered racial discrimination and physical abuse condoned by the state, including corporal punishment. It is clear that social policies do not extend to protecting children against the damaging impact of structural inequalities on their lives and their future life chances let alone liberating them from them.

'Same race' placements of children

Controversy has intensified since the 1980s, especially since the disruptions to everyday life in Romania and former Yugoslavia, over whether children should be fostered or adopted by families of a different ethnic group. Debate has been particularly fierce over whether black children should be placed with white families. An informed view suggests that both the extreme of insensitively ignoring issues and placing regardless, and the extreme of following an anti-racist orthodoxy and refusing to place unless the background of the child and the family matches perfectly, are less appropriate than an approach that takes account of the complexities of each situation before a decision is made (Gambe *et al.*, 1992, p. 62).

Where abuse occurs

Dempster (1993, p. 58) observes that although the majority of child sexual abusers are men, women tend to bear the burden when their children are abused. Most sexual abuse occurs within the household. Both girls and boys (to a lesser extent) are victims of sexual abuse. Experiences of sexual abuse affect children negatively in the present and in the future as adults (Showers *et al.*, 1983; Wyatt, 1985). The overwhelming majority of abusers are males known to the victim, and women in their role as mothers do not often collude with perpetrators of incest (Tamartch, 1986; Russell, 1986; Faller, 1988; Schlesenger, 1986; Nelson, 1987; Finkelhor, 1986; Hall and Lloyd, 1989; Horton *et al.*, 1990; Williams and Finkelhor, 1990). A survey of abusers in Scotland points to the need for services for perpetrators to be developed and the need to go much further in protecting children than teaching children to say 'no' (Dobash *et al.*, 1993, p. 132).

The treatment of the children involved in the Orkney child sexual abuse case remains controversial. Professionals tend to uphold the resilience of the law in Scotland.

It is thought that the basic premises upon which the childrens' hearing in Scotland is built remain valid in spite of the events in Orkney. Indeed, compared to the difficulties experienced south of the border, the strengths of the Scottish system appear to be vindicated. ... The major lesson of the Orkney case is that the whole system ultimately turns on the professionalism and integrity of those involved, social workers, reporters, judiciary and panel members. The case illustrates the limits of legal regulation of the exercise by them of the discretionary powers which are inevitable in any system of child care law. But the room for abuse, such as it is, would be even further diminished if the views of the children at the centre of the case were always taken into account when the children are sufficiently mature to understand the nature and purpose of the proceedings (Thompson, 1993, p. 177).

Against this must be set the critique by Beatrix Campbell (1995) of imbalances in investigatory mechanisms that enable perpetrators of abuse to go unchallenged. The inquiry report into multiple child abuse in nursery classes in Newcastle (Hunt, 1994) points to the failure of professionals and the authorities to act on the basis of a handful of complaints, and investigate the possibility of multiple abuse where there is access to a group of children.

Bandana Ahmad (1989) criticises both the coercive and the liberal approaches used in work with black families, the former because it simply involves removing children from families regarded as substandard and the latter because social workers striving to be seen as anti-racist may shy away from their duty to protect the child from abuse.

Since the 1980s, controversies over ritual abuse have emerged as issues. Jean La Fontaine (1994) reviewed 84 cases of alleged Satanic abuse between 1988 and 1992 in England and Wales, and found no evidence to substantiate them. Concern was expressed by some professionals at the unambiguous way in which the report dismissed the existence of Satanic abuse (*Community Care*, 9–15 June 1994, no.1020, p. 1). The continuing controversy over ritual abuse was given prominence by Tim Tate (1991) and dismissed in the report by La Fontaine in 1994. The findings on Satanic abuse attracted much controversy among professionals. La Fontaine was interviewed in June 1994 and suggested that cultural changes have helped to encourage allegations of ritual abuse.

The politically correct society creates a climate in which we are a bit nervous of standing up against it. Believing in Satanic abuse is promoted as politically correct in that it supports children, women and down-trodden against the powerful – the police, freemasons, all the other bogeymen. If you say you do not believe in the existence of Satanic abuse, you are accused of not believing in child sexual abuse and then of denying the Holocaust (Downy, 1994).

False memory syndrome is a term used by some accused parents, and therapists describing the mental state of their adult children, who accuse them of abusing them when they were children, an accusation they deny. The advocates and critics of the concept of false memory syndrome debate its existence strenuously. The situation is complicated because some people falsely allege that they have been abused and some parents strongly deny their abuse of their children. Also, it is difficult for social workers to gather testimony from survivors of abuse that is sufficiently coherent and substantial, or corroborated, to stand up in court and to comply with the *Memorandum of Good Practice* under the Criminal Justice Act 1991. Parents alleging the existence of false memory syndrome have formed the British False Memory Society, while its critics have founded Accuracy About Abuse.

Children with disabilities

In the Borough of Bromley, an internal report alleged the failure of residential child care to meet statutory requirements for children looked after by the local authority. The Association of Metropolitan Authorities (AMA) drew attention to the dramatic 65% increase in the numbers of children aged 10 to 14 with disabilities admitted to psychiatric hospitals. The AMA recommended more contact between child protection and disability services, and argued that black and ethnic minority children may receive inferior services, due to colour blindness, which is a tendency not to take due account of real differences in the circumstances of black and white children (*Community Care*, 9–15 June 1994, no.1020, p. 4).

Improving parenting and child care

A growing campaign to improve provision in care for children and young people, given the mounting proportion of women entering the workforce while engaged in child rearing, is reflected in the argument by Juliet Solomon (1987) for a reappraisal of the relationship between parents and children, particularly emphasising the need for fathers to spend more time with their children, for the working day to be shorter and for more flexible child care when children are younger. This observation was reinforced by a MORI survey carried out on the 150th anniversary of the birth of Dr Barnardo, which noted that 54% of fathers spend on average less than five minutes alone with their children per weekday (Barnardo's, 1995). However, the development of the marketplace for services for young children has not improved the quality or the quantity of provision. Melhuish and Moss (1991) conclude their international review of day care provision for young children with the comment that market forces cannot generate an affordable range of acceptable quality day care services, with adequately trained and well-paid staff working in high staff–child ratios, charging fees people can afford. Inevitably, in the absence of adequate services, less well-off parents contribute to a patchwork of local, often informal, childminding and similar arrangements, sometimes even leaving the children on their own (op. cit.).

There is a growing literature on the socialisation of children, with regard to imbalances of gender. Miedzian (1992) argues for measures to be taken to prevent violence among children and young people, especially boys from low socio-economic backgrounds who are more likely to engage in violence. She argues for provision for boys to be taught to resolve their conflicts in non-violent ways. She maintains that domestic violence and criminal behaviour would be affected positively if this were achieved, and suggests that these measures would have a positive impact on collective violence, provided they became an integral part of child rearing and a mandatory part of the education system. The implication of her argument is that violent punishment contributes to violence and that non-violent ways should be found of checking and disciplining children and young people.

References and further reading

Adams, R. (1991) *Protests by Pupils: Empowerment, Schooling and the State*, London: Falmer.

Adoption Act 1976, London: HMSO.

Adoption Agencies Regulations 1983, London: HMSO.

Adoption Agencies Regulations (NI) 1989, Belfast: HMSO.

Ahmad, B. (1989) Protecting black children from abuse, *Social Work Today*, 8 June.

Allen, N. (1992) *Making Sense of the Children Act: a Guide for the Social and Welfare Services*, London: Longman.

Aries, P. (1962) *Centuries of Childhood*, London: Jonathan Cape.

Barnardo's (1995) *The Facts of Life*, Barkingside, Barnado's.

Batty, D. (ed.) (1993) *HIV Infection and Children in Need*, London: British Agencies for Adoption and Fostering.

Bean, P. and Melville, J. (1990) *Lost Children of the Empire*, London: Unwin Hyman.

Butler-Sloss, E. (1988) *Report of the Inquiry into Child Abuse in Cleveland 1987*, Cm 412, London: HMSO.

Campbell, B. (1995) A question of priorities, *Community Care*, no.1082, 24–30 August, 18–19.

Carlebach, J. (1970) *Caring for Children in Trouble*, London: Routledge and Kegan Paul.

Carpenter, M. (1851) *Reformatory Schools for the Children of the Perishing and Dangerous Classes and for Juvenile Offenders*, London: Gelpin (reprinted 1968, London: Woburn Press).

Cattanach, A. (1993) *Play Therapy with Abused Children*, London: Jessica Kingsley.

Cattanach, A. (1994) *Play Therapy: Where the Sky Meets the Underworld*, London: Jessica Kingsley.

Children Act 1948, London: HMSO.

Children Act 1963, London: HMSO.

Children Act 1975, London: HMSO.

Children Act 1989, London: HMSO.

Children and Young Persons Act 1933, London: HMSO.

Children and Young Persons Act 1969, London: HMSO.

Cooter, R. (ed.) (1992) *In the Name of the Child: Health and Welfare 1880–1940*, London: Routledge.

Criminal Justice Act 1991, London: HMSO.

Dempster, H. L. (1993), 'The Aftermath of children sexual abuse: women's perspectives', in Waterhouse, L. (ed.) *Child Abuse and Child Abusers: Protection and Prevention*, Research Highlights in Social Work, no.24, 58–72, London: Jessica Kingsley.

Department of Health (1991) *Working Together under the Children Act 1989*, London: HMSO.

Department of Health (1994) *Review of the Children Act 1989* (second annual review), London: HMSO.

Department of Health (1995a) *Child Protection: Messages from Research*, London: HMSO.

Department of Health (1995b) *Health and Personal Social Services Statistics for England 1995 Edition*, London: HMSO.

Department of Health and Social Security and Welsh Office (1988) *Working Together: A Guide to Arrangements for Inter-agency Co-operation for the Protection of Children from Abuse*, London: HMSO.

Departmental Committee on the Adoption of Children (1972) (Houghton Committee), Report, London: HMSO.

Dobash, R.P., Carnie, J. and Waterhouse, L. (1993) Child sexual abusers: recognition and response, in Waterhouse, L. (ed.) *Child Abuse and Child Abusers: Protection and Prevention*, Research Highlights in Social Work, no.24, 113–135, London: Jessica Kinglsey.

Downy, R. (1994) Devil's no scapegoat, *Community Care*, 16–22 June, 8.

Doyle, C. (1990) *Working with Abused Children*, London: Macmillan/BASW.

Faller, K.,(1988) The myth of the collusive mother: variability in functioning of mothers of sexually abused children, *Journal of Interpersonal Violence*, vol. 3, no.2.

Finkelhor, D. (ed.), (1986) *A Sourcebook on Child Sexual Abuse*, London: Sage.

Franklin, B. (ed.) (1986) *The Rights of Children*, Oxford: Blackwell.

Frost, N. and Stein, M. (1989) *The Politics of Child Welfare: Inequality, Power and Change*, New York: Harvester Wheatsheaf.

Gambe, D., Gomes, J. Bijaykapur, B.J., Rangel, M. and Stubbs, P. (1992) *Improving Practice for Children and Families: a Training Manual*, Leeds: CCETSW.

Gillis, J. (1974) *Youth and History*, New York: Academic Press.

Gray, S., Higgs, M. and Pringle, K. (1995) *User centred responses to child sexual abuse: a radical proposal* (unpublished paper).

Griffiths, A. and Hamilton, D. (1984), *Parent, Teacher, Child: Working Together in Children's Learning*, London: Methuen.

Hall, L. and Lloyd, S. (1989) *Surviving Child Sexual Abuse*, London: Falmer.

Hall, S., Critcher, C., Jefferson, T., Clarke, J. and Roberts, B. (1978) *Policing the Crisis*, London: Macmillan.

Hawker, M. (1995) Let's scrap the guidelines, *Professional Social Work*, August 4.

Heywood, J.S. (1959) *Children in Care: the Development of the Service for the Deprived Child*, London: Routledge and Kegan Paul.

Hobsbawn, E. (1995) *The Age of Empire*, London: Weidenfeld and Nicolson.

Hoggett, B. (1993) *Parents and Children: the Law of Parental Responsibility*, 4th edn, London: Sweet and Maxwell.

Holman, B. (1988) *Putting Children First: Prevention and Child Care*, London: Macmillan and the Children's Society.

Horton, A.L., Johnson, B.L., Roundy, L.M. and Williams, D. (eds). (1990), *The Incest Perpetrator: a Family Member No One Wants to Treat*, London: Sage.

Hoyles, M. (ed.) (1979) *Changing Childhood*, London: Writers and Readers Co-operative.

Hunt, P. (1994) *Report of the Independent Inquiry into Multiple Abuse in Nursery Classes in Newcastle upon Tyne*, Newcastle upon Tyne City Council.

Industrial Schools and Reformatory Schools Act 1857.

King, M. (1995) Law's healing of children's hearings: the paradox moves north, *Journal of Social Policy*, vol.24, no.3, 315–340.

La Fontaine, J. (1990), *Child Sexual Abuse*, Cambridge, Polity Press.

La Fontaine, J. (1994) *The Extent and Nature of Organised Ritual Abuse*, London: HMSO.

Melhuish, C.E. and Moss, P. (eds) (1991) *Day Care for Children: International Perspectives*, London: Routledge.

Miedzian, M. (1992), *Boys Will Be Boys: Breaking the Link Between Masculinity and Violence*, London: Virago.

Millham, S., Bullock, R. and Cherrett, P. (1975), *After Grace – Teeth, a Study of the Residential Experience of Boys in Approved Schools*, London: Human Context Books.

National Children's Homes (1992) *The Report of the Committee of Inquiry into Children and Young People who Sexually Abuse Other Children*, London: National Children's Homes.

Nelson, S. (1987) *Incest – Fact and Myth*, Edinburgh: Stramullion.

NISW (1988b) *Residential Care: the Research Reviewed*, literature surveys commissioned by the Independent Review of Residential Care (Wagner Report Part II), London: HMSO.

O'Hara, G. (1993) Caring for Children and Families Infected and Affected by HIV/AIDS: a social work perspective, in Batty, D. (ed.), *HIV Infection and Children in Need*, 54–64, London: British Agencies for Adoption and Fostering.

Parton, N. (1985) *The Politics of Child Abuse*, London: Macmillan.

Parton, N. (1991) *Governing the Family: Child Care, Child Protection and the State*, London: Macmillan.

Piaget, J. (1948) *Le Language et la Pensee Chez L'Enfant*, Neuchatel and Paris: De la Chaux and Niestle.

Platt, A.M. (1969) *The Child Savers: the Invention of Delinquency*, Chicago and London: University of Chicago Press.

Plumb, J.H. (1973) Children: victims of time, in Plumb, J.H., *In the Light of History*, part 2, essay 5, 153–165, London: Allen Lane.

Pollock, L. (1987) *A Lasting Relationship: Parents and Children over 3 Centuries*, London: Fourth Estate.

Pringle, K. (1993) Review of Cooter, R. (ed.), *In the Name of the Child: Health and Welfare 1880–1940*, London: Routledge; in *Journal of Social Policy*, vol.22, part 3, July, 431–432.

Pugh, G. (1988) *Services for Under Fives: Developing a Co-ordinated Approach*, London: National Children's Bureau.

Randall, P. (1990) A child's eye view, *Community Care*, no.07, 29 March, 15–17.

Reformatory Schools (Youthful Offenders) Act 1854, London: HMSO.

Report of the Care of Children Committee (1946) (Curtis Report), Cmnd 6922, London: HMSO.

Report of the Committee of Inquiry into the Care and Supervision provided in relation to Maria Colwell 1974, London: HMSO.

Report of the Inquiry into the Removal of Children from Orkney in February 1991: Return to an Address of the Honourable the House of Commons dated 27 October 1992, XIV ([HC.] 195, 1992–93), London: HMSO.

Russell, D.E.H. (1986) *The Secret Trauma, Incest in the Lives of Girls and Women*, New York: Basic Books.

Save the Children Fund (1994) *Child Care in the Community*, London: Save the Children Fund.

Schlesenger, B. (1986) The Badgley Report on Sexual Offences against children, in Schlesenger, B. (ed.), *Sexual Abuse of Children in the 1980s*, London: University of Toronto Press,.

Schweinhart, L.J., and Weikart, D.P. (1980) *Young Children Grow Up: the Effects of the Perry Pre-School Programme on Youths through Age Fifteen*, monograph of the High Scope Educational Research Foundation, no.7, Ipsilante, Michigan: High Scope.

Showers, J., Farber, D., Joseph, J.A., Oshins, L. and Johnson, C.F. (1983) The sexual victimisation of boys: a three year survey, *Health Values*, no.7, 15–18 .

Social Services Inspectorate (1994) *Evaluating Child Protection Services: Findings and Issues*, London: HMSO.

Social Trends 26 (1996), London: HMSO.

Social Work (Scotland) Act, Edinburgh: HMSO.

Solomon, J. (1987) *Holding the Reins: Parents, Children and Nannies in their Search for Domestic Salvation*, London: Fontana/Collins.

Stedman Jones, G. (1984) *Outcast London, a Study in the Relationship between Classes in Victorian Society*, Harmondsworth: Penguin.

Tamartch, L.I. (1986) Fifty myths and facts about sexual abuse, in Schlesenger, B. (ed.), *Sexual Abuse of Children in the 1980s*, 3–15, London: University of Toronto Press.

Tate, T. (1991) *Children for the Devil: Ritual Abuse and Satanic Crime*, London: Methuen.

Thompson, J. (1993) Childrens' hearings – a legal perspective after Orkney, in Waterhouse, L. (ed.) *Child Abuse and Child Abusers: Protection and Prevention*, Research Highlights in Social Work, no.24, 166–177, London: Jessica Kingsley.

Thorpe, D.H. (1994) *Evaluating Child Protection*, Open University Press, Buckingham.

Waller, B. (1995) Too late to learn, *Community Care* ('Inside Community Care' supplement), 27 July–2 August no.1079, 1.

Waterhouse, L. (ed.) (1993) *Child Abuse and Child Abusers: Protection and Prevention*, Research Highlights in Social Work, no.24, London: Jessica Kingsley.

Williams, L.M., and Finkelhor, D. (1990) The characteristics of incestuous fathers, in Marshall, W.L., Laws, D.R., and Barbaree, H.E. (eds), *Handbook of Sexual Assault Issues, Theories and Treatment of the Offender*, New York: Plenum.

Wyatt, G. (1985) The sexual abuse of Afro-American and White-American women, *Child Abuse and Neglect*, vol.9, 507–519.

PART THREE

Adults' services

CHAPTER 6

Community care

This chapter deals with the NHS and Community Care Act 1990, which introduced quasi-markets and consequently new arrangements for co-ordinating and managing the delivery of community care. These measures make this the most significant legislation in the health and social care sector since the 1940s.

Context of community care

The NHS and Community Care Act 1990 created a structure for service delivery, based on markets in which statutory agencies shift from providing services to purchasing them from a range of largely independent – i.e. voluntary and private – providers. These markets are managed rather than free, in the sense that the government intervenes, for instance, by determining the nature and level of resources that local authority social services departments can allocate to the purchase of community care services. Under Section 46 of the Act, every local authority social services department must produce, and annually update, a plan, after consulting with other agencies, organisations, services users and carers, showing how it intends to meet people's community care needs (see an extract from the updating of one such plan, in document 11). While the impact of these changes on the quality of care has to be evaluated in the longer term, in the mid-1990s it is clear that the quality of services remains constrained by limited resources.

Concept of community care

The concept, policy and practice of community care have been the subject of public and professional debate for many years. Community care is much more than decarcerating people from mental hospitals and other institutions. It typically involves home care, housing, equipment and adaptations, primary health, community nursing, residential care, nursing home care, day centres, day hospitals, counselling for people having difficulty living independently, and services for carers. Not all work in the field of community care focuses on the needs of adults. Voluntary child care organisations provide a range of services that could be placed under this heading: family and community development centres, respite care, long-term work with disabled and profoundly disabled young people and their families. Some voluntary organisations also take on a role as advocates of the rights of children and families, and this may cut across, or even conflict with, their status as charities (see chapter 11).

The Percy Commission (HMSO, 1957) on mental health recommended increased community care, and some of its recommendations were incorporated in the Mental Health Act 1959. However, this Act did not abolish the large institutions that catered for mentally ill patients. Community care as an aspect of social policy in the 1960s meant decarceration, following the cost-cutting trend in the USA (see Scull, 1977). In Britain, discussion of the virtues of deinstitutionalising mental hospital patients was contained in a government publication in 1963 (Ministry of Health, 1963) which followed the Hospital Plan for England and Wales (Ministry of Health, 1962). This blueprint was half-hearted and did not lead to the implementation of community care in any coherent or widespread way. Kathleen Jones (1991, p. 155) observes that the plan 'lacked the conviction and force of the *Hospital Plan*, consisting only of general statements on the desirability of community care for physically and mentally disabled people and the elderly, and detailed returns from local authorities on the services they hoped to provide'. In Britain, despite pronouncements by governments, the practical development of alternatives to institutions tended to be left to the voluntary sector (Illsley and Jamieson, 1990, p. 92). A number of government reports in the 1970s, particularly in areas such as mental health and learning disability, emphasised community care as an alternative to continuing to maintain people in long stay hospital wards (see chapter 7). However, it was in the mid-1980s, with the publication of the Audit Commission Report *Making a Reality of Community Care* (1986), that the move towards hospital closure accelerated and the prospect that community care would be introduced became more real.

Bulmer (1993, p. 235) describes community care as resources 'outside formal institutional structures, particularly in the informal relationships of the family, friends and neighbours, as a means of providing care'. He points out that the word 'community' hardly captures the social basis of such care, but it seems strange that he should exclude formal structures, which could be in the statutory, voluntary or private sectors, from community care providers. Bulmer prefers the term 'social network' to 'community', the former including informal relationships in the family and with friends, neighbours and associates at work. (op. cit., p. 235) The values that the government wished to engender in its proposed legislation on community care were closely allied to those expressed in the All Party Commission on Citizenship set up in January 1989, which recommended in its report early in 1990 an enhanced role for the citizen. The Barclay Report (NISW, 1982, pp. xii–xiii) defines the 'community' as things shared, common interests and allegiances and local networks of relationships. Barclay recognised that formal and informal networks need to work together; partnerships are necessary between formal and informal carers. Barclay argued that social workers should take account of the networks of services users when they work with them. Thus, the concept of networking was linked with that of partnership: 'Clients, relations, neighbours and volunteers become partners with the social worker in developing and providing social care networks' (op. cit., p. 209).

Among the many factors that contributed to the NHS and Community Care Act 1990 were concern about the need to find alternatives to the institutionally based approaches to dealing with mentally ill people and to address the need for support in the community of an anticipated greatly increased population of elderly people over the next thirty years.

Extending community support for elderly people

There was growing concern in the 1980s about the anticipated imbalance in the proportion of older people in the population, as the absolute number of people aged 75 and over increased by about three-quarters of a million and the most heavy users of health and social services – people over 85 – doubled in number. The increase in residential provision that occurred since the creation of social services departments in the 1970s could not address the increased needs of older people in the community.

Research at the Personal Social Services Research Unit (PSRRU) in the University of Kent was developed in the light of moves in the USA, informed by experience of child care in the UK, to develop alternatives to long-term institutionally based care; it argued for a comprehensive approach to a total system of care, taking account of the complexity and long-term nature of people's needs, and provided a conceptual basis for policy and practice reforms – and particularly the principles and process of care management – incorporated in the NHS and Community Care Act 1990:

An appropriate response will require effective identification of cases in need, careful assessment, the organisation and coordination of care from a wide range of different sources (family, friends, intimate social networks, voluntary and statutory agencies) so that the care from each may be interwoven into a total system of care. Such an integrated system of care for a frail elderly person will not happen spontaneously, but will have to be consciously created. The active building, support and maintenance of a support network requires the development of effective case management with frail elderly people to ensure the coordination and performance of care tasks, in the way that would be expected in the care of vulnerable children (Challis and Davies, 1986, pp. 1–2).

This approach, making similar points to those made by Stevenson and Parsloe (1970) was geared to overcoming problems of co-ordination – fragmented services and the mismatch of provision and need; supporting, resourcing and complementing informal care by interweaving statutory with informal provision; raising the status of community care of older people; resolving problems of accountability of social services by clarifying roles and responsibilities within the health and social care sector (Challis and Davies, 1986, pp. 2–8) (for a discussion of the significance of Challis's work, see document 10, para. 2.2.4.).

Case management was an administrative device enabling the assessment of people's needs for residential services, until financial responsibility for residential and nursing home care – by then running at £10bn a year – was transferred to local authorities in April 1993. Then it was overtaken by the further reorganisation as community care was implemented.

Creation of internal markets in community care

In December 1986, Sir Roy Griffiths was appointed by the Secretary of State for Social Services 'to review the way in which public funds are used to support community care policy and advise on options which improve the use of these funds as a contribution to more community care'. The Griffiths Report was published in 1988 (Department of Health and Social Security, 1988). The Report dealt with two target groups: people returning to the community from institutions such as hospitals, and care of people by friends or relatives. Griffiths was not concerned with how community care should be funded. Many of the principles of Griffiths were incorporated into the 1990 legislation, but the details changed. The fundamental change, however, was not the principle of community care itself, but the introduction of the market economy into health and social care provision. The implications of that shift had more fundamental implications for the way professionals worked in the health and social care field.

Critical comment on the Griffiths Report by the Race Equal Opportunities Unit (REU) of the National Institute for Social Work (NISW) noted that the Report contained only one paragraph discussing multiracial perspectives. The REU commented that this was in the face of evidence that 'the concept of community care was not a new one in the black communities. The problem has been the abuse of this by white organisations which, in the absence of appropriate services to certain black user groups, have expected black families, community and voluntary organisations to provide care in the community however appropriate or inappropriate that has been' (NISW. REU, 1989, p. 1).

Caring for People 1989

The government published a White Paper on community care on 16 November 1989, entitled *Caring for People – the Next Decade and Beyond* (Department of Health, 1989b). The long delay before the publication of this White Paper was interpreted by many people as a sign that the government was hostile to the recommendations of the Griffiths Report. In the event, fears that responsibility for community care would be taken away from local authorities and transferred to health authorities were not realised. However, while both authorities retained certain responsibilities for aspects of community care, the restructuring of what became known as the mixed economy of welfare proved dramatic in its impact on the shape and operations of local services.

NHS and Community Care Act 1990

The advocates of community care as put forward by the NHS and Community Care Act praised the retention of administering care management by local authorities, the concept of individualised care plans and packages, and the centrality of service user choice and preferences to the devising and implementation of care plans. Further, there was support for the notion of improved evaluation, the introduction of quality assurance measures such as complaints procedures, and the notion of care management.

Implementation of community care

The White Paper proposals for the implementation of community care in April 1991 were delayed by the government when it announced in July 1990 that full implementation would not take place until 1993. Only the provisions relating to mental health and the new complaints procedures were to be implemented in full before then.

Attention was drawn to a major weakness of the Act by Sir Roy Griffiths. Shortly after the publication of the White Paper Griffiths said 'I had provided a purposeful, effective and economic four wheel vehicle but the White Paper has designed it as a three-wheeler, leaving out the fourth wheel of ring fenced funding' (*British Medical Journal*, vol. 300, p. 1187 quoted in Webb and Tossell, 1991, p. 119). A further criticism emerged more strongly after full implementation in 1993. This related to the impact of commercially driven values alongside those purely derived from human services values. The creation of internal markets in health and social care meant that private, voluntary and statutory service providers competed with each other to supply services, not purely on the basis of what would benefit clients the most, but on the basis of cost-effectiveness and value for money, which were not necessarily the same thing. Further, at an individual level, staff complained about the impact of the ethos of competition on their need to work collaboratively, across disciplines, professions and organisational boundaries. In the longer term, it was anticipated that the stimulation of private and voluntary sectors and a corresponding reduction in the public sector would have an impact on the store of expertise held centrally within the statutory organisations. It remained to be seen how far this would have a damaging effect on the quality of services being provided.

Enabling local authorities and community care

Since the mid-1980s 'enabling local authorities' have replaced 'providing local authorities'. Essentially, this change has involved enabling local authorities facilitating the provision of services by other agencies and organisations. In theory, enabling local authorities may adopt either market-based or collectivist approaches. In practice, the fact that the Conservatives were in power for so long after 1979 meant that market-based approaches were the norm. Compulsory competitive tendering from the late 1980s became a prominent way of providing local authority services (Elcock, 1993, pp. 164–165). Under the 1990 Act, social services departments in local authorities act as lead bodies; they and health authorities purchase community care services from providers whom they contract; they commission services by specifying needs, having established systems for bidding from potential service providers; contracts specify the costs (quantity) and standards (quality) of services; social services departments inspect services to ensure that they meet required standards (Elcock, 1993, p. 167).

Market-based and collectivist approaches share an enhanced concern with the service user as an individual consumer, rather than as a member of a wider community. Consequently, according to Elcock, 'concern with consumers may entail allowing discretion to service departments and service providers, which in turn produces relatively weak management at the organisation's centre'. Elcock rather optimistically points out that

in applying consumer reforms to local authority services we are dealing not with customers in the commercial sense but with citizens. Citizens have rights which they expect to be able to enforce and votes, which give them the ultimate sanction, if they do not like the way a local authority is run, of voting the councillors who control it out of office. Citizens' rights are being augmented and publicised through the publication of *The Citizen's Charter* (Prime Minister's Office, 1991) and related charters covering particular public services.

Elcock's description makes it sound easy for consumers to exercise political choices and influence the shape of services (Elcock, 1993, pp. 167–168), but the range of attempts made by local authorities to do this – from consumer research to decentralisation of services – by no means guarantees the outcome (Beresford and Croft, 1993).

Yet the NHS and Community Care Act 1990 required local authorities (Section 46) to consult with service users and carers in assessing community care needs, developing community care plans, setting local priorities and service objectives and developing local plans for delivering services collaboratively with health and housing authorities, as well as with the independent sector – voluntary and private providers of care – who were to provide 85% of services by the mid-1990s. The legislation changed the structure and organisation of the National Health Services (NHS) by introducing NHS Trusts and General Practitioner (GP) Fund-Holding Practices, and enables budget-holding GPs to opt out of the NHS. Family Practitioner Committees become Family Health Services Authorities. It made health authorities and local authority social services departments into purchasers of services from other providers they contracted to supply them.

The Act required health and local authorities to divest themselves of most of their assets and the majority of the services they provided. Their new role was as planners and purchasers of services. Health and local authorities as purchasers of services have two roles: the assessment of health and need in an area and the commissioning of health care services to meet that need. Under the NHS and Community Care Act 1990, the purchasers of health care – district health authorities, GPs holding their own budgets and local authority social services departments – assess the health and social care needs of their general populations of patients and other people and place service agreements or contracts with a variety of hospitals and community care services to ensure those needs are met.

The legislation established a mixed economy – through the statutory, voluntary, private and informal sectors – of care provision, partnerships with service users, patients and carers, choice of services, services that were accessible and quality assured, and minimum intervention consistent with promoting people's quality of life. The care programme approach (CPA), and the maintenance of registers for patients discharged from mental hospitals, were recommended in the White Paper *Caring for People* (Department of Health, 1989b, para. 7.7). Health Circular HC (90) 23 and Local Authority Social Services Letter LASSL (90) 11 implemented these recommendations by 1 April 1991. The CPA involves designing individual care packages to ensure that all patients accepted by specialist psychiatric services receive the care they need, using the keyworker approach (a keyworker being a nominated professional who co-ordinates the plan and the work with the person). In August 1993, the Secretary of State announced a ten-point plan to improve community care for mentally ill people, including the introduction of special supervision registers for patients considered most at risk and needing most support. These statements picked up the comment in the White Paper *Health of the Nation* (Department of Health, 1992) that patients most likely to relapse on discharge should not get 'lost', but the words 'support' and 'special supervision' were euphemisms for 'control', since this was a response to the media outrage over cases where discharged patients had murdered people (see chapter 7).

Continuing care provision includes long-term hospital care, NHS nursing care, acute, recovery, rehabilitation and respite care, community health care, and residential, nursing, respite and social care. Continuing care tends to be provided in areas such as the long-term, open-ended care of older people. The escalating costs of such provision have led local and health authorities to develop increasingly stringent criteria for people's eligibility. In some localities, local and health authorities compete with each other to shed responsibility for paying for people's continuing care. However, in the future the commissioning and contracting arrangements for some of these services may merge.

Legal basis for community care

While the major legislative reference point for community care is the NHS and Community Care Act 1990, other relevant legislation includes the Chronically Sick and Disabled Persons Act 1970, the Disabled Persons (Services Consultation and Representation) Act 1986, the Education Act 1981, the Education Reform Act 1988, the Local Government and Housing Act 1989, the Children Act 1989 and the Carers (Recognition and Services) Act 1995, due to be implemented in April 1996. This last Act requires social services departments to assess and take account of the needs of carers when determining the provision of community care services.

Approaches to community care

All approaches to community care are likely to fall within the legislative framework described above. Within this, the four main types of approach are identified in Fig. 4.1, chapter 4: protection, care, therapy and advocacy. Protection entails minimising or preventing risk to the person; care involves meeting a range of care needs; therapy may consist of a variety of treatments aimed at alleviating a condition, or modifying a person's response to circumstances; advocacy refers to action on behalf of or by the person, with the purpose of meeting personal needs. Advocacy services, largely in community care, are used by about 27% of social services departments, with a further third preparing to introduce advocacy provision (Valios, 1995, p. 7).

The process of care management involves a number of components clearly stated in government guidelines and generally referred to as occurring in sequence (Department of Health, 1991): informing potential services users about available services, assessing needs, devising a care plan, brokerage of necessary components and assembling the resources, implementing and reviewing the care plan. In general, authorities tend to draw a distinction between simple assessment, where a single item or service is required, and complex assessment where a range of resources may be required to meet physical, practical, psychological, emotional or social needs. The evidence suggests that assessment including a person's self-assessment in the light of personal history and experience, using a biographical approach, is likely to be more viable and satisfying in terms of meeting needs (Dant *et al.*, 1992).

Where a person needs a single service, such as shopping, because of inability to walk long distances carrying heavy loads, but otherwise is able to cope, it clearly makes sense to assess for maintaining maximum independence and provide a home shopping service, rather than to relocate the person in residential accommodation on the grounds that independent living is no longer sustainable.

Many authorities have shifted since the early 1990s from charging little or nothing for many community care services to imposing a partial or full cost charge. This may be means tested.

The variety and complexity of models of practice makes generalisation, and therefore general comment, difficult. This makes more essential than ever the activities of assessing, negotiating a care package, planning, implementing and reviewing. The main difference between care management and much informal caring may lie in the fact that care management involves the purposeful, planned, co-ordinated application of resources to a situation and/or need. At the reviewing and evaluating stage, Wilson (1993) points out the practical problems of collecting data incorporating users' and carers' perspectives into service development. Not least, this is because many people are inhibited from giving candid opinions.

Issues in community care

The lack of a single preferred model of best practice in the personal social services leaves some awkward questions to be answered. Who should receive community care? Who should be prioritised for services and why? What are the advantages and disadvantages of devolved budgets? Should care managers have a provider role as well as purchasing, or simply act as purchasers? (Davies, 1992). These questions enable a number of broad issues to be identified: whether community care is needs-led, user-led or simply resources-led, whether resources are adequate, problems of particular groups of carers, quality assurance through participation, problems of working together, pressure on smaller units and sustainability of services.

Needs-led, user-led or simply resources-led?

Government rhetoric in the late 1980s and early 1990s presented the implementation of community care as heralding a new era of quality services and enhanced choice by consumers. Yet critical commentators, including some groups of service users, tended to highlight the limitations of consumerism; they drew attention to the lack of real choice open to less mobile people and those without the resources to purchase adequate services. In the mid-1990s, local authorities found it increasingly difficult to sustain a range of provision to meet a diversity of human needs, and professionals still found it difficult to work together, across disciplinary, professional and organisational boundaries. The great variety of local patterns of organisation of health, housing and social services makes generalisation almost impossible. But three broad approaches to community care may be discerned: needs-led, user-led and service- or resources-led (Fig. 3.1, chapter 3). While no single approach operated to the exclusion of all others in a particular area, differences of emphasis can be discerned. These differences constituted boundaries, or parameters, within which community care evolved. The aim of the community care changes can be summarised in Michael Jarman's words, as from 'a service driven definition of needs to a needs driven definition of service' (Jarman, 1994, p. 6). The serious shortcomings in the quality of community care experienced by users and carers were scarcely addressed by the measures introduced by the Department of Social Services Inspectorate of the Department of Health in 1994 for evaluating progress on community care. These were criticised by directors and by user groups for focusing too much on issues from the point of view of policy development and neglecting other aspects (*Community Care*, no.1021, 16–22 June 1994, p. 1).

Research evaluating services confirms differences between the perceptions of purchasers and providers, service users and carers and professionals, and this is not surprising given their different interests. An evaluation of assessment in care management in social services departments by the SSI was positive and encouraging (Social Services Inspectorate, 1993), while Norman Warner's research for the Carers National Association which was published in 1994 was far more critical (Warner, 1994). The SSI noted that

moving from the service led to the needs led approach was a culture change for both professionals and potential users and carers. Despite the difficulties there were exciting examples of real change and flexibility in meeting user and carer needs. The skills required for assessment and the impact of work loads, given the greater expectation of involvement of service users and carers, still needed to be clearly established... there was a lack of clarity around the purpose of care planning. Care plans tended to be written mainly for service users with the more complex needs (SSI, 1993, p. 2).

Warner (1994), on the other hand, carried out a telephone survey of 420 carers throughout the UK and focus groups in Leeds and London. Ninety-five per cent of these carers were relatives of the person cared for, most were female and some of those cared for were 65 or over. Although 73% had heard of the community care changes, 74% had not received an assessment for the person they cared for since April 1993, and 55% did not know about assessments. Seventy-five per cent of carers who had been assessed said it had been hard to obtain an assessment, and 44% said they did not know how to complain. Of the carers who had received an assessment since April 1993, 22% still had not received any break from their caring during the year (op. cit., pp. 52–53).

The NHS and Community Care Act strengthened the voices of users although it did little to reconcile policy statements about user involvement with the reality that most users experienced, in terms of limited choice of services within limited budgets. Smale and Tuson (1990, p. 153) point out how long it has been since the Barclay Committee endorsed the Seebohm's reports recommendations regarding community-oriented provision (Committee on Local Authority and Allied Personal Social Services, 1968; NISW, 1982) and that a stated purpose of the Griffiths report was to provide the means for implementing the Barclay recommendations (Department of Health and Social Security, 1988). However, the White Paper *Caring for People* (Department of Health, 1989b) reduced the emphasis on informal carers, neighbourhood support and the local assessment of community care needs (Smale and Tuson, 1990, p. 153). The creation of internal markets inevitably focused attention on the financial and management aspects at the expense of the practice aspects of the implementation of community care (op. cit., p. 153).

Resources

The Audit Commission (1994) noted that authorities were running out of money to provide community care and that this was leading to shortfalls in services in many areas. The reasons for this included recent changes in the funding formula for distributing resources by government, which left some authorities with less money than they had anticipated, decisions at local level to allocate less money to social services, inadequacies in the local mechanisms for controlling resources, and a steadily rising demand for services. The report noted that service users complained often that the 'office hours' mentality of service providers militated against the provision of care when it was most needed, i.e. at night and during the weekends. The invidious practice of local authorities not recording unmet need – 45% of authorities did not do this in a survey by RADAR (1994) – makes it more likely that shortages of resources will adversely affect services (George, 1994, p. 26).

It is ironic that the separation of functions between purchasing and provision of community care services may lead to the same government that is promoting the development of community-based rather than institutional care – for example in the care of older people – funding a huge expansion of residential nursing homes (Illsley and Jamieson, 1990, p. 88).

A survey by the Labour Party of 40 local authorities found that 12 of these had no money left in their community care budgets, 24 were involved in rationing services and almost half were using funds that were earmarked for other services (*The Guardian,* 14 December 1994). *The Observer* reported that almost 40% of local authorities were reducing community care provision to try to ward off deficits in their budgets. It was anticipated that older people would be among the main casualties of this trend. In many areas, support services including shopping, cleaning, cooking and respite care were being cut. A third of directors of social services reported that many older people were dying within weeks of leaving hospital, implying that they had been discharged too soon. In Lancashire, home help provision was being reduced by a half. In Devon, an anticipated £8½ million pound deficit was leading to the rationing of services to exclude 'lower priority categories' of older people. Twenty thousand extra referrals had been received during 1994. In Dorset, services had been reduced by an average of a quarter in an attempt to address a project overspend of £3 million pounds, and referrals for elderly care had increased by 70% during the past twelve months (*The Observer,* 20 November 1994). A survey by the Association of Metropolitan Authorities (AMA) in 1994 found that the number of councils charging for home care services had increased from 72% in 1992–3 to 83% in 1993–4. The proportion of means-tested charges rose dramatically from 50% to 61% in the same period and reached 65% for respite care (op. cit.).

In February 1994, the Ombudsman condemned Leeds Health Authority for allowing a seriously incapacitated stroke victim to be discharged to a nursing home without financial support from the health authority. The Royal College of Physicians (RCP) (1994) was moved largely by this incident to note that one consequence of a four fold reduction of long stay beds was the impossibility of providing free NHS long stay care to all the people who may prefer it to private care.

Concern continued to mount in the 1990s, with a succession of reports critical of the failure of community care to protect people in the community. The case that attracted most media attention was that of the killing of Jonathan Zito by Christopher Clunis after his release from mental hospital (Ritchie *et al.*, 1994) (see document 14 for details). In 1995, the inquiry into the death of Jonathan Newby, a volunteer worker at the Oxford Cyrenian's Jacqui Porter House in Oxford, made many recommendations to improve the rigour of selection of volunteers and strengthen their training, support and supervision (Davies *et al.*, 1995). But such inquiry reports tended to indict specific aspects of practice rather than community care as a whole. Thus, the inquiry into the killing of Bryan Bennett by Stephen Laudat, who stabbed him 82 times, concluded that this act by a severely disturbed man could not be predicted; but the report was critical of hospital care at Kneesworth House, a private hospital in Hertfordshire, and of discharge arrangements for patients (Woodley, 1995).

The change to 'spot' contracts (tailor-made to single situations) from 'block' contracts (applicable to a group of care packages, facility, establishment or locality) raised a number of problems: whether the purchaser or the provider should carry the risk for unused services; how continuity of service in an establishment should be maintained; how stability and quality of non-establishment-based services could be assured. This implies a flexible approach to commissioning specific services from selected providers, so that the budget is not locked into service provision, but responds flexibly to the assessed needs of individuals. This leaves providers, and especially small providers in the voluntary and private sectors, to manage and quality assure the resultant ever-changing stream of individually tailored packages of services (Jarman, 1994, p. 7).

Problems of particular groups of carers

Policies of community care have exposed what informal carers have done for years, rather than creating a vast new army of carers (Sinclair *et al.*, 1990, p. 50). The increased burden of caring that falls on informal carers such as relatives and friends falls unequally on some groups, including women, people who themselves are in need of services, such as older and disabled relatives, and children and young people. There is a need to extend the participation not only of services users, but also of carers, in shaping the ways in which services can best respond to needs. A fundamental social, economic and cultural change is needed to address gender biases and unequal opportunities in caring for and by women (Finch and Groves, 1980).

Some informal carers, such as women, children and young people who care for a relative at home, experience particular problems. Ungerson (1987) has highlighted the situation of women carers caring for spouses, relatives and friends. If the burden of adult caring is largely hidden, that carried by young carers is even more so. Of over 640 young carers in contact with young carers' projects in Britain, the average age was 12, 60% lived in lone parent families and 1 in 10 cared for more than one person (Dearden and Becker, 1995). Becker argues that best practice initiatives to meet young carers' needs 'pursue a child-centred and children's rights approach, based on listening to and respecting young carers' own views and expressed needs. They promote the rights of young carers to be heard; to be respected and believed; to education; to recreation; to be consulted; to be protected from physical injury; to have access to information, advocacy, respite care; and to have greater choice and control over their own lives' (Becker, 1995, p. 17). The situation of young carers will be strengthened when the Carers (Recognition and Services) Act 1995 is implemented in 1996. It is estimated that about half of social services departments intend to employ a child care worker to carry out young carers' assessments and will carry out staff training on young carers' work (Valios, 1995, p. 6).

Quality assurance through participation

The Children Act 1989 and NHS and Community Care Act 1990 have set up new mechanisms to enable complaints to be made about services and to ensure they are inspected, intending thereby to strengthen the voices of professionals and service users in assuring the quality of services. However, this only touches the tip of the iceberg of the participation of people in community care planning, implementation and evaluation. There is a need to articulate what is an inherently political process from 'personal troubles to collective policy'. This is likely to involve developing and exchanging accounts of personal experiences, defining one's own needs, collaborating in assessments and negotiating decisions (Croft and Beresford, 1989, p. 16).

The NHS and Community Care Act 1990 and the Children Act 1989 required local authorities to set up and operate complaints and inspection procedures. On the whole, by the mid-1990s the complaints procedures of most authorities were exemplary. But shortcomings in their use were still apparent. An inspection of complaints procedures in five local authorities in 1993 indicated that complaints procedures were not being made readily accessible to all service users and carers, and were not being used to inform of changes in social services policies (SSI Department of Health, 1993, p. 4). Inspection units were required to be free-standing from the local authority, and undertook a range of registration and inspection functions regarding residential and day care adult and children's services provided by local authority or independent (private and voluntary) providers. Reports of SSI inspections of the work of inspection units (SSI/Department of Health, 1993, 1994) indicated varied success in achieving minimum standards. The latter inspection revealed that only two of the inspection units met all the standards set out by the SSI in terms of making explicit statements of service standards, publicising them and consulting providers and users about them, agreeing policy on sharing information between different parts of social services departments and for consulting service providers, recruiting suitably qualified staff to inspect children's homes and boarding schools, promoting the role of advisory committees, agreeing policies for making inspection reports available to the public in an appropriately accessible form, and agreeing how to ensure and demonstrate even-handed enforcement of inspection findings (SSI/Department of Health, 1994, pp. 2–3).

The Department of Health intended that, while elements of care management such as assessment were in effect contracted out by purchasers to providers, safeguards of the quality of these activities would be put in place. Official guidelines noted that the purchaser would have to monitor assessments and validate them to ensure their quality and consistency (Department of Health, 1991, p. 34). But this system for evaluating the quality of community care left significant scope for divergences of view. At the same time (see chapter 11), there was enormous variety in the ways authorities and services were structured and delivered in different parts of Britain. There was also unevenness in the delivery of services inherent in the diverse routes by which different groups of people come within the scope of community care. For example, a person with a mental health problem discharged from a mental hospital would immediately come into the ambit of care management through a community mental health team, whereas a statement of needs of a child with learning difficulties under the Education Act

1981 occurred in a process only passed on to community care when formal secondary education was completed.

Much could be learned from the experiences of different countries, acknowledging that the flow of knowledge and expertise is not only from the more affluent and developed countries to the rest. The KAPI – Open Care Centres for Elderly People – in Greece, with multi-professional staffing and to which older people have access as a social centre and a source of professional services (Hugman, 1994, pp. 163–166), are an example of a model of provision that could begin to address the challenge of providing flexible, user-responsive community care.

Problems of working together

Community care practice involves health and local authorities, especially housing and social services departments, collaborating to ensure that services are delivered at an appropriate standard to people who need them. Problems of working together have existed for many years. The organisational cultures of health and social services, for example, are very different; in many ways there is more compatibility between housing and social services. In fact, the local government reorganisation of 1996 is more likely to be followed by a convergence between housing and social services departments than between health and social services. Having said that, health – and within health, areas such as mental health – housing, disability and continuing care are areas that necessitate a high level of collaboration between social services, health and housing services. With health authorities pressured to meet performance targets in acute services, budgetary constraints have exacerbated demarcation disputes between health and social services over who pays for particular aspects of continuing care. Continuing care services tend to include nursing and residential homes for older people, people with mental health problems and people with physical or learning disabilities.

Just as murders carried out by discharged patients heightened issues concerning joint working between health and social services, so questions of responding to homelessness, inadequately housed people and people with special housing needs highlighted the necessity for joint working between housing and social services. Mearns and Smith (1994, pp. 194–195) have identified five trends in housing policy that apply with equal force in social services: the importance of independent living, enabling people to occupy housing that is not part of special needs provision but makes assistance available to disabled people (see also Morris, 1990); the need of older and disabled people for a network of specialist care and repair services, able to visit them and negotiate with them a package enabling them to respond to their own housing needs for repairs and adaptations; the necessity for support and encouragement for joint working between field-based housing and social services staff; the need to avoid the risk that focusing on staff collaboration becomes the priority rather than meeting service users' needs; the requirement to develop a geographically distributed continuum of housing options for people with a range of needs, not segregated from other housing provision and hence not stigmatising.

In a preliminary trawl in autumn 1995 of collaborative activity involving local authority social services departments, the author found that some social services departments purchase services such as occupational therapy from the housing department and health authority. Some departments such as education and libraries, planning and transportation, were set to merge in forthcoming local government reorganisation. Community care brought housing, social services and health much closer than they had been. Joint management of community resource teams for elderly mentally infirm people and community mental health teams, provision for substance misusers and joint mental health strategies were quite common. Collaboration between housing and social services took place in care and repair schemes and the provision of very sheltered housing. Planning between health and social services, in the words of one director of social services, has tended to be 'complementary if not yet integrated'. This euphemistically indicates the distance yet to be travelled before fully collaborative joint working can be achieved.

The United Kingdom Home Care Association (UKHCA), representing around 700 agencies, criticised the failure of local authorities to involve private domiciliary care agencies in the development of services. Among the factors militating against private provision, the UKHCA claimed, were arrangements for spot-purchasing rather than the block contracts providers needed in order to survive commercially, draconian penalty clauses, vague demands, delayed payments and inconsistent practices between different authorities (UKHCA, 1994). Within five years of the passing of the NHS and Community Care Act 1990 there were signs of a shift, supported by sections of the political Left (for example, in Labour-run Birmingham) and the Right (for instance, in Conservative-run Wandsworth), back towards allowing local government to take on the purchasing role, in health at any rate (Brindle, 1994). In 1993, David Knowles, then president of the Institute of Health Services Management, advocated in his inaugural address that the NHS surrender its role as purchaser of community care services.

In mid-1994, the Association of Metropolitan Authorities

(AMA) threw its weight behind proposals for this change to be tested in a number of pilot ventures throughout Britain. Jeremy Beecham, chair of the AMA, said:

> From a practical viewpoint, there is a feeling that local government is suited to this task because of its involvement in community care and environmental health, its responsiblity for so much of housing and education and its know-how in contracting-out services. From a democratic point of view, the case is irrefutable. The reformed NHS consists largely of unaccountable, unelected quangos and the public feel baffled and excluded. Replacing them with elected members, responsible to local residents for so many of the services affecting health, would turn what is now a national ill service into a genuine national health service (op. cit.).

Pressures on smaller units

There was evidence that the establishment of internal markets adversely affected voluntary and private organisations, especially the smaller ones. Despite the fact that legislation was designed to encourage the greater involvement of the independent sector, this was hampered in practice by a lack of resources and support for providers in small units. The contradiction between local authorities empowering people and keeping within their budgets creates pressure, restricting choice by service users and excluding smaller providers as economies of scale are sought by coalescing contracts for services (Clements, 1994, p. 22).

Sustainability

Melanie Henwood's (1994) study of the implementation of community care in five localities – two Shire Counties, one Metropolitan Borough Council, one Inner and one Outer London Authority – queried the sustainability of community care, in view of the lack of investment, unclear policies and inability of authorities to keep up with the demands on services and therefore to guarantee the future quality of community care. Staff were fearful of change and were experiencing burnout and 'change fatigue' as they coped with the implementation of community care in addition to existing duties. Henwood cited uncertainty over the division of responsibilities between health and social care, for example, when dealing with discharges from hospitals and long-term care, a lack of involvement of service users and carers, the under-involvement of GPs – some of whom were working against the legislation by using referrals to hospital to avoid working with social services departments – and underdevelopment of such alternatives to residential care as domiciliary services. She asked whether services were sufficiently commercially viable for private providers to be involved in future (Henwood, 1994). In the mid-1990s, it looks unlikely that the upswing in the economy forecast by the Conservatives and denied by Labour will occur, or that local government reorganisation will markedly improve the supply and the quality of community care services. On the other hand, as Le Grand and Bartlett (1993, p. 209) note in their case studies of quasi-markets, which include community care, it is too early to judge whether the community care reforms have succeeded or failed. The changes have incurred heavy transitional costs, there are problems of establishing a viable quasi-market (see chapter 11) and of resourcing an adequate range of services to meet needs. But Le Grand and Bartlett (1993, p. 209) conclude that it would be premature to evaluate the new approaches in isolation from those they have replaced. There may be problems in implementing community care, but there is insufficient evidence at this stage to justify abandoning it.

References and further reading

Association of Metropolitan Authorities (1994) *A Survey of Social Services Charging Policies 1992–94*, London: AMA.

Audit Commission (1994) *Taking Stock: Progress with Care in the Community*, London: HMSO.

Audit Commission Report (1986) *Making a Reality of Community Care*, London: HMSO.

Becker, S. (1995) Letter of the law, *Community Care*, no.1080, 3–9 August, 17.

Beresford, P. and Croft, S. (1993) *Citizen Involvement: a Guide for Change*, London: BASW/Macmillan.

Better Services for the Mentally Handicapped (1971) London: HMSO.

Brindle, D. (1994) The purse snatchers, *The Guardian,* 25 May, 12–13.

Bulmer, M. (1993) The social basis of community care, in Bornat, J., Pereira, M., Challis, D. and Davies, B. (1993) *Case Management in Community Care: an Evaluated Experiment in the Home Care of the Elderly*, Aldershot: Gower.

Children Act 1989 and the Carers (Recognition and Services) Act 1995, London: HMSO.

Chronically Sick and Disabled Persons Act 1970, London: HMSO.

Clements, L. (1994) Squeezed out, *Community Care,* no.1031, 25–31 August, 22–23.

Committee on Local Authority and Allied Personal Social Services (1968) *The Seebohm Report*, Cmnd 3703, London: HMSO.

Croft, S. and Beresford, P. (1989) User-involvement, citizenship and social policy, *Critical Social Policy*, issue 26, autumn, 5–18.

Dant, T., Carley, M., Gearing, B. and Johnson, M. (1992) Care for elderly people at home: the Gloucester project, in Morgan, K. (ed.) *Gerontology: Responding to an Ageing Society*, London: Jessica Kingsley.

Darvill, G. (1990) *Partners in Empowerment: the Networks of Innovation in Social Work*, London: National Institute for Social Work.

Davies, B. (1992) *Care Management, Equity and Efficiency: the International Experience*, Canterbury, Kent: PSSRU.

Davies, N. Lingham, R., Prior, C. and Sims, A. (1995) *Report of the Inquiry into the Circumstances Leading to the Death of Jonathan Newby on 9th October 1993 in Oxford*, Oxford: Oxfordshire Health Authority.

Dearden, C. and Becker, S. (1995) Young carers – the facts, *Community Care*, Sutton, Surrey. 17 November.

Department of Health (1989b) *Caring for People – the Next Decade and Beyond*, Cmnd 849, London: HMSO.

Department of Health (1991) *Implementing Community Care: Purchaser, Commissioner and Provider Roles*, London: HMSO.

Department of Health (1992) *Health of the Nation*, White Paper, London: HMSO.

Department of Health and Social Security (1988) *Community Care: an Agenda for Action* (Griffiths Report) London: HMSO.

Disability Discrimination Act 1995, London: HMSO.

Disabled Persons (Services Consultation and Representation) Act 1986, London: HMSO.

Education Act 1981, London: HMSO.

Education Reform Act 1988, London: HMSO.

Elcock, H. (1993), Local government, in Farnham, D. and Horton, S. (eds), *Managing the New Public Services*, 150–171, London: Macmillan.

Farnham, D. and Horton, S. (eds) *Managing the New Public Services*, London: Macmillan.

Finch, J. and Groves, D. (1980) Community care and the family: a case for equal opportunities, *Journal of Social Policy,* vol.9, 486–511.

George, M. (1994) Less money, more need, *Community Care,* vol.27, no.1040, 27 October–2 November, 26–27.

Henwood, M. (1994) *Fit for Change: Snapshots of the community care reforms one year on*, London: King's Fund Centre.

HMSO (1957) *Royal Commission on the Law Relating to Mental Illness and Mental Deficiency 1954* (Cmnd 169), The Percy Commission, London: HMSO.

Hugman, R. (1994) *Ageing and the Care of Older People in Europe*, London: Macmillan.

Illsley, R. and Jamieson, A. (1990) Contextual and structural influences on adaptation to change, in Jamieson, A. and Illsley, R. (eds), *Contrasting European Policies for the Care of Older People*, 83–94, Aldershot: Avebury.

Jamieson, A. and Illsley, R. (eds) (1990) *Contrasting European Policies for the Care of Older People*, Aldershot: Avebury.

Jarman, M. (1994) *Together Towards 2000: a perspective from the voluntary sector*, Paper presented to NCVCCO/ADSS North West Conference.

Jones, K. (1991) *The Making of Social Policy in Britain 1830–1990*, London: Athlone.

Le Grand, J. and Bartlett, W. (eds) (1993) *Quasi-Markets and Social Policy*, London: Macmillan.

Local Government and Housing Act 1989, London: HMSO.

Mearns, R. and Smith, R. (1994) *Community Care: Policy and Practice*, London: Macmillan.

Mental Health Act 1959, London: HMSO.

Ministry of Health (1962) *A Hospital Plan for England and Wales*, London: HMSO.

Ministry of Health (1963) *Health and Welfare: the Development of Community Care*, Cmnd 1973, London: HMSO.

Morgan, K. (ed.) (1992) *Gerontology: Responding to an Ageing Society*, London: Jessica Kingsley.

Morris, J. (1990) *Our Homes Our Rights: Housing, Independent Living and Physically Disabled People*, London: Shelter.

NHS and Community Care Act 1990, London: HMSO.

NISW (1982) *Social Workers: their Roles and Tasks* (Barclay Report), London: National Institute for Social Work/Bedford Square Press.

NISW. Race Equality Unit (1989) Submission in Response to the White Paper on Community Care, London: NISW.

Prime Minister's Office (1991) *The Citizen's Charter,* London: HMSO.

RADAR (1994) *Disabled People Have Rights,* London: RADAR.

Report of All Party Commission on Citizenship (1990) House of Commons, London.

Ritchie, J.H., Dick, D. and Lingham, R. (1994) *The Report of the Inquiry into the Care and Treatment of Christopher Clunis,* London: HMSO.

Royal College of Physicians (1994) *Ensuring Equity and Quality of Care for Elderly People,* London: RCP.

Scull, A. (1977) *Decarceration,* Englewood Cliffs, NJ: Prentice Hall.

Sinclair, I., Gorbach, P., Levin, E., Neill, J. and Williams, J. (1990) Community Care and Residential Admissions: Results from Two Empirical Studies, in Jamieson, A. and Illsley, R. (eds) *Contrasting European Policies for the Care of Older People,* 37–48, Aldershot: Avebury.

Smale, G. and Tuson, G. (1990) Community social work: foundation for the 1990s and beyond, in Darvill, G., *Partners in Empowerment: the Networks of Innovation in Social Work,* London: National Institute for Social Work.

Social Services Inspectorate (1993) *Inspection of Assessment and Care Management Arrangements in Social Services Departments, Interim Overview Report,* London: SSI. London East Inspection Group.

SSI/Department of Health (1993), *Social Services Department Inspection Units: the First 18 Months,* a report on 10 inspection units inspected in 1992/1993, London: Department of Health.

SSI/Department of Health (1994) *Social Services Inspection Units: Report of an Inspection of the Work of Inspection Units in 27 Local Authorities,* London: HMSO.

Stevenson, O. and Parsloe, P. (1978) *Social Services Teams: the Practitioners' View,* London: HMSO.

UKHCA (1994) *Progress and Problems with Contracting,* London: UKHCA.

Ungerson, C. (1987) *Policy is Personal: Sex, Gender and Informal Care,* London: Tavistock.

Valios, N. (1995) Survey reveals lack of services for young carers, *Community Care,* no.1080, 3–9 August, 6–7.

Warner, N. (1994) *Community Care: Just a Fairy Tale?* Report of a UK research survey commissioned by Carers National Association, London.

Webb, R. and Tossell, D. (1991) *Social Issues for Carers: A Community Care Perspective,* London: Edward Arnold.

Wilson, G. (1993) Evaluating the contribution of participants in community care assessment and planning, *Journal of Social. Policy,* vol.22, no.4, 507–526.

Woodley, L. (1995) *The Woodley Report,* London: East London and The City Health Authority.

CHAPTER 7

Mental health and disability

This chapter examines how the work of the personal social services relates to people with mental health problems and disabled people, with some reference to people with learning disabilities. The circumstances in which the needs of some adults come to the notice of the personal social services vary from self-referral to referral by professionals and/or other agencies. The fact that this chapter deals with work with disabled people and people with mental health problems means that it includes work with some adults whose circumstances may be problematic, in the sense that they may feel oppressed by those around them. This is a difficult area to highlight, since some people justifiably feel that even the fact that they are singled out for services of one kind or another reinforces any stigma they already experience. Understandably, many people receiving services described in this chapter never experience being labelled or stigmatised. Yet, taken as part of the broad field of community care, work with adults exceeds in volume the area of social work with children. Social services provided through local authorities for adults use approximately a half to three-fifths of the budget.

Context of mental health and disability

From treatment to empowerment

The tensions between the treatment and empowerment paradigms are particularly significant in fields such as mental health and learning disability, where medical and social perspectives underlie negotiations about whether health or social services should take the lead in shaping services and practice. Historically, medical practitioners have dominated mental health and 'mental handicap', yet most of the critical perspectives on these areas have been introduced from outside the medico-treatment paradigm. Mental hospitals are a prototype of the largely medicalised and Western-dominated societal response to the range of mental health problems people experience throughout their lives. The organisation Survivors Speak Out, founded in 1986, is one manifestation of the hostility of former patients in mental hospitals to being stigmatised simply because of their previous hospitalisation (Adams, 1996, pp. 59–60). Service users in mental health and disability, for example, have played a leading role in campaigns against discrimination and oppression. The disability movement has been particularly active in promoting the empowerment of disabled people, rather than the perpetuation of their oppression through the imposition of the stigma of disablement for impairments they may have. While impairment is a term referring to a medical condition, disability is held by disabled activists to denote the negative impact on them of the label of disablement. Activists have drawn attention, for example, to the diminution of the personhood (see chapter 8 for discussion of concept of personhood) of the individual implicit in using terms such as 'the disabled', as though the aspect in which the person is impaired has become that person's identity. Addressing this criticism and also the point that services should be provided *with* and not *for* people, the Barclay Report (NISW, 1982, p. 35) observes that 'an attempt must be made to see people and their needs as a whole and to take account of their view about what services, if any, are provided'. However, changing the language of disablement does not remove the reality of the oppression of disabled people. The word 'disability' and its derivatives are used here in recognition of this fact.

Some adults requiring the personal social services are reluctant to, or ambivalent about, being in touch with a social services agency and accepting help, for two particular reasons. First, older people may associate social services with national assistance, or even the Poor Law; they may have had contact with services at a time when the values of the Poor Law were visible in the attitudes of some workers. Second, their needs may be in areas such as disability; they may resent being labelled as inadequate or a problem, and simply want their particular needs addressed.

Disability: a contested area

To spend this chapter debating the categorisation of the knowledge informing policy responses to aspects of disability would be complex, but could risk missing the point, which is that what underlies critiques of labels such as 'subnormality', 'retardation', 'mental handicap', 'learning difference', 'impairment', 'being intellectually challenged' is a struggle by people experiencing the misuse of power: they are aware of the oppressiveness of being 'disabled', whether at the level of the society, the organisation, the group, the household or the individual. So, the designation of the territory of this chapter is inherently problematic, since the way it is labelled is held by critics, including the disability movement, to be part of the problem of the oppression of disabled people themselves. This chapter recognises this and deals first with aspects of disability as a whole, with particular regard to physical impairment. Then, because it is easier to make links between social policy responses to learning disability and mental health if they are dealt with together, the following sections address these two under single headings. But in no sense does this imply that learning disability does not warrant being addressed in its own right.

Impairment and disability

Disability is a largely hidden aspect of society, in that the majority of the population experience some form of impairment, and an unknown number experience the stigma of disability. As implied above, disability refers to the labelling of a person through oppression – the abuse of power in society, at structural, institutional, group and individual levels (document 12). Social work with disabled people needs to take on board the impact on them of oppression. Although pressure groups such as the Disablement Income Group (DIG) were active as long ago as the 1960s, since the 1980s various organisations, mainly in the voluntary sector, have taken up issues concerning the rights and empowerment of disabled people.

The Chronically Sick and Disabled Persons Act 1970 was a milestone in the history of services for disabled people. It amended 39 existing Acts of parliament on behalf of disabled people, imposed new duties on 12 departments of state and local authorities and became a model of such legislation for many other countries. It required local authorities to spend much more than previously on cash benefits and services, in the form of home visits, assessments and aids and adaptations in the home. Between 1970 and 1980 public spending on services and benefits for disabled people increased tenfold to £3.03 billion (Alf Morris, 1994). But attitudes to disabled people remained largely unchanged (Brandon, 1995, p. 7).

In 1985, only 8% of disabled people over 60 in Britain were in residential or institutional care (Pringle, 1995, p. 107). Informal care is characterised by men being relatively privileged, people living alone receiving most formal care (op. cit., p. 110), and discrimination against female married carers reflecting the wider gendered division of labour and cultural societal norms (op. cit., p. 111).

Alf Morris (1994), reflecting on the Civil Rights (Disabled Persons) Bill concerning the rights of disabled people, which failed to pass through the House of Commons in the early summer of 1994, noted that between 1945 and 1964 there was no mention of services for disabled people in the manifestos of any political party and not one debate in the Commons on disability. But this Bill at least succeeded in putting the issue of full civil rights for disabled people onto the political agenda. 'No one even knew how many disabled people there were in Britain. They were treated not even as second-class citizens, more as non-people: seen or heard only by their families or, if in institutions, by those who controlled their lives' (A. Morris, 1994).

Mental health and learning disability

While the history of mental health provision in Britain extends over many centuries (Jones, 1960), provision for people with learning disability, or 'mental handicap' as it was known, in anything like a modern form does not predate the 1960s. The Mental Deficiency Act 1913 set up 'colonies' for 'mental defectives' regarded as needing to live in institutions. The Mental Health Act 1959 was a milestone in the history of mental health services, in the sense that it was intended to shift from incarcerating people who were mentally ill and 'mentally handicapped' people to providing support to enable them to live in the community. Unfortunately, this Act did not achieve this change, for reasons largely associated with a lack of appropriate resources to develop community-based provision. This, in retrospect, is ironic, since from the late 1980s cost-saving was to provide a major motivation for closing down mental hospitals. The movement towards community care in mental health did not develop purely on the grounds of finance, although Thatcherite policies associated with reducing the dominance of state and public sector provision were as prominent in mental health as in other aspects of the human services. Technological and ideological factors were also important: technological change through the development of drugs that enabled people's behaviour to be controlled for relatively long periods outside the hospital; ideological opposition to the mental hospital as an institution.

Advances in medication were significant at different levels. They led to practical changes, in the flexible treatment now provided for, say, schizophrenic people who only needed to attend an outpatients' clinic for a top-up injection or prescription every week or fortnight, rather than living on the ward. But more important from the point of view of professional power, they provided a means by which the medico-treatment paradigm could transfer into the community. Advances in community care could be made in the face of opposition to the great power of hospital-based medical professionals, who experienced the loss of their practice base as hospitals closed, or by providing a rationale for that practice to be relocated in the community. The medical model of treatment was more vulnerable in the community, since the social dimension was more apparent in closer proximity. But there is little doubt that advances in medication were one mechanism enabling the shift to the community as the main site for tensions between medical and social models to be worked out.

Ideological opposition to the mental hospital as an institution gathered strength from the early 1960s. It would be misleading to overplay the contribution to this area of individuals, since history in any case is a social construction, only one dimension of which is represented in a narrative that gives prominence to great people. The task is to understand why some ideas are picked up at one time and not at another. In this respect, it is instructive to juxtapose the work of three people against some key aspects of mental health and learning disability: Erving Goffman, Wolf Wolfensberger and Ronald Laing. Goffman's work in the 1960s – notably the series of essays published in the wake of his study of a single mental hospital in Washington DC (Goffman, 1967) and to a lesser extent his book on stigma and exclusion (Goffman, 1968) – provided a basis whereby many critics of hospital-based treatment could develop research, commentary and alternative practice. Wolfensberger's primary contribution was originally in the field of what was then termed 'mental handicap', now generally referred to as 'learning disability', although the designation of this area of work is contested, not least by people who are intellectually challenged themselves. Wolfensberger's work spans the period from the early 1960s to the mid-1990s, since he is still an active proselytiser of concepts as this book is being written. His impact in Western countries began with 'normalisation' (Wolfensberger, 1972), an ideological position from which he later moved to 'social role valorisation' (SRV) (Wolfensberger, 1982), which he tends to designate as a social science theory; currently his work lies in the area he describes as 'deathmaking of socially devalued people' (Wolfensberger, 1994). Laing's contribution as a psychiatrist to what became known as 'anti-psychiatry' began with his critical reflections on his practice with schizophrenic patients (Laing, 1962) and led to a broad-based anti-psychiatry movement in Western countries, which neither disappeared nor survived beyond the decade as a separate area of practice, but was absorbed into psychiatric practice along with other critiques (Clare, 1976).

Between the 1950s and the 1990s, ideas about what constitutes best practice have been transformed: from institutional to residential care; from purpose-made accommodation in the community to ordinary living in normal housing; and from bricks and mortar provision to a service provided *with* as well as *for* people. Prior to the 1960s, people with learning disabilities either lived at home with their families or were warehoused on a long-term basis in institutions. The gradual change from institutional provision to hostels and staffed and unstaffed group homes and 'core and cluster' facilities in the community in the 1970s still led to people being housed in purpose-built or adapted 'ghetto'-style establishments. The emphasis in the 1970s was on training people, as the route out of learning disability, or mental handicap as it was termed at the time.

Pauline Morris's research into the appalling conditions in many long stay hospitals helped to stimulate the government publication *Better Services for the Mentally Handicapped* (DHSS, 1971). This product of some Labour Party politicians' commitment to community-based social democracy (see also chapter 10 for parallels in responses to delinquency) was not adopted and implemented wholesale. It came at a time when the newly created local authority social services departments were spending money developing their own largely specialist establishments catering for people with learning disability. When local authority budget cuts followed the crisis of escalating oil prices in the Middle East in the winter of 1973-4, the social services did not have the spending power and health services could not challenge the power of medical professionals. During the 1970s, although Wolfensberger's ideas on normalisation were gaining ground, local authority training and rehabilitation day centres symbolised the dominance of a model of learning disability in which 'mental handicap' was framed as a problem of individual deficit, which could be made up through training from professionals, to enable the individual to function normally in society. Wolfensberger applied the concept of normalisation to the field of learning disability in the 1960s, then replaced it with social role valorisation. Meanwhile, research continued to imply that closure rather than reform would be the most productive next step for the hospitals dealing with 'mentally handicapped' people (Jones *et al.*, 1975). But it was the 1980s before a significant change occurred in practice. The early 1980s saw the publication of several government reports emphasising the necessity for community care (DHSS, 1980, 1981a, 1981b) and building on the previously neglected recommendations of the Jay Committee (The Jay Report, 1979). This report had recommended adopting ordinary housing for people with disabilities, based on notions of rationality of choice and advocacy, an idea with growing currency at the time (King's Fund Centre, 1980). Pilgrim and Rogers argued even before 1990 the need to improve the quality and quantity of housing, support for informal carers, real 'asylum', improved access through public transport to public services and fully financed community care services (Pilgrim and Rogers, 1989, p. 9). These initiatives foreshadowed Jenny Morris's argument that decarceration of disabled people will only result in institutionalisation within the community unless the experience of the independent living movement is acknowledged and people have housing that enables them to develop their independence and civil rights (Morris, 1994b, p. 44).

The ten-year All Wales Strategy (AWS) for developing services for mentally handicapped (as they were described then) people was published in 1983. It was founded on principles of full involvement of service users and carers. Genuine attempts were made to involve service users, carers and, where necessary, an advocate, in the development of the community care process (McGrath and Grant, 1992). The All Wales Strategy (Welsh Office, 1982) was a testing ground for many of these ideas and experiences, partly because politicians needed to invest in Wales to build up support in an area neglected for so many years; also, policy and practice could proceed largely from scratch, rather than having to adapt existing facilities. The learning disability field also benefited from the factors identified above in the mental health field, which applied also to the development of community care through the hospital closure programme.

Despite the gathering momentum of the hospital closure programme from the late 1980s, other forms of custodialisation increased. For example, an increasing number of people with learning disabilities were in prison in the 1990s, following the closure of locked wards in mental hospitals. More insidiously, the organisation Resicare campaigned (see Cox and Pearson, 1995) with some success in the mid-1990s to keep open former 'mental handicap' hospitals, under the appealing label of 'village communities'. This title did not endear them to professionals, who tended to regard them simply as institutions with the addition of marginal facilities such as a small shop. Critics of care villages emphasise the negative consequences of creating ghettos and the risk that they are alien to the values and principles of personalised care underpinning community care (Mapp, 1994, p. 27).

Alternatives to institutions for mentally ill people

The mental hospital system, which dominated the response to people with mental health problems for 150 years in Britain, has been almost completely removed. The development of new drugs such as tranquillisers and anti-depressants made it possible to treat many more acute cases successfully and to discharge many mentally ill people, such as schizophrenics, and older confused people to the community once they had established a pattern of self-medication or medication by carers. But criticism has continued for many years of shortcomings in community-based support of people with chronic conditions and the revolving door effect, where increasing numbers of patients repeatedly return to the hospital. Discharging patients does not ensure that their problems become redefined as social and are given support by the community-based social services rather than hospital-based medical services.

The impact of the Mental Health Act 1983 and the hospital closure programme on decreasing the numbers of patients going into institutions has been countered by increased re-admission rates, and the use of the Act as though the community is an extension of the mental hospital (Bean and Mounser 1993, p. 166).

The arguments for a Community Treatment Order suggest that social control could be extended from the hospital into the community, reversing the traditional role of the hospital as the area for treatment and the community for back-up. The Compulsory Treatment Order (CTO) would enable patients to be compulsorily treated in their own homes, an activity that raises all kinds of issues and practical problems. It is hard to see also how the hospital function of providing protection of people from themselves could easily be transferred into the community.

The Blom Cooper inquiry (Blom Cooper, 1995) recommended that the Mental Health Act of 1983 be overhauled on the grounds that the legislative framework for community care, with its mandatory care plans, should be applied to people with mental health problems. The government reacted coolly to this, the general view being that the recently introduced structure of supervision orders and supervision registers should be adequate to cope with the situation.

The fact that mental health problems involve services in a range of residential and community settings across the statutory, voluntary, private and informal sectors makes professional responses complex to co-ordinate and problematic to deliver. One of the most vulnerable transitions for a person with mental health problems is from the residential setting to community care. Lack of adequate community care services have been a source of concern for many years, surfacing in a series of inquiry reports (e.g. Ritchie *et al.*, 1994; Davies *et al.*, 1995; Woodley, 1995). A study of 51 people with schizophrenia discharged in West Lambeth, London found that their contact with social workers had decreased against their wishes. In the first year after discharge, 17 had regular contact with social workers, compared with seven after four years (Conway *et al.*, 1994). Common problems include loneliness and depression. Research estimates the chances of a person with severe mental health problems committing suicide within a month of discharge from hospital as 200 times higher for men, and 130 times higher for women, than the general population (Goldacre *et al.*, 1994).

Mental hospitals: new roles beyond warehousing

Hospital-based mental health practices have remained among the clearest examples of how not to treat people in the entire human services. Significantly, Erving Goffman selected an anthropological study of a mental hospital to illustrate how the institutional culture subverted the formal purpose of treatment in total institutions. Goffman's (1967) research imported into the training of staff a critical, sociological view of the institution, as a means by which relatively large numbers of people could at best be treated, but at worst were warehoused, disciplined and dehumanised, by a relatively small and powerful staff group. Mental health policy and practice in Britain have struggled against the legacy of its large Victorian institutions, which exemplify these structures, attitudes and practices. Longstanding criticisms, publicised in the media, have exposed weaknesses in the regimes and treatment of patients in several mental hospitals, notably the special hospital of Rampton. Since 1961, almost a dozen major reports criticising special hospitals in particular, and mental hospitals in general, have been published. The SSI has played an increasingly active role in furthering decarceration, but public pressure has been important in forcing critical scrutiny of conditions and shortcomings in medical and nursing practice, particularly in the special hospitals (see document 15).

There are four special hospitals, dealing with patients who are a danger to themselves or others, as well as serious offenders under Section 37 or 45 of the Mental Health Act 1983: Ashworth (formerly Moss Side and Park Lane), Broadmoor and Rampton in England and Carstairs in Scotland. These institutions were subject to Home Office control and now are managed through the Special Hospitals Services Authority (SHSA), a quango set up in October 1989 representing the Department of Health and the Home Office.

The Glancy Report in 1974 dealt with security in psychiatric hospitals, including special hospitals (Department of Health and Social Security, 1974). The Butler committee was set up in the wake of the murders committed by Graham Young and Terry Iliffe after their release from Broadmoor. During the collection of evidence for the Butler Report, several patients carried out a protest on the roof of Broadmoor which attracted enough attention for the formation of the Broadmoor Public Action Committee. When the interim report of the Butler Committee was published (Home Office/Department of Health and Social Security, 1974), Lord Butler pointed out that the committee produced this interim report largely because they were appalled by conditions in Broadmoor (Cohen, undated, p. 98). The full report of the Butler committee was published subsequently (Home Office/Department of Health and Social Security, 1975, Cmnd 6244). Conditions in Broadmoor continued to cause concern in the 1970s and there was mounting pressure for investigation to be carried out (Cohen, undated, p. 98). In 1977, the Department of Health commissioned a plan for a new 100 bed wing from its own designers and the team studied how Broadmoor worked for several weeks, finally producing a very critical report which was never published, but is discussed in Cohen's book (Cohen, undated). In 1980 the All-party Parliamentary Committee on Mental Health reported on the situation in Broadmoor, following allegations of ill treatment by both former staff and patients (Report of All-party Mental Health Committee, 1980).

The acceleration of the hospital closure programme in the late 1980s led to a complementary but altogether different set of problems. A series of serious crimes committed by people released from mental hospitals in the early 1990s fomented public and media pressure for further reforms. The most influential incident was the murder of Jonathan Zito. The report into the treatment of Christopher Clunis described a cumulative series of failures and omissions by different people and agencies from his first hospital attendance in July 1987 until he stabbed Jonathan Zito in December 1992 (Ritchie *et al.*, 1994; Woodley, 1995) (document 14).

Circumstances such as the Zito case fuelled public and professional concern and led to increased political pressure for action to be taken to increase measures to control mentally disordered patients, particularly when released from mental hospitals to the community. The Reed Committee, a joint Department of Health/Home Office review of services for mentally disordered offenders, was set up in 1990 and completed its work by issuing 11 advisory reports in 7 volumes between 1992 and 1994 and a final summary report in 1994 (Department of Health/Home Office, 1994). It was followed by a series of circulars from the Home Office and Department of Health, attempting to implement new, more stringent guidelines for the supervision of mentally disordered offenders, in and out of custody.

A community treatment order (CTO) or a community supervision order (CSO) were proposed at different times from the early 1980s. The sheer practical problems of implementation meant that neither would ensure the compulsory supervision of a patient formerly in a hospital, now living in the community. The principle of such a compulsory order is controlling, even punitive, and at the very least intrusive. But, as Bean and Mounser (1993, p. 79) admit, it would have the benefit of offering a rationale for community-based practice to psychiatrists losing their base as hospitals close. However, the stigmatising consequences for former patients would be more difficult to justify. Controversial proposals made by the government for strengthening community supervision, i.e. control, of such patients are due to be debated when the Mental Health bill comes before Parliament in the Session of 1995–96.

Legal basis for mental health and disability work

All work in these areas is subject to the NHS and Community Care Act 1990, to the extent that it comes under the heading of community care. Additional legislation applies to particular areas referred to below.

Legal basis for work with disabled people

The statutory duties of local authority providers of social services for disabled people are contained in the National Assistance Act 1948, the Chronically Sick and Disabled Persons Act 1970, requiring all local authorities to keep a register of disabled persons in their area, and the Disabled Persons (Services, Consultation and Representation) Act 1986, superseded in some respects by the Disability Discrimination Act 1995. Blind people's needs were addressed originally in the Blind Persons' Act 1920 requiring local authorities to make provision for the welfare of blind people, were transferred to section 29 of the National Assistance Act, which also addressed the circumstances of deaf people. Duties are carried out under the legislation by social workers, mobility officers, home teachers, technical officers and occupational therapists; some provision, for people with sensory impairments for example, involves workshops for their employment (SSI, 1988, p. 47). Local authorities have not always met their full responsibilities to provide, for example, physical aids to mobility in the disabled person's home under the 1970 Act, and the 1986 Act has not been implemented fully.

Legal basis for mental health work

The major legislation for work with people with mental health problems is the Mental Health Act 1983. The NHS and Community Care Act applies specifically to mental hospitals, for example, in their move towards becoming NHS trusts. However, difficulties that arose in 1995 in the granting of trust status may be attributable to their holding some 'politically sensitive' offenders, such as the 'Moors' murderer Ian Brady. Special hospitals are provided for 'mentally disordered' people subject to detention under the Mental Health Act 1983 (MHA), which is the main basis for the majority of court disposals, save those where an offender is found not guilty by reason of insanity under the M'Naughton Rules Criminal Procedures (Insanity and Unfitness to Plead) Act 1991. Mental disorder is the terminology of the Act, but is not a precise definition; it refers to people requiring detention because their behaviour is deemed challenging or disordered. Home Office Circular 66/90 requires inter-agency collaboration to be maximised in work with mentally disordered offenders. Acute medium secure facilities include some regional secure units (RSUs) and some more local. The main options are an order for psychiatric treatment Section 37(3) MHA; a probation order with condition of residence or psychiatric treatment as an alternative to a hospital order; a hospital order Section 37 as alternative to a restriction order Section 41 or a custodial sentence; an interim hospital order Section 38; or a guardianship order Section 37.

In April 1994, the government introduced supervision registers for people with mental illness deemed to be a risk either to themselves or to others. A multi-professional assessment process commonly precedes decisions, and reviews, of circumstances where people are on such supervision registers. Such multi-professional work is underpinned by Home Office Circular HO 12/95 and detailed in guidelines on inter-agency working (Home Office and Department of Health 1995).

Approaches to mental health and disability work

The major stated policy change has been from a service-led to a needs-led approach; professionals have worked since 1993 within the new framework of purchase and provision of the NHS and Community Care Act 1990; service users, carers and advocates have stronger voices, individually and collectively, than at any previous time.

With the exception of initiatives in the fields of mental health and disability, such as in the London Borough of Hounslow where grants are given to a group for, and run by, disabled people, for them to allocate to services they target, the health and social care sector in general is prone to reflecting the societal stigmatisation of people and carers, rather than empowering them to deal with their circumstances and gain the resources to meet their needs. The patchy nature of services, the dominance of the medical model and the tendency for their professional providers to reflect patronising and at worst downright stigmatising societal attitudes, are features of the field. Voluntary organisations, self-help and self-advocacy groups carry out much work to counter this tendency. The four main approaches identified are protection, care, therapy and advocacy (see Fig. 4.1, chapter 4).

Protection

In the mental health field, the term 'protection' applies most readily to approaches involving medication and physical security. Secure accommodation has been provided traditionally in many mental hospitals, regional secure units and in the four Special Hospitals which protect people from both self-harm and harming others. Most of the locked wards in the mental hospitals have now disappeared, since the bulk of the hospitals themselves have been closed. Many critics have argued for the closure of the Special Hospitals and for the development of more local secure accommodation so that people can retain their links with their family and locality.

Care

Approaches to mental health and disability in the community are prone to the general criticism that they lack the element of 'care'. There is an increasing tendency in the mental health field to rehabilitate the term 'asylum' and indicate that its former meaning of a refuge denotes a function of some benefit. The process of closing hospitals is lengthy and complex and involves staff and patients in many problems of transition. There is some concern also that a by-product of the hospital closure programme will be the reduction or disappearance of refuges of this kind for people with mental health problems. Some small communities set up during the heyday of the anti-psychiatry movement, such as the Philadelphia Association (Gibbons, 1988, p. 187) have fulfilled this function for many years.

The inherently problematic nature of work with disabled people in general is illustrated by the controversy over whether people with learning difficulties should be accommodated in what are euphemistically called village communities or through community care. Agencies and professionals are beginning to acknowledge the importance of advocacy, self-advocacy and the growing strength of user-led movements, which form a counterpoint to professionally led approaches. The health and social services sectors have incorporated some of the experience of disabled people themselves in their own guidelines on practice, in areas such as community care.

Pointing to cases where disabled people have received inadequate housing because social workers have received inadequate training in housing law, Jenny Morris (1994a, p. 23) quotes Michael Oliver: 'If you can't access rights, then they aren't worth anything.'

Therapy

There may be a role for residential mental health facilities for people recovering from drug or alcohol misuse. In Synanon, a community-based approach based on self-help residential groups, which began in the USA and has spread to Britain (Adams, 1996, p. 123), various therapeutic techniques based on encounter groups are used to challenge people's substance misuse.

Three pilot projects undertaken in Birmingham, Kirklees and Liverpool by NACRO for three years from July 1993 were intended to encourage effective co-operation between people working in the criminal justice system and the health and social services, to ensure that the continuing treatment and care needs of mentally disordered offenders were met (Home Office, Mental Health Foundation and NACRO, 1994).

Advocacy

Despite the fact of multi-professional involvement in the mental health field, the concept of advocacy crosses professional boundaries quite smoothly. The language of advocacy for healthcare professionals does not differ significantly from that employed in social work. The four functions of advocacy for nurses identified by Sines (1995, p. 447) include: guarding people's rights; preserving their values; championing social justice in care provision; and conserving people's best interests. Similarly, Holmes (1995, p. 448) argues that nurses with learning disabled people should avoid the excuse that people with profound impairments cannot act as self-advocates, and should struggle to develop their practice.

In mental health, there can be little doubt of the significant role played in the past 20 years in Britain by journalists, and latterly by user groups themselves, in ensuring that critical issues regarding the quality of mental health services to patients and their friends and relatives are addressed. Undoubtedly, user groups themselves contributed to the widespread acceptance among politicians of all parties of the principle now being practised in some areas, of allocating directly to disabled people themselves the cash to buy services – an example of convergence between the supporters of the empowerment of service users and right-wing adherents to the extension of the voucher principle of entitlement to social services. The growth of the self-advocacy movement in the mental health field may be attributable in part to the fact that too little attention is paid to the views of service users about their mental health needs (Rogers *et al.,* 1993). Survivors Speak Out plays an influential role in shaping user involvement, and contributions to policy and practice, in the mental health sector.

A large-scale survey of mental health services through the experiences of users was reported on by Rogers *et al.* (1993). They concluded that a good deal of work is still needed to convince the government of the need to meet users' needs in personal and social rather than in medical terms, and to reduce the tendency to stigmatise people with mental health problems to the extent that they are unable to live normal lives in the community.

Issues in mental health and disability work

Rather than engaging in the technical aspects of policy and practice surveyed above, this final section focuses on two key issues: problems as metaphors and the empowerment of service users.

Problems as metaphors

The collision between government ideology in the personal social services and the value base of critical academics and practitioners surfaces in some areas more than others. Certain differences between the life experiences of people become metaphors for aspects of the human condition. Clearly, mental health and disability, especially learning disability, stand near the centre of debates about how far societal responses simply reinforce oppression and stigmatise (Goffman, 1968) rather than valuing and empowering people. Susan Sontag's brilliant analysis captures the imagery associated with fears about different afflictions in different historical periods. Cancer, she argues, despite the inaccurate view that it is a modern disease (Sontag, 1991, p. 71), is the modern version of tuberculosis – itself the plague of Victorian times. Just as historically certain mental health problems and disabilities were felt to be a sign of divine judgement on an individual (op. cit., p. 131), so HIV/AIDS mobilises group and societal homophobia and racism in particularly virulent forms.

AIDS is a favourite concern of those who translate their political agenda into questions of group psychology: of national self-esteem and self-confidence. Although these specialists in ugly feelings insist that AIDS is a punishment for deviant sex, what moves them is not just, or even principally, homophobia. Even more important is the utility of AIDS in pursuing one of the main activities of the so-called neo-conservatives, the Kulturkampf against all that is called, for short (and inaccurately), the 1960s. A whole politics of 'the will' – of intolerance, of paranoia, of fear of political weakness – has fastened on this disease (op. cit., pp. 148–149).

In this light, perhaps, social policy responses to mental health and disability revisit perspectives on the reshaping of the personal social services (see chapters 1 and 3 especially), particularly concerning consumerist assumptions of free will and choice, in the light of implicit moral judgements about what impaired people (whom society has disabled), or people who are experiencing serious mental health problems, may expect in terms of services from the state. What they should not expect is the oppressive message conveyed in the Government's proposed Mental Health Bill in autumn 1995 (see below).

Empowering service users

The World Health Organisation (WHO) locates mental health within a total approach to health in its 1986 declaration quoted by Fernando (1991, p. 209), that 'a state of complete physical, mental and social well being and not merely the absence of disease or infirmity, is a fundamental human right ... whose realization requires the action of many other social and economic sectors in addition to the health sector.' Mental health policy and practice in Britain illustrates a form of professional imperialism that has seen the colonisation of this aspect of people's lives by healthcare professionals. A similar form of psychiatric imperialism, through the application of Western-dominated approaches to psychiatry across the world, has been criticised as being 'ill conceived and destructive to other cultures' (op. cit., p. 170). Critics allege that mental health policies and practices need to be restructured so that service users and carers can take power and control over resources from the authorities and the professionals. Psychiatry needs to become global, in the sense that the promotion of mental health at all levels – the individual, the family and community – needs to be taken in conjunction with the economic and political issues associated with the exploitation and inequality in societies. Radicals assert the indivisibility of policies at the international (macro) and individual (micro) levels. For example, Fernando (1991, p. 208) argues that racism adversely affects people's self-confidence if they are viewed as racially inferior; it is 'seriously divisive in multiracial and multicultural communities; it is a barrier to social harmony generally', so its eradication 'is a *sine qua non'* of any mental health programme.

There was widespread opposition from service users and professionals to the government's proposals that the Mental Health Bill, due to go before Parliament during the 1995–96 session, should include provisions to impose on people with mental health problems living in the community, without their necessary consent, conditions requiring that they should live in a specified place and attend specified activities at specified times. This chapter ends, therefore, on a negative note as far as empowering service users in a key area of mental health is concerned. The medical professionals remain in their seats of power. In the disability field, community care planning has led to enormous efforts by some local authority social services departments to consult service users and carers and in some cases hand over resources to them, and thereby the power to determine what services they need. But the advocacy and self-advocacy movements still struggle against an enormous weight of discriminatory structures and practices (Oliver, 1990; Brandon, 1995). In the latter half of the 1990s, the impact of the Disability Discrimination Act 1995 on the significant individual, organisational and societal oppression experienced by disabled people remains to be tested.

References and further reading

Adams, R. (1996) *Social Work and Empowerment*, Basingstoke: BASW/ Macmillan.

Bean, P. and Mounser, P. (1993) *Discharged from Mental Hospitals*, Basingstoke: MIND/Macmillan.

Blind Persons' Act 1920, London: HMSO.

Blom Cooper, L. Hally, H. and Murphy, E. (1995) *The Falling Shadow: One Person's mental health care 1978–1993*, London: Duckworth.

Brandon, D. (1995) *Advocacy*, Birmingham: Venture Press.

Brown, H. and Smith, H. (1992) *Normalisation: a Reader for the Nineties*, London: Routledge.

Chronically Sick and Disabled Persons Act 1970, London: HMSO.

Civil Rights (Disabled Persons) Bill, London: HMSO.

Clare, A. (1976) *Psychiatry in Dissent*, London: Tavistock.

Cohen, D. (undated) *Broadmoor*, London: Psychology News Press.

Conway, A.S., Hale, A.S. and Melzer, D. (1994) *The Outcome of Targeting Community Mental Health Services: Evidence from the West Lambeth Schizophrenic Cohort*, London: St Thomas's Hospital,.

Cox, C. and Pearson, M. (1995) *Made to Care*, London: Resicare.

Customs and Excise Management Act 1979, London: HMSO.

Davies, N., Lingham, R., Prior, C. and Sims, A. (1995) *Report of the Inquiry into the Circumstances Leading to the Death of Jonathan Newby on 9th October 1993 in Oxford*, Oxford: Oxfordshire Health Authority.

Department of Health (1992) *The Health of the Nation – a Strategy for Health in England*, Cmnd 1986, London: HMSO.

Department of Health and Social Security (1971) *Better Services for the Mentally Handicapped*, London: HMSO.

Department of Health and Social Security (1974) *Revised Report of the Working Party on Security in NHS Psychiatric Hospitals* (Glancy Report), London: DHSS.

Department of Health and Social Security (1975) *Better Services for the Mentally Ill*, London: HMSO.

Department of Health and Social Security (1980) *Mental Handicap: Progress, Problems and Priorities. A Review of Mental Handicap Services in England since the 1971 White Paper*, London: HMSO.

Department of Health and Social Security (1981a) *Care in Action: a Handbook of Policies and Priorities for the Health and Personal Social Services in England*, London: HMSO,

Department of Health and Social Security (1981b) *Care in the Community, a Consultative Document on Moving Resources for Care in England*, London: HMSO.

Department of Health/Home Office (1994) *Review of Services for Mentally Disordered Offenders* (Reed Report), Cmnd 2088, London: HMSO.

Disabled Persons (Services, Consultation and Representation) Act 1986, London: HMSO.

Drug Trafficking Offences Act 1986, London: HMSO.

Fernando, S. (1991) *Mental Health, Race and Culture*, London: Macmillan.

Gibbons, J. (1988) Residential care for mentally ill adults, in NISW (Sinclair, I., ed.), *Residential Care: the Research Reviewed* (Wagner Report Part II), 159–197, London: HMSO.

Goffman, E. (1967) *Asylums: Essays on the Social Situation of Mental Patients and other Inmates*, Harmondsworth: Penguin.

Goffman, E., (1968) *Stigma: Notes on the Management of Spoiled Identity*, Harmondsworth: Penguin.

Goldacre, M., Seagroat, V. and Hawton, K. (1994) *Suicide After Discharge from Psychiatric Inpatient Care*, Oxford: University of Oxford.

Heron, A. and Myers, M. (1983) *Intellectual Impairment: the Battle against Handicap*, London: Academic Press.

Holmes, A. (1995) Self-advocacy in learning disabilities, *British Journal of Nursing*, vol.4, no.8, 448–450.

Home Office (1988) *Tackling Drug Misuse – a Summary of the Government's Strategy*, London: HMSO.

Home Office and Department of Health (1995) *Mentally Disordered Offenders: Inter-agency Working*, London: HMSO.

Home Office/Department of Health and Social Security (1974) *Interim Report of the Committee on Mentally Abnormal Offenders*, Cmnd 5678, London: HMSO.

Home Office/Department of Health and Social Security, (1975) *Report of the Committee on Mentally Abnormal Offenders* (Butler Report), Cmnd 6244, London: HMSO.

Home Office, NACRO and Mental Health Foundation (1994) *The NACRO Diversion Initiative for Mentally Disturbed Offenders: an Account and an Evaluation*, London: Home Office.

Jay Report, The (1979) *Report of the Committee of Enquiry into Mental Handicap Nursing and Care*, Cmnd 7468, London: HMSO.

Jones, K. (1960) *Mental Health and Social Policy*, London: Routledge and Kegan Paul.

Jones, K., Brown, J., Cunningham, W.J., Roberts, J. and Williams, P. (1975) *Opening the Door: a Study of New Policies for the Mentally Handicapped*, London: Routledge and Kegan Paul.

King's Fund Centre (1980) An Ordinary Life. *Comprehensive Locally-based Residential Services for Mentally Handicapped People*, London: King's Fund Centre.

Laing, R.D. (1962) *The Divided Self*, Harmondsworth: Penguin.

Malin, N., Race, D. and Jones, G. (1980) *Schemes for the Mentally Handicapped in Britain*, London: Croom Helm.

Mapp, S. (1994) Village people, *Community Care*, 4–10 August, no.1082, 27.

McGrath, M. and Grant, G. (1992) Supporting needs-led services: implications for planning and management systems (a case study in mental handicap services), *Journal of Social Policy,* vol.21, 171–197.

Medicines Act 1968, London: HMSO.

Mental Deficiency Act 1913, London: HMSO.

Mental Health Act 1959, London: HMSO.

Mental Health Act 1983. London: HMSO.

Misuse of Drugs Act 1971, London: HMSO.

Morris, A. (1994) A Lost Opportunity, *The Guardian*, 11 July 1994.

Morris, J. (1994a) Rights muddle, *Community Care,* no.1026, 21–27 July, 22–23.

Morris, J. (1994b) Community care or independent living? *Critical Social Policy,* issue 40, vol.14, no.1, 24–45.

Morris, P. (1969) *Put Away: a Sociological Study of Institutions for the Mentally Retarded*, London: Routledge and Kegan Paul.

National Assistance Act 1948, London: HMSO.

NISW (1982) *Social Workers: their Roles and Tasks* (Barclay Report), London: National Institute for Social Work/Bedford Square Press.

NISW (1988) *Residential Care: the Research Reviewed* (Wagner Report Part II) Sinclair I., ed., London: HMSO.

Oliver, M. (1990), *The Politics of Disablement. Critical Texts in Social Work and the Welfare State,* London: Macmillan,.

Pilgrim, D. and Rogers, A. (1989) Radical mental health policy, *Critical Social Policy*, issue 25, summer 4–17.

Pringle, K. (1995) *Men, Masculinities and Social Welfare*, London: UCL Press.

Report of All-party Parliamentary Committee on Mental Health (Broadmoor Report), London: HMSO.

Report of Normansfield Inquiry, Cmnd 7537, London: HMSO.

Ritchie, J.H., Dick, D. and Lingham, R. (1994) *The Report of the Inquiry into the Care and Treatment of Christopher Clunis*, London: HMSO.

Rogers, A., Pilgrim, D. and Lacey, R. (1993) *Experiencing Psychiatry: Users' Views of Services*, London: MIND and Macmillan.

Scull, A. (1977) *Decarceration*, Englewood Cliffs, NJ: Prentice Hall.

Shearer, A. (1972) *Normalisation?* Discussion paper no. 3, London: Campaign for the Mentally Handicapped.

Sines, D. (1995) Empowering consumers: the caring challenge, *British Journal of Nursing*, vol.4, no.8, 445–448.

Social Services Inspectorate (1988) A Wider Vision: the management and organisation of services for people who are blind or visually handicapped, London: Department of Health.

Sontag, S. (1991) *Illness as Metaphor* and *AIDS and its Metaphors*, Harmondsworth: Penguin.

Welsh Office (1982) *The Development of Community Care for Mentally Handicapped People.* Report of the All-Wales Working Party on Services for Mentally Handicapped People, Cardiff: Welsh Office.

Wolfensberger, W. (1972) *The Principle of Normalisation in Human Services*, Toronto: National Institute on Mental Retardation.

Wolfensberger, W. (1982) Social Role Valorisation: A proposed new term for the principle of normalisation, *Mental Retardation*, 21(6), pp. 234–239.

Wolfensberger, W. (1994) A personal interpretation of the mental retardation scene in light of the 'Signs of the Times', *Mental Retardation*, vol.32, no.1, February, 19–33.

Woodley, L. (1995) *The Woodley Report*, London: East London and The City Health Authority.

CHAPTER 8

Group care

In dealing with aspects of people's experiences through their life course, it is arguable that to work with different age groups – such as older people – separately, mirrors and reinforces ageist societal definitions and responses to them. There is a strong argument also for not mirroring the segregation from the community of people who live in institutions, by devoting a separate chapter to residential and day care. But the counter-argument is that the unique context and nature of residential provision merits particular attention.

This chapter examines group care for children and aspects of work with older people, with some references to services for disabled adults and adults with mental health problems, although these have been dealt with in chapter 7. It deals with debates and issues in the field of group care, in a context where the definitions of childhood and ageing remain problematic. Group care is the widely used term adopted here to refer to the part of the continuum of provision – day care and residential – that excludes fieldwork.

Context of group care

The life course and social policy

The definitions of childhood, youth and ageing as life stages are social constructions. This is not to deny the value of examining the impact on people of physiological and psychological changes throughout the life course. Neither does it lessen the significance of cultural differences that make generalisations about ageing and policy responses to ageing within the UK, to say nothing of across Europe as a whole, very difficult (Jamieson, 1990, p. 5). But it is undeniable that some divisions in society – between wealthy and poor people, employed and unemployed people, disabled and non-disabled people – are reflected in different social responses to children, young people and older people. Ageist attitudes are widespread, particularly at these extremes of the life course. The age below which young people are regarded as dependent on adults and unable to take responsibility for running their own lives has increased; a third of young people are likely to pass straight from school to higher education by the year 2000 and thus will enter the labour market at a minimum age of 22 years.

International demographic trends affecting the life course

The age at which children become adults has progressively been raised since the early nineteenth century (see chapter 5). Many developing countries are young, in that the proportion of children and young people in the population, as well as absolute numbers, have risen rapidly in the last quarter of the twentieth century. Ageing older populations are a feature of many developed countries in most of Europe and the USA, contributed to by an increasing absolute number of people aged 65 or over, an increased proportion of older people and increased life expectancies at birth (Hugman, 1994, p. 1).

The need for residential care for older people is increased by several factors: the growing proportion of older people, and especially people aged over 85; the consequent growth in the number of disabled people and those suffering from dementia; increasing numbers of elderly people living alone; the decreasing proportion of potential care givers, especially women in their forties, relative to the number of elderly people; the increasing proportion of women working in their forties; increased migration of people, which decreases the likelihood that care can be provided by relatives; the fact that the demand for residential care comes not only from elderly people themselves, but also from their relatives and from professionals (Sinclair, 1988, pp. 245–247).

The legacy of the Poor Law Amendment Act of 1834 and attitudes to old age shape policy responses to older people. Throughout much of the twentieth century, former workhouses continued to be used as residential homes for older people. Ageist attitudes inform responses to children and older people alike. At the 'upper end' of the life course, Scrutton (1989, pp. 15–16) identifies several myths associated with ageism: the myth of chronology – the notion that once people reach a certain age they automatically become part of 'the elderly' population; the myth of ill health – the assumption that growing older necessarily involves becoming more ill and deteriorating irreversibly and untreatably; the myth of mental deterioration – the notion that people's mental faculties become slower and more senile as they grow older; the myth of inflexible personality – that people's personalities change with age, so that they become more intolerant, inflexible and conservative; the myth of misery – that older people are unhappy because they are old; the myth of rejection and isolation – that society rejects older people and is uncaring towards them and that they prefer to 'disengage' from life, i.e. withdraw into themselves; the myth of unproductive dependence – that older people are not productive because they are not in paid employment and so are dependent on other people.

The fact that people, including older people themselves, regard old age, infirmity and dependence as so inextricably related is a feature of ageist attitudes. The notion that growing old necessarily involves disengaging from life and becoming a problem – in the sense of a burden on other people and on healthcare facilities – is as much socially constructed (Hugman, 1994, p. 2) as the view that adolescence can be defined as a period when youthful personalities undergo an inevitably difficult transition to adulthood (Adams, 1991, p. 201). It is not difficult to construct a list of comparable statements based on 'myths' about childhood and young person-hood that complements those about older people made above. Such perspectives on human growth, development and ageing emphasise fairly stereotypical features of childhood and growing older, such as the growth and development associated with youth and the deterioration associated with becoming older. But they tend to neglect the aspects of people's life courses that contradict these trends and the different ways in which the life course is viewed in different societies.

Historical aspects of group care

Enormous changes have taken place since the beginning of the nineteenth century in the formal arrangements in Britain for caring for poor, disabled, older and mentally ill people. Provision in the nineteenth century centred on residential institutions such as workhouses for paupers, hospitals for sick people and asylums for those considered mentally ill, as well as outdoor relief. Reformatories, orphanages and children's homes dealt with the nurturing and disciplining of children. Until the 1950s, however, children in care, mentally ill people and older people requiring residential care could all expect to be housed in large, probably Victorian institutions, whose regimes owed more to regimentation and discipline than to meeting the need of the individual to be cared for. Often treatment was a mixture of controlling or curbing people's behaviour with a strong element of moral or religious reform, sometimes linked with education or training (Parker, 1988, p. 4).

Size of the group care industry

Clough's (1982) wide-ranging book about residential establishments includes those for children as well as adults. He notes that 3% of the population of Britain lived in some kind of residential institution at the beginning of the 1980s (op. cit., p. 1).

Residential care for older people in Britain is provided mainly by hospitals, nursing homes and residential homes, since restrictions on combining independent residential and nursing homes in the non-public sector were removed in 1984, although they can still be provided separately (Knapp, 1989, p. 248). Between 1977 and 1985 the number of homes in all sectors increased from just over 5700 to just over 9600. Between 1977 and 1981 there was a 14.6% increase, and between 1981 and 1985 there was a 45.2% increase. The number of residents was 169,435 in 1977, 183,710 in 1981 and 218,243 in 1985 (op. cit., p. 248). In the same period, the market share of the private sector increased from 14% to 33% (op. cit., p. 249).

The rapid growth of residential child care from the nineteenth century may be attributable to economic and social factors associated with the increasing dislocation and stresses experienced by children and families as a consequence of rapid industrial growth and urban development.

The children of many wealthy and privileged people in Britain from the fourteenth century attended boarding schools, which were the forerunners of today's public schools and also of residential child care institutions. In 1987, 127,250 were in independent, i.e. private or public schools; 7750 were in local authority maintained boarding schools 27,600 were in boarding schools for those with special needs such as learning or behavioural difficulties; 20,000 were in residential care and 34,000 were in foster homes, out of 70,000 in care, or looked after by the local authority (Kahan, 1991, pp. 139–140). Between 1980 and 1990, the proportion of children who were fostered increased from 37% to nearly 60%, while those in community homes with education declined from 5.5% to 1.9%. During the same period, the number of children in care declined by a third, from about 90,000 to around 60,000 (documents 7 and 8). While residential education and residential care overlap in some respects, the former largely caters for the belief that some children benefit from education away from home, whereas the latter acts as a substitute in the case of the inability of parents and other adults with parental responsibility to provide adequate care for the child at home.

Women form the bulk of the increased number of older people in residential care. According to the 1981 census, psychiatric wards and nursing homes for people with mental disorders account for about 46,000 older people, other hospitals and nursing homes about 47,000 and homes for older and disabled people about 174,000 (Sinclair, 1988, p. 249). Most of these people were accommodated in local authority accommodation until the 1990s. The implementation of the NHS and Community Care Act 1990 has not meant that the reduction of the numbers of older people catered for in residential settings has been accompanied by a corresponding increase in domiciliary services (op. cit., p. 251).

As the numbers of children and adults catered for and the range of residential institutions have grown, so the occupations involved in work with people, and the infrastructure of central and local government administering them, have proliferated. Between 1881 and 1911 in Britain, the number of women employed in central and local government increased from 7000 to 76,000 (Hobsbawm, 1995, p. 201). Traditionally, the residential care of children out of the family has been the responsibility of largely untrained, mainly female staff. In 1977, 67% of staff in children's homes were women (Howe, 1986). The Utting Report (1991) confirmed the need for massive staff development in this sector. Residential care, first of children then of older people as the workhouses were replaced by old people's homes and nursing homes, became an alternative occupation for a growing workforce of unqualified women, seeking an alternative occupation to staying at home or employment in service, the latter job being not as universally available as before due to the spread of labour-saving devices in the home (Hobsbawm, 1995, pp. 200–201). In the 1990s, it is still not compulsory for care staff in residential and day care to be trained, only around 20% being qualified in the early 1990s (Kahan, 1991, p. 149), and pay has been commensurately poor. The low status of the workforce engaged in group care was reinforced by the fact that from the 1950s to the 1980s, training for fieldwork staff was generally full-time and became increasingly concentrated in the universities (between the 1970s and about 1990, leading to the Certificate of Qualification in Social Work (CQSW)), whereas that for care workers in residential and day care took place on a part-time, work-based basis and was linked mainly with colleges of further and higher education (from the mid-1970s to about 1990, leading to the Certificate in Social Service (CSS)). The force of these points was not lessened by the decline in the residential sector in the 1980s referred to above.

Shortcomings of residential life

In general, research into the defects of residential life far exceeds that extolling its virtues. In 1962, Townsend's research into old people's homes found serious shortcomings in them (Townsend, 1962); in effect, the shadow of the workhouse still hung over many establishments. Many subsequent attempts were made to raise standards of residential care. Since the mid-1980s, there has been growing concern about the contribution, and the quality, of the private sector in residential provision for older people. The question is whether the private sector can provide acceptable hotel-style accommodation or whether homes must remain essentially as places of last resort (Sinclair, 1988, p. 245).

Between the 1940s and the 1970s, children's homes could be very disciplinarian (Joyce, 1955; Millham *et al.*, 1975). There were long-standing weaknesses in the treatment of children while in residential care and leaving care. Other, less obviously rigid, regimes have their shortcomings. But the ideology of the pseudo-family promoted by the Curtis Report (Report of the Care of Children Committee, 1946), on which many were based, has since been scrutinised critically (Aymer, 1992).

On occasions, children themselves have taken action in response to poor conditions. The riot at Carlton approved school was sparked off by the children's protests about harsh and inflexible conditions going unheeded by staff (Adams, 1991, p. 46).

Many children have experienced abuse in children's homes, and research indicates on one hand that such children are prone to absconding, and on the other hand that problems arising from children's responses to residential care can create further problems, making their need for continued residential care a self-fulfilling prediction (Millham *et al.*, 1978).

Older people traditionally have tended to be consulted about the shaping of policy and practice rather less than their carers and the people who professionally care for them. Booth's survey of homes for older people found marked differences in the rates at which residents deteriorate and die in different homes, but failed to find correlations between this and differences between the management of the homes and the caring practices of staff. But the research was based largely on a postal questionnaire completed by the managers of homes, so the findings of the study were dependent largely on the perceptions of heads of homes and did not appear to acknowledge the likelihood that residents' perceptions would differ from those of staff (Booth, 1985, p. 205). In terms of methodology, Booth's research contrasts with that of Clough (1981), which involved questionnaires administered to staff, interviews with residents and participant observation in a home for older people.

Bearing the cost of care

Since the 1980s, local authorities have tended increasingly to pay voluntary and private providers for residential services for children.

Less than 1.5% of places in residential care for older people were provided by the private sector in 1981, compared with 37% in 1994 (Department of Health, 1995, p. 78). At least 60% of people in private residential care pay for their own care (Sinclair, 1988, p. 251). Until the 1990s, there was generally more public provision of residential care for older people in poorer districts, and a predominance of private provision in relatively affluent areas (op. cit., p.

252). The changes in funding arrangements for services for older people introduced in 1993 reduced the role of local authorities to that of regulating the funding of voluntary and private provision and gatekeeping the access of service users and carers to, for example, residential and day care provision in a much-decreased public sector. Most older people, apart from those who are disabled or mentally ill, would not live in a residential home as a matter of choice. This is because they regard it as involving them losing independence and privacy, and bringing them into company that they would not otherwise choose.

Residential provision for older people has been somewhat problematic in the wake of the NHS and Community Care Act 1990. Joint planning between health, housing and social services has been found very difficult to achieve (op. cit., p. 254). The Audit Commission (1986) found that a consequence of rate-capping and arrangements made to shift resources from London hospitals and to transfer the burden of care from hospitals to social services departments was to exacerbate the existing difficulties of joint planning and management of community care (Sinclair, 1988, p. 254). Shortages of resources have made the task of shifting the balance of provision from residential to domiciliary care even more difficult.

Legal basis for group care

Chapters 4 and 5 deal with the major legislation affecting personal social services provision for children and young people, with the additional note that boarding education has been governed since the 1940s by the Education Act 1944, the Children Act 1948 and, latterly, the Children Act 1989; provisions for children with special needs have been updated from the Education Act 1981 by the Education Act 1993.

Work with adults who are regarded as vulnerable and in need of personal social services may refer to a wide range of legislation over and above the NHS and Community Care Act 1990, including the following: National Assistance Act 1948, Disabled Persons (Employment) Act 1958, Mental Health Act 1959, Health Services and Public Health Act 1968, Chronically Sick and Disabled Persons Act 1970, Supplementary Benefits Act 1976, Mental Health Act 1983, Health and Social Services and Adjudications Act 1983, Registered Homes Act 1984, the Disabled Persons (Services, Consultation and Representation) Act 1986 and the Registered Homes (Amendment) Act 1991.

Work with older people is likely to fall within the framework of care planning embodied in the NHS and Community Care Act 1990. The National Assistance Act 1948 was an attempt to shift the provision for older people from the shadow of the workhouse to residential care. In the 1940s, much of the residential care for older people was still provided in public assistance institutions. The Registered Homes Act 1984, implemented on 1 January 1985, required local authorities to ensure that facilities in the private and voluntary sectors met the standards laid down in the statutory sector. The Registered Homes (Amendment) Act 1991 extends responsibilities of social services departments to small homes with fewer than four residents, in the independent sector. In a pattern common to much legislation in the human services, such legislation forms part of a package of circulars and codes of practice issued by government departments, which follow a process of consultation between service providers and officials, beginning in the Department of Health, formerly the Department of Health and Social Security).

Approaches to group care

The four main approaches identified in Fig. 4.1, chapter 4 are protection, care, therapy and advocacy. Needs-led assessment is seen by many professionals as a key to identifying types and levels of intervention to protect older people and support carers.

However, approaches to group care of children have tended to focus on protection and care rather than therapy and advocacy. This reflects shortages of resources and staff expertise, and the lack of momentum towards self-advocacy among groups and organisations involving children – other than the National Association of Young People in Care (NAYPIC), catering for children in the care of the local authority – and involving older people as a whole.

Many local authorities publish charters of standards for group care, as part of a range of services. Unfortunately, the lack of adequately qualified care staff in the sector makes these difficult to realise in practice.

Protection

Approaches to child protection dealt with in chapter 5 – through child protection conferences and child protection registers – apply also in group care settings. The local authority may provide residential accommodation – with foster parents or adoptive parents – or may arrange for a child to attend a family centre, perhaps with one of the parents, to ensure the protection of the child.

Protective work with adults and older people regarded as vulnerable may take the form of services such as social work support and advice, rehabilitative, adult training, occupational, recreational and cultural activities for people with disabilities.

Warden-supported, sheltered and a range of similar housing schemes are increasingly important, in the growing recognition of the cross-bracing necessary between housing and social services.

Increasing attention has been paid to the problems of elder abuse, particularly since professionals and the public became more sensitised by publicity surrounding child abuse scandals. But the reminiscence from the early years of the twentieth century, to Ronald Blythe by a villager in *Akenfield*, the anonymised Suffolk community (Blythe, 1975, p. 23), concerning the older relative who was locked in a cupboard all day to prevent her wandering when the family members went off to work on the land, is a reminder that elder abuse is probably as traditional in many countries (Hornick *et al.*, 1992, pp. 301–335), as child abuse. In Britain, elder abuse was considered important enough to be highlighted in the matters of public concern raised by the annual report 1993/4 of the chief inspector of the SSI (see document 3). *Confronting Elder Abuse* is a report based on SSI research in two London boroughs, and provides practice guidelines on tackling elder abuse (SSI, 1993). The study of elder abuse has been enriched since the late 1980s by research and theories informing professional responses to it. Phillipson *et al.*, (1995) have located the growing awareness of the significant incidence of abuse of older people in the wider context of perspectives on older people in society, as well as examining strategies for addressing the problems of abuse.

Sometimes protective work may be more overtly controlling. The local authority may exercise legal powers to have a person considered to be at risk of self-harm, or otherwise incapable of managing through mental disorder (the legal terminology used in the Mental Health Act 1983), removed to residential accommodation – a residential home or nursing home – or hospital. It is insufficient for the professional to judge that the person is living in filthy surroundings; she or he may choose to live that way. The person must be shown to be incapable of self-care. It may arise that relatives and friends put pressure on the local authority to have an older person taken into residential accommodation, but the person is unwilling; in such circumstances, professionals have to take due account of the wishes of the older person and any carers in making an assessment of needs.

Care

The above services also provide the basis for care; the boundary between protective and caring work is often blurred at the point where minimising risk to the person overlaps with providing care (Brearley and Hall, 1982). Care staff often work in collaboration with other disciplines and professions, such as occupational therapists, teachers, nurses and social workers. Status differences and the variety of occupational cultures may obstruct multi-professional work of this kind. Physically ill people or people recuperating after operations, for example, may attend day centres and have meals provided. A high proportion of older people experience disabilities for which the provision of physical aids – in which a short period in group care may contribute to the assessment – may make the difference between loss of independence and maintaining independence.

Increasing attention given by employers to maintaining a safe, accident-free working environment, in the light of the Health and Safety at Work etc. Act 1974, makes more difficult the task of sustaining a person-oriented programme in the home, day care or residential setting. Codes of practice governing the health and safety of workers, service users and carers may contradict the goal of maintaining a person's independence, since this will involve taking calculated risks (op. cit.). The kinds of pressures the contract culture of the marketplace imposes on service providers are likely to militate against such risk-taking.

It may be difficult to maintain the boundary between professional and personal relationships in care work, perhaps when there is a large age gap, or power imbalance, between staff and service user. Care staff may work in a quasi-parental role. They may also relate to much older, or much younger people, as would a relative or friend. Given that more than three-quarters of care staff are untrained, abuse of residents by staff is likely to occur when boundaries round the professional role are unclear, or staff cross them inappropriately.

Therapy

Therapeutic activities take place in the context of increasingly rationed services. Inevitably, services for older people have to manage a tension in enabling them to adjust realistically to their circumstances while not being oppressed. It should not be assumed that older people will necessarily become less dependent. However, it is likely that they will experience more traumas in particular areas as they grow older. For example, they are more likely than younger people to experience the loss of significant people, the loss of their own role as parents, the loss of employed status, the loss of financial status that goes with it, declining physical abilities and the increasing consequences of poor health. Some older people will want to talk about the growing prospect of losing control of what is going to happen to them, and also the likelihood of long-term illness or approaching death. Others will not want to discuss these matters. Some older people feel that younger people deny them the opportunity to air their feelings about these issues.

Biographical approach

One approach to working with children and with older people involves gathering with them a picture of their life history. This may contribute to the process of assessment, which in any case should be carried out *with* the person and not 'on' the person. Life story-books may be constructed with children and family trees with older people. While these may be used to further medico-treatment, it is more likely that professionals using such approaches will employ them to empower people. A biographical approach to assessing a person's circumstances gives them the opportunity to reflect on their experiences and to evaluate the past, the present and the future prospects of their life (Dant *et al.*, 1989) and to use the products of that reflection as they wish. Constructing a biography with an older person may have negative aspects, but can also be an exciting, pleasurable and rewarding experience, both for the older person and for the worker. Particular attention may be paid to the relationships the older person has with other people, the groups and networks to which she or he relates and what she or he identifies as needs.

Counselling

Sometimes, individual counselling is a necessary part of work with an older person. The onset of serious or even terminal disease, or the need to choose whether to have a major but risky operation in order to prolong active life, are situations that may require counselling. Material help, perhaps in the form of aids and adaptations, may also be necessary.

There may be a tendency for interaction with another individual to lead to an undue focus on the precise negative memories and experiences from which it could help the older person to escape. 'Any work undertaken on an individual basis should always focus attention on the broader social context in which the individual lives' (Scrutton, 1989, p. 78).

Reality orientation and reminiscence work

Reminiscence work and reality orientation, as O'Sullivan (1990) notes, can be criticised as an imposition by professionals on the independence and self-determination of older people. Nevertheless, they have formed part of many programmes of work with older people. It may be necessary to deal also with the impact of the loss of physical and emotional relationships, the consequences of alcohol, illness, depression, loss, growing confusion, abnormal grieving, chronic grieving and preparation for death. There is also an increasing issue concerning euthanasia. Older people who are dying have particular needs, including physical, medical, emotional and financial needs. On the whole, work consists of trying to ensure that the dying person has retained as much responsibility for control of the situation as possible. Often, this will be in the face of attempts by carers to take control away from the dying person. This may not only emphasise the dependence of the dying person, but may also reduce their status as a person. Elisabeth Kübler-Ross (1982) suggests that work with dying people, whether younger or older, needs to recognise that they are likely to pass through five successive stages, more or less in sequence depending on the situation: denial, anger, bargaining, depression and acceptance. She gives moving illustrations of her sensitive techniques in breaching the wall of silence, and, in many British homes, repressed feelings and communication, which prevent people from dealing with dying. Often, the struggle of a dying person to accept death is made more difficult when professionals are fixated in the medico-treatment paradigm, which seeks cure rather than care. Stoddard (1979, pp. 7–8) points to the pre-medieval tradition of hospices to caution against regarding the hospice movement as having begun either with the Irish Sisters of Charity in mid-nineteenth century Dublin, or in the 1960s with the work of Dr Cicely Saunders (Saunders, 1959). On the other hand, hospices do not, and should not, monopolise care provision for working with people who are dying. A range of palliative care services needs considering and evaluating (Goddard, 1993).

Advocacy

Frost and Stein develop a matrix as a theoretical and political basis for developing policy and practice in work with children and young people. This involves charting the cumulative impact of different dimensions of oppression (social class, gender, age, ethnicity and so on), and also proposes that power is relational – a person is more, or less, powerful in comparison with someone else – and that power presupposes resistance (Frost and Stein, 1992, pp. 162–163). Widespread illustrations of the pervasive character of resistance to imposed institutional requirements exist in the area of schooling, but, not surprisingly perhaps, they are not publicised by adults (Adams, 1991).

Hockey and James (1993) place residential work with children and with older people in the context of the structural relationships, notably power imbalances, between young and old people in residential care and the professionals and carers involved with them, and identify modes of resistance by people to processes that infantilise them: through direct confrontation between people and their carers, through the empowerment of people, through carers recognising the dangers of infantalisation, through self-help groups involved in political activity and through the developments of movement asserting the rights of citizenship for all people. Hockey and James assert that departures from the full achievement of personhood reflect deviations from people achieving a degree of fulfilment to match their place in the life course.

The circumstances of some people make some form of advocacy desirable or even necessary. This may consist of professional or peer, individual or collective advocacy. For example, older people with mental health problems including people with Alzheimer's disease, are prone to being defrauded while their money is looked after. Relatives or friends may take on responsibility for managing the affairs of a patient (Brayne and Martin, 1993, p. 272). A report by the House of Commons Public Accounts Committee in August 1994 discovered major inefficiencies in the Lord Chancellor's department involving a failure to update information on patients and to visit patients whose accounts were run privately, but for whom the Lord Chancellor's department maintained overall responsibility (House of Commons Committee of Public Accounts, 1994). The then Secretary of State Virginia Bottomley announced in August 1994 that Community Care Charters would be introduced throughout England in 1996, to set standards for the quality and speed of service for people being cared for in their own homes or in residential homes.

Issues in group care

This section considers the main issues arising in group care: sustaining people's rights, charging for services, quality of services, and the education and training of staff. These are associated with the vulnerability of purposes associated with maximising the quality of life, and therefore the independence, of service users and carers, as contrasted with the stable, priority purposes associated with maintaining services.

Sustaining people's rights

Although this issue applies to all settings, the issues concerning children's rights are selected for comment here. Statements concerning the rights of children (Rosenbaum and Newell, 1991) and legislation asserting the rights of children (Children Act 1989) have not done away with wrongs done to children, as is shown by the continued succession of inquiry reports into child abuse. Some incidents occur because social workers have failed to intervene, others involve abuse by staff themselves. Some incidents involve abuse in the name of treatment, as occurred in 'Pindown' (see document 6). There was much public and professional concern about the use of what became known as the Pindown regime in Staffordshire residential homes for children. Pindown was a method of behaviour control involving humiliating and degrading treatment, often in solitary confinement. MPs, child care specialists and councillors called for an independent inquiry. In the wake of a Granada Television documentary entitled 'Pindown', on 25 July 1990, Staffordshire County Council announced an independent inquiry with the aim of evaluating Pindown and 'to allay public concern and maintain public confidence in the social services department and its protection of the interests of children and young persons and of the general public' (Levy and Kahan, 1991, pp. 1–2). Incidents such as Pindown apparently do not increase the will of the government to make training for group care staff compulsory, and to make resources available to ensure that this happens. This gives a clear message to this area of the human services about the low priority attached to the interests of children and older people in need of specialist care.

It can be demonstrated that a person's right to having the transitions in and out of group care managed so as to meet personal needs is especially vulnerable. A study following a group of 16–18 year olds out of care over a two and a half year period explored their experiences, future hopes and their adjustment. It identified acute housing problems, made worse by the introduction of the Supplementary Benefit (Amendments) Miscellaneous Provisions Regulations at the end of April 1985. Young people leaving care were likely to be unemployed and living on supplementary benefits, therefore on the edge of poverty (Stein and Carey, 1986, p. 175). The study found that residential care tended not to supply young people with the long-term family experience they had previously lacked. The researchers concluded that 'in comparison with young people who had not been in care, our young people were more likely to be unemployed, to lack educational qualifications, to be living in poverty, to change accommodation frequently and to be confused about their pasts and unsettled in their present relationships. At its worst the state had become an added burden rather than a supportive parent' (op. cit., p. 179).

Such research points to the need for attention to be given to the material, emotional and social aspects of people's needs, throughout, and especially during transitions to and from residential care.

It also highlights the irrelevance of policies that segregate practice in one area from that in another. For example, social policy changes are necessary in the social security system to ensure that people leaving residential care, at whatever age, can secure good, affordable housing and have their material needs met, as well as being assured access to a supportive network of relationships.

Charging for services

The introduction in 1983 of guidelines from the DHSS on the ceilings to be set for the highest reasonable charge for suitable accommodation in the locality led to rapid increases in charges by residential homes and nursing homes in the private sectors to the maximum rather than the average (Knapp, 1989, p. 250). There is debate about whether the rapidly increasing numbers of private residential homes opening in the 1980s to meet the new demands once social security entitlements were available for many elderly people were offering accommodation to people who needed it but could not gain access to it formerly, or to people who would have required it in any case. Bradshaw and Gibb found that only a small proportion of recently admitted residents of private and voluntary homes were inappropriately placed in residential care, but other people have expressed doubts about that finding (Knapp, 1989, p. 251; Bradshaw and Gibb, 1988). Clearly, there is a trade-off between people's desire to find the most suitable accommodation and their ability to pay. The trend of government policy in the 1990s towards loading the cost of services on the consumer rather than on the provider, via mechanisms such as means testing, makes it less likely that older people will make choices purely on the basis of their needs.

Quality of services

The Department of Health emphasises that the quality of services depends on high-quality assessments and case management (Department of Health, 1989c). But quality is a product of many other contextual factors, including the overall resourcing of the service, the level and training of staffing and the extent to which the service is organised around meeting users' rather than the organisation's needs. Knapp (1989, p. 251) lists other components of a quality service as including the integrity of assessments (whether they take account of the wishes of the service user and carer), whether placements are appropriate, how quality of care is to be assured (the effectiveness of placements) and how accountabilities to the service user, the carer and the public are to be maintained. Thus, the provision of quality group care remains problematic.

Education and training of staff

The Utting Report (1991) found that the proportion of staff in residential child care possessing relevant qualification had been static for ten years. The Warner Report (Committee of Inquiry into the Selection, Development and Management of Staff in Children's Homes, 1992) recommended the introduction of a new workplace-based, modular diploma concerned with group care of children and young people at an equivalent level to the Diploma in Social Work, as the main professional qualification for staff who worked in residential care with children. Warner also recommended that National Vocational Qualifications (N/SVQs) should tackle the training needs of staff in residential child care. In 1993, the government had instituted a review of the Diploma in Social Work to be completed by 1995, based on a statement of occupational standards intended to be compatible with N/SVQs in care work. This emphasis on occupational standards rather than N/SVQs at Dip SW level could be interpreted as an attempt by the Care Sector Consortium to back off from the much-criticised label of N/SVQs, which had become attached to the lower grade staff at care assistant level.

The quality of group care is unlikely to be improved without increased resources and enhanced requirements for the education and training of staff, of which there is as yet little sign.

References and further reading

Adams, R. (1991) *Protests by Pupils*, London: Falmer.
Audit Commission (1986) *Making a Reality of Community Care*, London: HMSO.
Aymer, C. (1992) Women in residential work: dilemmas and ambiguities, in Langan, M. and Day, L. (eds), *Women, Oppression and Social Work: Issues in Anti-discriminatory Practice*, 186–200, London: Routledge.
Blythe, R. (1975) *Akenfield*, Harmondsworth: Penguin.
Booth, T. (1985) *Home Truths: Older People's Homes and the Outcomes of Care*, Aldershot: Gower.
Bradshaw, J. and Gibb, I. (1988) *Public Support for Private Residential Care*, Aldershot: Gower.
Brayne, H. and Martin, G. (1993) *Law for Social Workers*, 3rd edn, Oxford: Blackstone.
Brearley, C.P. and Hall, M.R.P. (1982) *Risk and Ageing*, London: Routledge and Kegan Paul.
Children Act 1948, London: HMSO.
Children Act 1989, London: HMSO.
Chronically Sick and Disabled Persons Act 1970, London: HMSO.

Clough, R. (1981) *Old Age Homes*, London: Allen and Unwin.

Clough, R. (1982) *Residential Work*, London: BASW/Macmillan.

Committee of Inquiry into the Selection, Development and Management of Staff in Children's Homes (1992) *Choosing with Care* (Warner Report), London: HMSO.

Dant, T., Carley, M., Gearing, B. and Johnson, M. (1989) Care for elderly people at home: the Gloucester Project, in Morgan, K. (ed.) *Gerontology: Responding to an Ageing Society*, London: Jessica Kingsley.

Davies, B.P. (1986) *Matching Resources to Needs in Community Care*, Aldershot: Gower.

Department of Health (1989c) *Case Management in Community Care*, London: HMSO.

Department of Health, (1990) *Framework for Local Community Care Charters in England*, London: HMSO.

Department of Health (1993), *Diversification and the Independent Care Sector*, London: HMSO.

Department of Health (1995) *Health and Personal Social Services Statistics for England 1995 Edition*, London: HMSO.

Dickenson, D. and Johnson, M. (eds) (1993) *Death, Dying and Bereavement*, London: Sage.

Disabled Persons (Employment) Act 1958, London: HMSO.

Disabled Persons (Services, Consultation and Representation) Act 1986, London: HMSO.

Education Act 1944, London: HMSO.

Education Act 1981, London: HMSO.

Education Act 1988, London: HMSO.

Employment in the public and private sectors (1994) *Economic Trends*, no.458, 98–105.

Frost, N. and Stein, M. (1992) Empowerment and child welfare, in Coleman, J.C. and Warren-Anderson, C. (eds,) *Youth Policy in the 1990s: the Way Forward*, 161–171, London: Routledge.

Goddard, M.K. (1993) The importance of assessing the effectiveness of care: the case of hospices, *Journal of Social Policy*, vol.22, no.1, 1–17.

Goffman E. (1967) *Asylums*, Harmondsworth: Penguin.

Gottesmann, M. (ed.) *Residential Child Care: an International Reader*, London: Whiting and Birch.

Health and Safety at Work etc. Act 1974, London: HMSO.

Health and Social Services Adjudications Act 1983, London: HMSO.

Health Services and Public Health Act 1968, London: HMSO.

Hobsbawm, E. (1995) *The Age of Empire 1875–1914*, London: Weidenfeld and Nicolson.

Hockey, J. and James, A. (1993) *Growing Up and Growing Old – Ageing and Dependency in the Life Course*, London: Sage.

Hornick, J.P., McDonald, L. and Robertson, G.B. (1992) 'Elder abuse in Canada and the United States: prevalence, legal and service issues, in Peters, R. DeV., McMahon, R.J. and Quinsey, V.L. (eds), *Aggression and Violence throughout the Life Span*, 301–335, London: Sage.

House of Commons Committee of Public Accounts (1994) *Looking After the Affairs of People with Mental Incapacity*, 39th Report of the Committee of Public Accounts, London: HMSO.

Howe, D. (1986) The segregation of women and their work in the personal social services, *Critical Social Policy*, no.15, 211–235.

Hugman, R. (1994) *Ageing and the Care of Older People in Europe*, London: Macmillan.

Jamieson, A. (1990) Informal care in Europe, in Jamieson, A. and Illsley, R. (eds), *Contrasting European Policies for the Care of Older People*, 3–21, Aldershot: Avebury.

Jamieson, A. and Illsley, R. (eds) (1990) *Contrasting European Policies for the Care of Older People*, Aldershot: Avebury.

Joyce, C.A. (1955) *By Courtesy of the Criminal: the Human Approaches to the Treatment of Crime*, London: Harrap.

Kahan, B. (1991) Residential care and education in Great Britain, in Gottesmann, M. (ed.) *Residential Child Care: an International Reader*, 138–156, London: Whiting and Birch.

Knapp, M. (1989) Private and voluntary welfare, in McCarthy, M. (ed) *The New Politics of Welfare: an agenda for the 1990s?*, 225–252, Basingstoke: Macmillan.

Kubler-Ross, E. (1982) *Living with Death and Dying*, London: Souvenir Press.

Levy, A. and Kahan, B. (1991) *The Pindown Experience and the Protection of Children: the Report of the Staffordshire Child Care Inquiry 1990*, Stafford: Staffordshire County Council.

Mental Health Act 1959, London: HMSO.

Millham, S., Bullock, R., Cherrett, P. (1975) *After Grace – Teeth, a Study of the Residential Experience of Boys in Approved Schools*, London: Human Context Books.

Millham, S., Bullock, R., Hosie, K. (1978) *Locking Up Children*, Farnborough: Saxon House.

Morgan, K. (ed.) *Gerontology: Responding to an Ageing Society*, London: Jessica Kingsley.

National Assistance Act 1948, London: HMSO.

NHS and Community Care Act 1990, London: HMSO.

NISW (1988a) *Residential Care: a Positive Choice*, Independent Review of Residential Care (Wagner Report Part I), London: HMSO.

NISW (1988b) *Residential Care: the Research Reviewed*, Literature surveys commissioned by the Independent Review of Residential Care (Wagner Report Part II), London: HMSO.

O'Sullivan, T. (1990) Responding to People with Dementia, *Practice*, Vol.4, No.1, 5–15.

Parker, R.A. (1988) An historical background to residential care, in NISW, *Residential Care: the Research Reviewed*, Literature surveys commissioned by the Independent Review of Residential Care 3–38. (Wagner Report Part II), London: HMSO.

Phillipson, C., Biggs, S. and Kingston, P. (1995) *Elder Abuse in Perspective*, Buckingham: Open University Press.

Poor Law Amendment Act 1834, London: HMSO.

Registered Homes (Amendment) Act 1991, London: HMSO.

Registered Homes Act 1984, London: HMSO.

Report of the Care of Children Committee (1946) (Curtis Report) London: HMSO.

Report of the Working Party on Security in NHS Hospitals (1973) chaired by Dr J. Glancy (The Glancy Report), London: DHSS.

Report on Mentally Abnormal Offenders (1975) (Butler Committee) Interim Report, Cmnd 5689, London: HMSO.

Report on Mentally Abnormal Offenders (1975) (Butler Committee) Final Report, Cmnd 6244, London: HMSO.

Report of Normansfield Inquiry, Cmnd 7537, London: HMSO.

Ritchie, J.H., Dick, D. and Lingham, R. (1994)*The Report of the Inquiry into the Care and Treatment of Christopher Clunis,* London: HMSO.

Rosenbaum, M. and Newell, P. (1991) *Taking Children Seriously: a Proposal for a Children's Rights Commissioner,* London: Calouste Gulbenkian Foundation.

Saunders, C. (1959) *Care of the Dying,* London: Macmillan.

Scrutton, S. (1989) *Counselling Older People: a Creative Response to Ageing,* London: Edward Arnold.

Sinclair, I. (1988) Residential care for elderly people, in NISW (1988b) *Residential Care: the Research Reviewed,* Literature surveys commissioned by the Independent Review of Residential Care (Wagner Report Part II), 241–291, London: HMSO.

Social Services Inspectorate (1986) *Inspection of the Implementation of the Registered Homes Act 1984 Stage 1: the Impact on Registration Authorities,* London: Department of Health and Social Security.

Social Services Inspectorate (1993) *Confronting Elder Abuse,* London: HMSO.

Social Services Inspectorate/Department of Health (1993) *Report of an Inspection of Management and Provision of Social Work in the Three Special Hospitals, July–September 1993,* London: Department of Health.

Stein, M. and Carey, K. (1986) *Leaving Care,* Oxford: Blackwell.

Stoddard, S. (1979) *The Hospice Movement,* London: Jonathan Cape

Supplementary Benefits Act 1976, London: HMSO.

Townsend, P. (1962) *The Last Refuge: a Survey of Residential Institutions and Homes for the Aged in England and Wales,* London: Routledge and Kegan Paul.

Utting, Sir W. (1991) *Children in the Public Care: a Review of Residential Child Care* (Utting Report), London: HMSO.

PART FOUR

Criminal and youth justice services

CHAPTER 9

Criminal justice

This chapter examines the principal features of criminal justice policy and practice in Britain that have a bearing on the personal social services, highlighting the key issues and controversies associated with them.

Context of criminal justice

Changing penal policies

The moves made in Britain towards developing more flexible custodial measures such as parole (Home Office, 1988b) and alternatives to custody through such measures as community service orders and suspended sentences since the 1950s have had so little impact on the ever-rising numbers of people in prisons that they merely serve to underline the fact that the centrality of Britain's criminal justice policies remains its prison system. The past 200 years have seen an unparalleled increase in the use of imprisonment in Britain, in common with the USA, which now has more than five million people in prisons and the highest proportion of its population behind bars of any country in the world. This is in marked contrast with countries such as the Netherlands, where public tolerance of enlightened criminal justice policies is relatively high.

Crime may be rising; but of the near fourfold rise in people found guilty of an indictable offence in England and Wales, 1951–1994, less than one fifth were women (Social Trends 1996, pp. 162–63). Also, this does not distinguish serious from minor offences. The various gaps between the actual, and probably always unknown, incidence of crime and the efforts of police to catch and courts to process people thought to be involved in crime make even more complex the difficulties of deciding how to sentence convicted offenders. Since the Home Secretary announced a 27-point law and order crackdown in October 1993, the number of people in prison has hovered around 50,000. Changes in criminal justice policy and practice – notably in the Criminal Justice Acts 1982 and 1991 and the Criminal Justice and Public Order Act 1994 – reflect the dominance of the Conservative party over British politics from 1979 at least until the end of 1995, when this book was being written. These changes have affected all parts of the criminal justice system – the courts, the prisons and other institutions such as special hospitals – and the roles of participants in criminal justice, including sentencers, offenders and victims, prisoners' families, custodial staff, probation and social work agencies, researchers and reformers. They have particularly affected sentencing policies and practices.

The rationale for imprisonment in the mid-Victorian era was the reform of the individual. This ideal remained undimmed when the Gladstone Committee reformed the prison system in 1895 (Departmental Committee, 1895). The rehabilitationist ideal was still alive in the White Paper of 1959, which stated: 'The constructive function of our prisons is to prevent the largest number of those committed to their care from offending again' (quoted in Stern, 1989, p. 15) and in borstal institutions for young offenders (Bishop, 1960; Gibbens, 1963). The collapse of the rehabilitationist justification for imprisonment over the following 15 years anticipated the decline of the treatment paradigm in social work. The struggle to find an appropriate philosophy to justify imprisonment occupied professionals and critics (Bottoms, 1990). Attempts were made to frame future policy and practice around the principle of justice, for offenders and for those associated with them. In some parts of the system, notably therapeutic work with sex offenders and in probation work, attempts to retain the rehabilitative ideal continued.

Changes in the legal basis for criminal justice include the shift from treatment to justice rationales for sentencing. This was in the wake of an unlikely convergence of right-wing proponents of 'law and order' and radical critics of the use of the medico-treatment model as a rationale for, and to inform the practice of, criminal justice sanctions (Walker, 1991).

Not surprisingly, in view of the range of stakeholders in the criminal justice system, penal policy often displays somewhat complex and contradictory characteristics. Thus, the second half of the twentieth century has witnessed the abandonment of capital punishment in the Murder (Abolition of the Death Penalty) Act 1965 and corporal punishment in the Criminal Justice Act 1948. But debates about their efficacy and desirability in certain circumstances remain. A majority of the public would support a return to the death penalty for certain types of offences. While the use of dietary punishment has been increasingly discredited, within institutions, isolation cells and physical constraints such as immobilising jackets are still in use in the mid-1990s. Segregation and special units, like that in Barlinnie Prison (Cooke, 1989), remain controversial methods of containing offenders in institutions who are seen as either a risk to themselves or a danger to others (Bottomley and Hay, 1991). A sceptic could argue that data from research by Dr Eric Cullen (1994) – head of research at Grendon prison – concerning the effectiveness of aspects of the treatment regime in

Grendon, Britain's leading treatment-oriented prison, in reducing criminality could be used by the Home Office even before its publication, to justify the continued prison building programme in the face of European Union directives that prison populations should be reduced. A report from the National Audit Office in July 1994 stated that the cost of the government's prison building programme had overrun by £78.9 million. The prison modernisation programme had begun in 1980. It constituted the largest investment in prison building since the mid-nineteenth century, involved building 21 new prisons (11,000 new places) and 7500 extra places at existing prisons as well as in-cell sanitation throughout much of the system. In the mid-1990s, the Home Office stated its intention that the next six prisons would be built and financed by private agencies (*The Guardian*, 20 July 1994, p. 3).

Explanations for criminality: no consensus

More fundamentally, if less visibly, the knowledge base of criminology has been recast in keeping with a shift in the centre of gravity of discourse about social policy and politics, away from Marxist and neo-Marxist analyses of crime and delinquency and societal responses to them and towards social democratic ideas based on 'left' realism (Stenson and Brearley, 1991, p. 223). The thrust of left realism towards empowering local citizens, particularly those traditionally excluded from local politics on account of their low social status, poverty and political marginality, creates problems for theorists wishing to align it with the left and distinguish it from simplistic policy claiming to solve the crime problem (op. cit., p. 225).

Traditionally, criminology operated apart from issues central to social work, such as discrimination against black people in the criminal justice system, against poor people and against unemployed people. Also, the practice of social work and probation work in the criminal justice system tends to engage with the negative features of custodial conditions, and the impact of a range of custodial and non-custodial measures on offenders, their relatives and other networks, and on the life chances of offenders and those who depend on them subsequent to their sentence by the court. Criminal justice services cannot be detached from the social context in which crime problems arise. The prison and other disposals are located in a society where poverty, unemployment, housing shortage, inequalities, urban riots and white collar crime are features of the total situation in which crime arises and is responded to. Divisions and inequalities in society are reflected in the population of women (Carlen, 1983; Carlen *et al.,* 1985; Morris and Wilkinson, 1988) and black prisoners (Crow and Cove, 1984). As Hudson puts it, 'while legal theory might be able to tell us what is the appropriate punishment for the crime before the court, and whilst criminology might be able to tell us that, and even sometimes why, the black defendant is more likely to end up in prison than the white defendant, we need to transcend these perspectives if we are to be able to understand why the mentally disturbed man and the homeless woman are more likely to be arrested and brought to court than to be given treatment or accommodation' (Hudson, 1993, p. 6).

Hudson distinguishes between what she calls the run-of-the-mill offences committed by perfectly free, perfectly rational people who offend for instrumental reasons, for which the concurrent criminal justice systems is best adapted, and other offences out of economic urgency, or provoked by racism, abuse, helplessness, despair, illness or addiction. She argues that the filtering mechanisms that failed to exclude people in the latter categories mean that 'rational, consistent legal justice cannot by itself fulfil the requirements of social justice' (op. cit., p. 200). The adoption of a new realism about responses to crime in society grew from the early 1980s (see Taylor, 1982 and chapter 8 of Lea and Young, 1984). It represented a shift towards a 'realist' perspective by some radical criminologist members of the National Deviancy Conference of the 1960s, who had developed the most fully articulated Marxist criminology in Britain in the early 1970s (Taylor *et al.*, 1973). New realist criminology was influenced by feminist critiques and attempted to take on board both the reality of public fears, especially among older people, about crime, and the incidence of criminal violence in the home and sexual harassment of women. Ironically, this brought realist criminology close to the territory occupied by the Right, since at a superficial level it seemed as though both radicals and conservatives advocated a just-deserts approach to sentencing.

It would be a mistake to regard criminology as having reached a position where it addresses issues of gender adequately. Commentary and research often acknowledge its lack of attention to women (see for example the focus on male deviance in Willis (1978) and Corrigan and Frith (1976)), but do not critically reflect on the significance of this. Gender should not be regarded as synonymous with women's issues, however, since researchers and workers in criminal justice have yet to tackle in an even-handed way the issues of masculinity and femininity which permeate questions of the causation of, and responses to, adult and youth crime. For example, there is a need for greater awareness of the processes leading a significant proportion of men to offend while the overwhelming majority of women are law-abiding. Significant progress has been made since the 1980s (Heidensohn, 1989, p. 99) on the basis of ethnographic and other research into female criminality, gender and criminal justice and gender-based crimes, and, associated with this, in criminological theory (Howe, 1994). There are also the longstanding issues for families associated with the consequences of men being sent to prison (Morris, 1965).

Problems of the prison population

Concerns about the excessive number of prisoners incarcerated (Rutherford, 1986), controversy about the treatment of particular groups of prisoners such as IRA prisoners in Northern Ireland (Adams, 1994, chapter 4), remand prisoners (King and Morgan, 1976) and the growing number of prisoners who do not have access to the treatment they need, are attested to by the proportion of prisoners with mental health problems. NACRO (1993) highlights the excessive number of mentally disordered offenders who, because they are sent to prison, do not receive the mental health services to which they are entitled. Mentally disordered offenders have occupied an uneasy borderland between treatment and punishment for more than a century (Criminal Lunacy (Departmental) Commission, 1882), were the focus of the Butler Committee (Home Office/Department of Health and Social Security, 1975) and, as chapter 7 indicates, are still subject to particular scrutiny in the mid-1990s.

Prison conditions in the British penal system have been criticised for many years. Almost half of the prisons in Britain, and 90% of the local prisons, were built before 1900. Conditions in them have often fallen far short of minimum standards in the European Union (Council of Europe, 1973), to say nothing of those advocated by critics in Britain (Casale, 1984). In an example that was replicated many times in other inspection reports during the 1980s and early 1990s, the report of the HM Chief Inspector of Prisons on Preston Prison in Lancashire was highly critical: 'it was as if nothing had changed since the 1960s', with an 'abysmal' regime. His Honour Judge Tumin concluded that 'establishments with impoverished regimes and poor conditions which failed to gain the co-operation of the majority of staff to improvements may lend themselves to being taken over by private companies, particularly if the cost of their operation is disproportionate to the performance delivered' (*The Guardian*, 28 July 1994).

Problems of security, secrecy and accountability

There is a tension between maintaining accountable penal institutions and keeping prisons secure. The arguments for the latter may be used, rather insidiously, to undermine the former. Security concerns have been prominent in the prison system for nearly 30 years, since Mountbatten was called in after the escape of the spy George

Blake, late in 1966, partly as a means of giving enhanced public and Home Office attention to the allocation of increased public money to boost the security of Britain's ageing prisons (Home Office, 1966). The abolition of capital punishment, plus a trend towards judges giving longer sentences, often with recommendations of a minimum period to be spent in prison, meant a growing population of long-term prisoners considered to be a security risk. Although Mountbatten's proposals for a single high-security prison on the Isle of Wight were abandoned at the time – on the grounds that it would create a 'no-hope' atmosphere among staff and prisoners in that institution – in favour of the creation of a number of top security facilities within a number of prisons, in 1995, in the wake of a number of escapes from prisons, the Home Secretary revived this proposal.

On 29 September 1972, the Franks committee reported, recommending that Section 2 of the 1911 Official Secrets Act, empowering courts to imprison civil servants for disclosing information, be repealed. The committee recommended that Section 2 be limited to items of national concern. However, as Cohen and Taylor (1976) noted, in a study of prison secrecy, several years later secrecy and violations of human rights in prisons were still widespread. But it is the lack of public accountability of the prison system that militates against improvements in conditions in prisons. Crown immunity has meant for many years that when, for example, buildings, food or hospital conditions fail to meet the Food Act 1984 or the Health and Safety at Work Act 1974, the officials responsible cannot be taken to court (Stern, 1989, p. 79). While logic and basic quality assurance require that the prison system be made more directly accountable to the public and through legislation (Maguire *et al.*, 1985), the combined effects of the power of the Home Office and medical professionals over the years (Sim, 1990) have been to curtail independent critical scrutiny of key aspects of the prisons, such as the quality of healthcare.

The complaints of many prisoners from the 1960s that their grievances had not been responded to, increasing concern among critics of the penal system, a number of protests by prisoners and prison riots (Adams, 1994), the growth of the prisoners' organisation Preservation of the Rights of Prisoners (PROP) (Fitzgerald, 1977), and – most important from the point of view of the Home Office – the increasing applicability in Britain of standards of justice in the penal system specified in the rest of the then European Community, led to attention being paid to the processing of complaints from prisoners (Home Office, 1987) as well as the adjudication of alleged offences committed by prisoners in custody (Home Office, 1985; Fitzgerald, 1985).

Privatisation and agency status

The Prison Service acquired the status of an Executive Agency on 1 April 1993. This gave the officials running prisons, from the Director General as chief executive to prison governors, more autonomy than before and set up a series of contracts by which penal establishments would receive agreed resources to enable them to meet specified operational objectives. Despite assurances to the contrary, the government encouraged increased involvement of the private sector in supplying services such as prison education and catering, and a number of contracted out, privately run, penal establishments came into operation, with more planned. In the mid-1990s, Britain was still the only country in Europe to have private prisons. This form of marketisation of the penal system (Ryan and Ward, 1989) blurs traditional boundaries between statutory, voluntary, private and informal sectors and introduces a bizarre commercial dimension to criminal justice which means, in effect, that while the victims of crime suffer and offenders are punished, private companies make a profit out of the consequences of sentencing. The fact that the Prison Service, formerly part of the Civil Service, now has agency status still allows many staff to continue with their former work. Budgets are devolved, for example, to governors of penal establishments. Contracts form the basis of agreements between governors and government departments for the provision of specified services. Whilst these contracts may be primarily with the Home Office, facilities are subject to inspection by other relevant bodies. For example, the mother and baby unit at Styall prison in Cheshire is subject to inspection by the Social Services Inspectorate. Private organisations contribute an increasingly international dimension to criminal justice services, the trend towards privatisation in Britain relying increasingly on international penal corporations, following the trend in the USA (op. cit.). The creation of internal markets in the penal system, as in community care, gives prisoners and their families – like service users and carers – the status of customers alongside the general public (Player and Jenkins, 1994, p. 27). It meshes with other government initiatives, notably towards time limited contracts, for instance, for clerks to justices and in policing. Senior police officers expressed concern at their ACPO Conference in July 1994 that the government might be seeking to privatise the police. There were also concerns at the erosion of police responsibilities and the rapid growth of the private security industry, including self-help community defence initiatives. While it could be argued that the core of police duties is relatively small in terms of searching, arresting and detaining citizens, bearing arms and exercising force, and having full access to criminal records and criminal intelligence, the view of many senior police officers was that this did not take account of the fact that many core police tasks are extremely labour-intensive and that many ancillary and core tasks are multi-functional and interdependent (Morgan, 1994).

Towards punishment in the community

Proposals in 1988 to introduce curfews for offenders were opposed by NAPO, and, although they were incorporated in the Criminal Justice Act 1991, most sentencers resorted to them only halfheartedly. More significantly, the Criminal Justice Act 1991 reflected government pressure towards making probation orders themselves into punishment in the community. The Green Paper *Punishment, Custody and the Community* (Home Office 1988a) set out the government's proposals for greater use of non-custodial options, but at the same time suggested that the procedures for breaches of community service orders would be tightened. It also proposed a new supervision and restriction order that could involve compensation, reparation, community service, judicial supervision, attendance at a day centre or restriction of liberty using 'tagging' or electronic monitoring. The government persisted in its attempts to establish the tagging of offenders, attempting in 1995 to run a pilot scheme for evaluation, which was hampered by technical shortcomings in the equipment used.

The Home Secretary made moves in 1994–95 towards detaching probation work from social work, and aligning it with the government's vision of the criminal justice system's post-rehabilitative, controlling and, where necessary, punitive role; this included the revamping of the probation order as an aspect of punishment in the community.

Legal basis for criminal justice services

The criminal courts – Magistrates and Crown courts, plus the Court of Appeal (Criminal Division), High Court and the House of Lords – deal with sentencing and appeals respectively. Sentences range from absolute and conditional discharges and binding over at one extreme, through financial penalties, probation, attendance centre and community service orders, to imprisonment at the other extreme (Home Office, 1990). Unlike other countries such as the Netherlands, in Britain there are no laws laying down minimum standards for imprisonment (Stern, 1989, p. 78). However, the probation service has adopted national standards for supervising offenders in the community (Home Office, 1992). Since World War II, there has been a steady stream of legislation directly governing the criminal justice system, as well as many other Acts that affect it indirectly. The following are the main laws: Criminal Justice Act 1948, Criminal Justice Act 1961, Children and Young Persons Act 1969, Criminal Justice Act 1972, Criminal Law Act 1977, Criminal Justice Act 1982, Police and Criminal Evidence Act 1984, Sporting Events (Control of Alcohol etc.) Act 1985, Prosecution of Offences Act 1985, Drug Trafficking Offences Act 1986, Public Order Act 1986, Firearms Act 1988, Criminal Justice Act 1991 and Criminal Justice and Public Order Act 1994.

The Criminal Justice and Public Order Act 1994 took away the right of an arrested suspect to silence, made a life of travelling or squatting illegal in many circumstances, and targeted raves and out-door parties for preventive action by the police.

Approaches to criminal justice work

The contemporary societal, and political, preoccupation with using the criminal justice system as a mechanism by which to punish offenders directly makes it difficult to reconcile the content of this section with any of the four approaches set out in Fig. 4.1 (chapter 4). One way of addressing this debate is to reframe control and custody, and locate them with prevention, in the context of protection of the public. Because this book is concerned with the aspects of criminal justice that fall within the ambit of the personal social services, brief reference is made here to work of a broadly protective and therapeutic nature.

Protective approaches

Crime prevention

The preoccupation of politicians and professionals with the conundrum of how to curb increases in the incidence of recorded crime has led to a growing emphasis on developing strategies for preventing crime. Heidensohn (1989, p. 175) categorises these into those based on the individual, the community and the physical environment. Individual approaches stress the adoption by people of a more security-conscious lifestyle, for example, involving marking property to attempt to reduce the incidence of burglary and theft. Community approaches, such as neighbourhood watch schemes, owe more to faith in untested assumptions about the benefits of mutual surveillance than in empirical evidence about the effectiveness of such schemes in reducing the incidence of crime. Approaches based on the physical environment hark back to ecological criminology of the Chicago school of criminology in the interwar years. They presume a cause and effect relationship between the design of a locality and the incidence of crime in it, reminiscent of Oscar Newman's attempts to design crime out of housing estates by maximising the amount of space overlooked by neighbours (Newman, 1972).

The rapid growth of the private security industry attests to the ability of commercial opportunists to identify a lucrative market for a growing range of products, employing traditional physical bolts and bars and the increasingly sophisticated means of electronic surveillance and protection.

Locking up prisoners

Another approach to protection is based on containment. Measures to curb prisoners' behaviour include a range of physiological and physical means, from the widespread use of drugs such as tranquillisers to isolating prisoners, individually and in groups, within prisons. The negative impact on prisoners of security units within prisons has been the subject of critical attention ever since Cohen and Taylor (1972) carried out their classic, undercover study. The growth of layers of security within establishments has been referred to as a 'Chinese box' effect, from which prisoners who offend against the discipline code while inside may find it difficult ever to extricate themselves (Cohen, 1977).

Therapeutic approaches

While indirect work of a therapeutic nature may be undertaken with the families (or in the circumstances of serious, traumatic crime the victims) of offenders, on the whole, therapeutic work with offenders in custody is very marginal to the central activities of controlling, supervising, monitoring, occupying and training people, whether in or out of custody. The probation service carries out the vast bulk of supervisory work with offenders in the community, often under the auspices of aftercare and supervision. Work with offenders takes place in the context of the strategies adopted by the state in response to crime.

The probation service has responsibility for court reports, throughcare, and a range of alternatives to custody in its work with adult and young offenders. There is a tension in the role of the probation service between rehabilitationist treatment and fulfilling the justice and control requirements of the criminal justice system. Attempts have been made by the Home Office over the years to clarify the trajectory of probation work, as in 1984, with the Statement of National Objectives and Priorities (SNOP). SNOP gives significant emphasis to the role of the probation service in maximising the number of offenders kept out of custody. Whitehead (1990) has studied in detail the implications of such an approach. The latent values of the probation service tend to surface whenever changes, either in sentencing or in the role and training of probation officers themselves, are mooted. The former can be seen in the adverse reaction of many probation staff to the introduction of community service orders, which were, rightly, viewed as having no social work content but simply as punishment in the community (Williams, 1995, p. 2). The latter is evident in the furore over what may loosely be described as a further Home Office initiative, in the proposals of the Dews Report (Dews and Watts, 1994). This was instigated and endorsed by Michael Howard, Home Secretary, in 1995, to replace university-based professional education as part of the Diploma in Social Work with employment-based training, segregated from what he saw as the ruinous influence of social work. The debate, however, goes deeper than a simple dichotomy between a right-wing Home Secretary and social work/probation values. The identity of probation officers is inherently contested, as is evidenced by the argument of Mike Nellis that criminology would make the basis of a more appropriate training than social work for probation officers (Williams, 1995, p. 5). The other factor is the thrust of the Home Office towards strengthening the role of probation officers in punishments in the community.

Growing importance has become attached to cognitive work (McGuire and Priestley, 1985) with offenders, including more serious offenders such as violent and sex offenders, to reduce or eliminate their offending behaviour. Cognitive approaches are not simply offence-focused but involve broader problem-solving (Raynor *et al.,* 1994, p. 75); they stand out as placing choice and control in the hands of the offender, in contrast with some psychotherapy and methods based on behavioural psychology.

A feature of social work in the criminal justice systems is the extent to which joint work takes place between social workers and other professionals, such as in prisons, where schemes may exist for probation and other prison staff to co-work or collaborate, or in the community. Terry Thomas (1993) has explored the differences and similarities between the role of police and social workers and some of the problems and conflicts that arise in joint work as a result. The codes of practice for police that originally came into force on 1 January 1986 and were afterwards revised in accordance with the Police and Criminal Evidence Act 1984, para. 67 (7), relate to four areas: police officers exercising statutory powers of stop and search, police officers searching premises and seizing property found on persons or premises, police officers detaining and questioning persons, and the identification of persons by police officers. The revised code came into force on 1 April 1991. The existence of these codes of practice is one reflection of the tension between providing the police with clarifying boundaries with professions such as social work guidelines and maintaining safeguards for the rights of citizens – adults and children – in the community.

Roles of probation and social work staff in criminal justice and social services

It would be easier to deny the organic link between probation and social work than to work through the complexities of their inter-relationship. There is no simple dichotomy between punishment and help/support, in the roles of either probation or social workers. The shift of the government towards punishment as the rationale for criminal justice policies in the 1990s is paralleled by struggles of probation services towards a positive, yet realistic, philosophy for work with offenders in the post-rehabilitation era (Whitehead, 1990, p. 19).

Social workers are called on as much as ever as agents of social control in areas such as youth justice, work with children and families, mental health and community care. For example, they make a key contribution to decisions about whether mentally ill people should remain in the community, whether an abusing adult should be excluded from the family home, and whether children would better be brought up away from their birth parents.

Issues in criminal justice

Inequalities in criminal justice

There has been increasing debate since the 1970s about the alleged discriminatory treatment received by various groups – notably black people, women, and the families and children of prisoners – in the criminal justice system. Evidence for the discriminatory treatment of black people has come from penal reform groups such as NACRO (1991) (see also document 9), while some commentators have urged caution about broad-based assumptions based on inadequate statistics concerning the incidence of black people in prisons (Harris, 1992).

Increasing concern has been evident since the 1980s about the handling of cases of suspected rape of women. Police and other professionals have received enhanced training in counselling rape victims. The treatment of rape victims in the process of giving evidence in court has been criticised on the grounds that the victim can be made to feel like an offender when cross-questioned as a witness. The disproportionate representation of women in some parts of the criminal justice system, notably prison, for some categories of offences, has been the subject of campaigns by reformers (Carlen, 1983).

The negative consequences of imprisonment of the main householder for other members of the family, notably children, have increasingly been recognised (Shaw, 1987, 1992).

Power, penal politics and practices

Among many facets of power that underlie controversies and debates over criminal justice policy and practice, three forms of power struggle are being fought out between different stakeholders in the penal system in the 1990s: first, between the Home Secretary and similarly aligned Conservative politicians and senior officials in and linked with the Prison Service, including the Chief Inspector of Prisons Judge Stephen Tumin, whose term in office came to an end in October 1995; second, between professionals within and around prisons, notably prison officers, governors, prison officers and probation staff; third, between staff and prisoners.

A groundswell of discontent from within and without (see, for example, criticisms from the Prison Officers Association, the Governors of prisons, penal reform organisations and Labour and Liberal Democratic politicians) has arisen in the 1990s in relation to the running of the prison system in Britain. This increased throughout much of 1995, following the two prison riots on 2 and 3 January at Everthorpe in Humberside and the escape of prisoners from Parkhurst Prison on the Isle of White and from Whitemoor prison. The POA complained that a lack of resources was responsible for the staff shortage which, in their view, led to the prison riots. Other sources, including prisoners and their families, maintained that the riots occurred because of a tightening of discipline, including the re-introduction of peepholes in cell doors and a general lack of freedom in the regime of many prisons, not just Everthorpe, as part of the Home Secretary's commitment to making prison sentences more rigorous and punitive. In the wake of the escape of three prisoners from Parkhurst prison early in January 1995, which followed widespread concerns about security lapses in Whitemoor prison in 1994, six staff at Parkhurst were removed from their posts and transferred to other duties. The following month saw increasing criticism of the performance of the director general of the Prison Service, and on 16 October 1995 it was announced that the Home Secretary had sacked him.

Throughout the history of prisons, prisoners have resisted their imprisonment (Adams, 1994). Different explanations for rioting have been advanced. The Home Office's research has tended to downplay the experience of prisoners, particularly long term prisoners (Cohen and Taylor, 1972). Yet it is undeniable that riots often signal prisoners' own responses to both conditions in, and the condition of, imprisonment that they are suffering. It has been noted that 'Prisons have been likened to bombs; secure containers with an explosive mixture inside' (Player and Jenkins, 1994, p. 27). Ironically, the prolonged riot at Strangeways prison in 1990 achieved more in a month than 100 years of activity by prison reform organisations, since it led to the inquiry into the riot by Lord Justice Woolf. Although Woolf's report (Woolf, 1991) addressed the liberal agenda of how to reform prisons rather than the radical agenda of abolishing the 80% of them that only warehouse minor offenders, it is the most significant statement of the agenda for further necessary prison reforms in Britain to have been made in the twentieth century.

Criminal justice policy and social justice

Hudson (1993) argues that some adjustment is needed in the balance between the criminal justice system punishing people on the one hand and helping them on the other, applying the law on the one hand and meeting social needs on the other, addressing collective interests and satisfying individual circumstances. While the purpose of the law is to contribute to guaranteeing the well-being of citizens, 'penal policy should bear in mind that it is but one strand of social policy and that all social policy should be directed towards the attainment of social justice' (op. cit., p. 200).

There is little doubt of the strong tide of punitive over-reaction in the Conservative government in the mid-1990s, led by Michael Howard, Home Secretary. Whether other more reasonable views would prevail subsequent to a Cabinet reshuffle is difficult to judge. What is evident is that this tendency runs against the vast body of research findings confirming the pointlessness of excessive use of punitive sanctions, particularly imprisonment, as a means of curbing crime in society. Against this, informed professional and critical opinion points to the gains to be derived by the stakeholders in criminal justice from developing a positive rationale for the use of imprisonment and other sanctions in the criminal justice system, apart from any notion of punishment (Adams, forthcoming). A corollary of this could involve bringing together the quartet of interests with a stake in the enterprise of criminal justice – the victims of crime, the families of prisoners, offenders and the staff working with them – to work out how contractual relationships in criminal justice could be better deployed than currently, in order for all parties to realise at least some of their claims for benefit and/or compensation. In the process, the issue of advocacy for these different interests – at present not very well articulated in criminal justice – would also need to be addressed.

References and further reading

Adams, R. (1994) *Prison Riots in Britain and the USA*, Basingstoke: Macmillan.

Adams, R. (forthcoming) *The Abuses of Punishment*, Basingstoke: Macmillan.

Bishop, N. (1960) Group work at Pollington Borstal, *Howard Journal,* vol.10, no.3

Bottomley, A.K. and Hay, W. (eds) (1991) *Special Units for Difficult Prisoners*, Centre for Criminology and Criminal Justice, Hull: University of Hull.

Bottoms A.E. (1990) The aims of imprisonment, in Garland, D. (ed.), *Justice, Guilt and Forgiveness in the Penal System*, Paper no.18, Centre for Theology and Public Issues, Edinburgh: Edinburgh University.

Brody, S. (1976) *The Effectiveness of Sentencing: a Review of the Literature,* Home Office Research Study no.35, London: HMSO.

Carlen, P. (1983) *Women's Imprisonment*, London: Routledge and Kegan Paul.

Carlen, P., Hicks, J., O'Dwyer, J., Christina, D. and Tchaikovsky, C. (1985) *Criminal Women*, Cambridge: Polity Press.

Casale, S. (1984) *Minimum Standards for Prison Establishments*, London: NACRO.

Children and Young Persons Act 1969, London: HMSO.

Cohen, S. (1977) Prisons and the future of control systems: from concentration to dispersal, in Fitzgerald, M. *et al.* (eds), *Welfare in Action*, Milton Keynes: Open University.

Cohen, S. and Taylor, L. (1972) *Psychological Survival: the Experience of Long Term Imprisonment*, Harmondsworth: Penguin.

Cohen, S. and Taylor, L. (1976) *Prison Secrets*, London: National Council for Civil Liberties and Radical Alternatives to Prison.

Cooke, D.J. (1989) Containing violent prisoners: an analysis of the Barlinnie Special Unit, *British Journal of Criminology*, vol.29, no.2, 129–143.

Corrigan, P. and Frith, S. (1976) The politics of youth culture, in Hall, S. and Jefferson, T. (eds), *Resistance through Rituals*, London: Hutchinson.

Council of Europe (1973) *Council of Europe Standard Minimum Rules for the Treatment of Prisoners*, Strasbourg: Council of Europe.

Criminal Justice Act 1948, London: HMSO.

Criminal Justice Act 1961, London: HMSO.

Criminal Justice Act 1972, London: HMSO.

Criminal Justice Act 1982, London: HMSO.

Criminal Justice Act 1991. London: HMSO.

Criminal Justice and Public Order Act 1994, London: HMSO.

Criminal Law Act 1977, London: HMSO.

Criminal Lunacy (Departmental) Commission (1882) *Report of the Commission to Inquire into the Subject of Criminal Lunacy*, Cmnd. 3418, London: HMSO.

Crow, I. and Cove, J. (1984) Ethnic minorities and the courts, *Criminal Law Review*, 413–417.

Cullen, E. (1994) Grendon: the Therapeutic Prison that Works, *Therapeutic Communities* Vol. 15, No. 4, pp. 301–310.

Departmental Committee (1895) *Report from the Departmental Committee on Prisons* (Gladstone Report), Cmnd 7702, Parliamentary Papers, vol.56.

Dews, V. and Watts, J. (1994) *Review of Probation Officer Recruitment and Qualifying Training* (Dews Report), London: HMSO.

Drug Trafficking Offences Act 1986, London: HMSO.

Firearms Act 1988, London: HMSO.

Fitzgerald, E. (1985) Prison discipline and the courts, in Maguire, M., Vagg, J. and Morgan, R. (eds), *Accountability and Prisons: Opening Up a Closed World*, London: Tavistock.

Fitzgerald, M. (1977) *Prisoners in Revolt,* Harmondsworth: Penguin.

Fitzgerald, M. and Sim, J. (1982) *British Prisons,* Oxford: Blackwell.

Fitzgerald, M. *et al.* (eds) (1977) *Welfare in Action:* Milton Keynes: Open University.

Food Act 1984, London: HMSO.

Franks Committee (1972) The Departmental Committee on section 2 of of the Official Secrets Act 1911, 4 volumes, London: HMSO.

Garland, D. (ed.) *Justice, Guilt and Forgiveness in the Penal System,* Paper no. 18, Centre for Theology and Public Issues, Edinburgh: Edinburgh University.

Gibbens, T.C.N. (1963) *Psychiatric Studies of Borstal Lads,* Oxford: Oxford University Press.

Harris, R.J. (1992) *Crime, Criminal Justice and the Probation Service,* London: Tavistock/Routledge.

Health and Safety at Work etc. Act 1974, London: HMSO.

Heidensohn, F. (1989) *Crime and Society,* London: Macmillan.

HM Chief Inspector of Prisons (1994) *Report of an Inspection of Preston Prison,* London: Home Office.

Home Office (1966) *Report of the Inquiry into Prison Escapes and Security* (Mountbatten Report), Cmnd 3175, London: HMSO.

Home Office (1979) *Report of the Committee of Inquiry into the United Kingdom Prison Services* (May Committee), Cmnd 7673, London: HMSO.

Home Office (1985) *Report of the Committee on the Prison Disciplinary System* (Prior Report), Cmnd 9641, London: HMSO.

Home Office (1987) *A Review of Prisoners' Complaints,* a report by HM Chief Inspector of Prisons, London: HMSO.

Home Office (1988a) *Punishment, Custody and the Community,* Cmnd 424, London: HMSO.

Home Office (1988b) *The Parole System in England and Wales,* Report of the Review Committee (Carlisle Report), Cmnd 532, London: HMSO.

Home Office (1990) *The Sentence of the Court: a Handbook for Courts on the Treatment of Offenders,* London: HMSO.

Home Office (1992) *National Standards for the Supervision of Offenders in the Community* (published jointly with Department of Health and Welsh Office), London: HMSO.

Home Office Circulars: 114/1983, *Manpower, Effectiveness and Efficiency in the Police Service;* 14/1985, *The Cautioning of Offenders,* London: Home Office.

Home Office/Department of Health and Social Security (1975) *Report of the Committee on Mentally Abnormal Offenders* (Butler Report), Cmnd 6244, London: HMSO.

Howe A. (1994) *Punish and Critique: towards a Feminist Analysis of Penalty,* London: Routledge.

Hudson, B.A. (1993) *Penal Policy and Social Justice,* London: Macmillan.

King, R. and Morgan, R. (1976) *A Taste of Prison: Custodial Conditions for Trial and Remand Prisoners,* London: Routledge and Kegan Paul.

Lea, J. and Young, J. (1984) *What is to be Done About Law and Order? Crisis in the Nineties,* Harmondsworth: Penguin.

Maguire, M., Vagg, J. and Morgan, R. (eds) (1985) *Accountability and Prisons: Opening Up a Closed World,* London: Tavistock.

McGuire, J. and Priestley, P. (1985) *Offending Behaviour: Skills and Stratagems for Going Straight,* London: Batsford.

Morgan, R. (1994) Paying the big bill, *The Guardian,* 4 August, 22.

Morris, A. and Wilkinson, C. (1988) (eds) *Women and the Penal System,* Cropwood Conference Series 19, Institute of Criminology, Cambridge: University of Cambridge.

Morris, P. (1965) *Prisoners and Their Families*, London: Allen and Unwin.

Murder (Abolition of the Death Penalty) Act 1965.

NACRO (1991) *Black People's Experiences of Criminal Justice*, London: NACRO.

NACRO (1993) *Community Care and Mentally Disturbed Offenders*, Mental Health Advisory Committee Policy Paper 1, London: NACRO.

Newman, O. (1972) *Defensible Space: People and Design in the Violent City*, London: Architectural Press.

Official Secrets Act 1911, London: HMSO.

Player, E. and Jenkins, M. (1994) *Prisons After Woolf: Reform through Riot*, London: Routledge.

Police and Criminal Evidence Act 1984, London: HMSO.

Prosecution of Offences Act 1985, London: HMSO.

Public Order Act 1986, London: HMSO.

Punishment, Custody and the Community (1988) Green Paper, Cmnd 424, London: HMSO.

Raynor, P., Smith, D. and Vanstone, M. (1994) *Effective Probation Practice*, Basingstoke: BASW/Macmillan

Reiner, R. and Cross, M. (1991) *Beyond Law and Order: Criminal Justice Policy and Politics into the 1990s*, London: Macmillan.

Rutherford, A. (1986) *Prisons and the Process of Justice*, Oxford: Oxford University Press.

Ryan, M. and Ward, T. (1989) *Privatization and the Penal System: the American Experience and the Debate in Britain*, Milton Keynes: Open University Press.

Shaw, R. (1987) *Children of Imprisoned Fathers*, London: Hodder and Stoughton.

Shaw, R. (1992) *Prisoners' Children: What are the Issues?* London: Routledge.

Sim, J. (1990) *Medical Power in Prisons: the Prison Medical Service in England 1774–1989*, Milton Keynes: Open University Press.

Social Trends 26 (1996), London: HMSO.

Sporting Events (Control of Alcohol etc.) Act 1985, London: HMSO.

Stenson, K. and Brearley, N. (1991) Left realism in criminology and the return to consensus theory, in Reiner, R. and Cross, M., *Beyond Law and Order: Criminal Justice Policy and Politics into the 1990s*, 223–247, London: Macmillan.

Stern, V. (1989) *Imprisoned by our Prisons: a Programme of Reform*, London: Unwin Hyman.

Taylor, I. (1982) *Law and Order: Arguments for Socialism*, London: Macmillan.

Taylor, I., Walton, P. and Young, J. (1973) *The New Criminology: for a Social Theory of Deviance*, London: Routledge and Kegan Paul.

Thomas, T. (1993) *The Police and Social Workers*, 2nd edn, Aldershot: Gower.

Walker, N. (1991) *Why Punish?* Oxford: Oxford University Press.

Whitehead, P. (1990) *Community Supervision for Offenders*, Aldershot: Avebury.

Widdicombe Report (1986) *The Conduct of Local Authority Business*, Cmnd 9797, London: HMSO.

Williams, B. (ed.) (1995) *Probation Values*, Birmingham: Venture Press.

Willis, P. (1977) *Learning to Labour: how Working Class Lads Get Working Class Jobs*, London: Saxon House.

Woolf, Lord Justice (1991) *Prison Disturbances April 1990: Report of an Inquiry by the Rt. Hon Lord Justice Woolf (Parts I and II) and His Honour Judge Stephen Tumin (Part II)*, Cmnd 1456, London: HMSO.

CHAPTER 10

Youth justice

This chapter considers the historical context and legal basis for youth justice work, as well as the main approaches and issues that arise.

Context of youth justice

Youth justice work, involving probation officers and social workers, is located in an area of continuing public concern and media controversy. Much of the debate revolves around the linked issues of more or less continuous rises in some categories of recorded juvenile crime since the 1950s in Britain, and the question of how society should respond to this. The commonly stated view that there is a 'flat earth' plateau in the crime figures in Britain over the past century and a half (Pearson, 1975, 1983) needs qualifying in the light of evidence about changes in crime rates since World War II. The Home Affairs Committee (1993) noted that only 10% of juveniles are cautioned or found guilty of full indictable offences involving violence. Although it has been known for many years that most young people commit offences at some time (Belson, 1975), it is not known precisely why most of these will cease offending by the time they are adult. Three explanations of rising recorded juvenile crime are common: it may be viewed as a feature of the crime statistics and policing rather than of the incidence of crime itself; it may be seen as a sign of deteriorating parenting manifested in young people's behaviour; critics of Conservative government policies may view it as one of the economic and social consequences of government policies aggravating long-term unemployment, hastening the fragmentation of working class neighbourhoods and creating a generation of young people with little hope of achieving jobs or prosperity through legitimate social activities. Although the 1980s witnessed a move towards the community rather than the use of custody in dealing with youth crime, there was an increasing tendency to view a group of persistent young offenders as needing tougher measures. This culminated in the plans made in 1993 by the government to introduce a small number of custodial centres with stricter regimes.

It is a simplification and distortion to characterise the official responses to delinquency in terms of the polarised themes of welfare and punishment. It is also not true to imply that the past 150 years have simply seen an uncomplicated and marked movement from more punitive to less punitive measures for dealing with young offenders. However, a powerful campaign to separate the facilities for children from those of adults, and to preserve measures for caring for and protecting children alongside those for punishment, was conducted in the mid-nineteenth century.

Historical aspects of responses to youth crime

Child offenders are a little-discussed aspect of youth justice. A small minority of child offenders have often committed grave offences such as murder, for which, if adults, they would have received sentences of 14 years or more. The fact that some cases such as that of Mary Bell, convicted as a child murderer, achieve notoriety in the media makes work with the individual more difficult, since therapeutic and rehabilitative programmes may need to be developed with a view to the eventual release of the individual. Child murderers may occupy secure provision for many years before they are released as adults. They may have been sentenced at an age when the kinds of therapeutic programmes of confronting offending behaviour that have been developed for adults are not appropriate for work with them. Work with child offenders also presents many issues concerned with meeting their developmental needs and equipping them for life in the community that they have never known as adults.

Despite the huge media coverage of the small minority of serious crimes committed by a tiny number of child and young offenders, such crimes are untypical of youth crime in general. Unfortunately, though, responses to youth crime reflect societal values and the presumptions of adults rather than research evidence. Consequently, children continue to be locked up inappropriately. Two examples are the remanding of juveniles to prison and the use of secure units. As long ago as the 1850s, Mary Carpenter's campaign to set up children's reformatories was stimulated in part by her desire to remove children from adult prisons. Between April and September 1990, 374 juveniles were on remand in prison, awaiting trial, on the alleged grounds that there was no alternative accommodation (Thompson, 1995, p. 12). At that time, there were only ten local authority secure units in England and none in Wales, but despite the stated intention to improve that situation, a joint report by the National Association for the Care and Resettlement of Offenders (NACRO) and the Association of Chief Probation Officers (ACPO) indicates that from October 1993 to September 1994, 1478 juveniles, mainly boys accused of burglary, 'joyriding', robbery and violence, were remanded to prison (NACRO/ACPO, 1995). In part, this trend was facilitated by the fact that the criminal justice legislation of 1994 made easier the sentencing to secure accommodation of children aged 10 to 14 (Thompson, 1995, p. 13).

Research shows that the way children going into care are treated, rather than any inherent characteristics of their personalities or behaviour, leads to some of them finishing up in secure provision (Millham *et al.*, 1978). There is little need within the child care system for an expansion in the number of secure places (Harris and Timms, 1993), while there may be some need for short-term secure remand facilities and secure treatment facilities in certain geographical areas. It is also necessary to distinguish between different functions of security and to separate the functions of finding shelter for some children for intensive care and custody for others. It may be difficult for staff to fulfil these different functions for children housed together. Milham *et al.* (1978, p. 188) argues that improved alternatives to custody and short-term shelter would prevent many children currently housed there from finding their way into residential care.

There is a striking contrast between the conditions of young people housed in different kinds of custodial facilities. There is a tendency to draw attention to the superficial resemblances between, for example, the facilities and costs of keeping young people at Eton or Harrow and in a young offenders' custody unit. However, the regime of the former works in favour of maximising the education and development of the young person, while in the latter staff roles may reflect a far less positive and much more punitive of custodial, merely warehousing, set priorities and roles.

The personal social services – usually this means social workers employed by the local authority social services department – have responsibility for: liaising with police before a decision to charge a child or young person; ensuring that an 'appropriate adult' is present during questioning; making the arrangements where the juvenile is to be remanded in local authority accommodation; preparing a social enquiry report or pre-sentence report before the court makes an order; and triggering the social services to act to protect a child at risk, for example, of physical or sexual abuse (Brayne and Martin, 1993, chapter 5). In carrying out these tasks, professionals, and particularly those in local authorities, are likely to refer to a range of legislation that extends back more than 60 years, to the Children and Young Persons Act 1933.

The history of policy and practice regarding juvenile offenders since statutory provision for containing them in residential reformatories began in 1854, and industrial schools in 1857, has been over-simplified in the twin goals of providing care (love) and control (punishment). This division is still widely regarded as part of the inheritance of youth justice and child care, although it is doubtful whether the words used in the 1990s hold the same connotations as they did more than a century ago. The Probation of

Offenders Act in 1907 created probation, the Children Act of 1908 was known as the Children's Charter, and the Prevention of Crime Act in 1908 created borstal training for 16–21 year olds. Borstal training involved a sentence of between 1 and 3 years in custody, depending on how the young offender responded to treatment, plus a period of supervision of at least 6 months. Borstal training was intended to provide reformation for offenders, as was preventive detention for habitual criminals, which was introduced at the same time under the Prevention of Crime Act.

Between the wars, the most significant legislation affecting young offenders was the Children and Young Persons Act 1933, which contained many of the recommendations of the Malony committee (Home Office Departmental Committee on the Treatment of Young Offenders, 1925). Up to World War II there was a trend away from using custodial institutions in general, and after World War II the 1948 Criminal Justice Act reflected a change in attitude towards young offenders, perhaps partly following an increase in recorded juvenile crime in the war years. This expressed the somewhat contradictory response to young offenders by introducing attendance centres, remand centres and support for probation hostels as well as abolishing corporal punishment on one hand, while introducing a detention centre order, intended to be a short custodial sentence, containing a deterrent element of punishment. The first detention centre opened in 1952.

The fact that the 1948 measures targeted at children and young people were not entirely punitive was emphasised not just in the Criminal Justice Act but also in the passing of the Children Act 1948, which aimed to end the practice of putting children in need of care in approved schools along with offenders. Local authority children's departments were set up to develop residential care resources and staffing to deliver fostering and adoption services – the beginning of social work services exclusively for children.

The Ingleby committee reported in 1960 and the Children and Young Persons Act of 1963 raised the age of criminal responsibility to 10. The Longford Report (Labour Party Study Group, 1964) was largely a Labour Party response to the Ingleby Report. The government White Paper *The Child, the Family and the Young Offender* followed many of the significant recommendations of the Longford Report, such as family courts and the abolition of juvenile courts, but was abandoned in favour of the White Paper, *Children in Trouble,* the Children and Young Persons Act 1969.

The Children and Young Persons Act 1969 was the benchmark, and in retrospect the high-water mark, of the application of the treatment paradigm in youth justice. The intention was to phase out detention centres and borstals for juveniles and replace them with intermediate treatment. It is doubtful whether there was ever a consensus about this, as the swing back towards law and order in the 1970s indicates. The expenditure committee report (House of Commons, 1975) criticised the Children and Young Persons Act 1969 for not making a clear distinction between children who need care and those who need more control and an element of punishment. The White Paper of 1980, *Young Adult Offenders*, was followed by the Criminal Justice Act of 1982. The manifesto of the Conservative Party in 1979 promised to strengthen sentencing powers regarding juveniles and young adults in the 1980 White Paper. It included the stated re-introduction of a small number of detention centres, and the experiment with tougher regimes in two of these – Send and New Hall – began in 1980. There were contradictory pressures on the government – political, general public, media, professional, academic – towards more punitive, inevitably custodial, measures and away from the spiralling expense of custody. The evaluation of the short sharp shock showed it to be a failure (Thornton *et al.*, 1984). Magistrates preferred youth custody. Despite this, the government extended the regime briefly to all parts of the system of detention. The Criminal Justice Act 1982 decreased the detention centre sentences from 3 months to 21 days and from 6 months to 4 months. Imprisonment for offenders under 21 was abolished and borstals were replaced by a Youth Custody Order at Youth Custody Centres. The minimum for this was 4 months and one day, and the maximum was 6 months. At around the same time, Circular LAC 83 (3) issued by the Department of Health and Social Security encouraged local authorities to support alternatives to custody by making grants available for intermediate treatment programmes. This circular also addressed the need for work with persistent offenders and serious offenders to be better co-ordinated at local level, between agencies. The Criminal Justice Act 1988 introduced a new sentence of detention in a Young Offender Institution (YOI), separate detention centres disappearing and being amalgamated with young custody centres to become YOIs. Courts could decide how long the sentence was to be for young people aged 15 and over.

Ironically, the move towards adoption of what became the justice approach in some ways had coincided with what radical reformers had been advocating in their critique of welfare approaches to delinquency. One of their main criticisms had been that the more professionals were involved in delving into the backgrounds of children and young people who became delinquent, the more likely it was that the net of professional intervention would be widened and more young people would be sucked into the youth justice system (Thorpe *et al.*, 1980). By the late 1970s the use of community-based sentences for juvenile offenders had declined and custodial sentences had increased. This had at least as much to do with changing sentencing practices as it did with any shifts in the nature of juvenile crimes being committed (Hagell and Newburn,

1994, p. 14). In so far as criminal justice legislation since 1970 has affected children and young people, its emphasis has been on developing more control and punishment for juveniles and young offenders themselves, as in the Criminal Justice Act 1982, and on sanctioning parents as the adults responsible for children's offending, as in the Criminal Justice Act 1991. Yet, during the 1980s, there was a significant decline in the use of custody for juveniles, partly because the number of young males aged 14 to 16 declined by almost a fifth and partly because strategies to divert young people from court and from custody were actually working under the Thatcher government (op. cit., pp. 15–16).

After the murder of James Bulger in 1993, the government focused more on what were viewed as persistent young offenders. The government was more unwilling than even its predecessors to listen to advice from researchers and professionals concerning the ineffectiveness of long sentences as a means of deterrence, either of the offender or of other potential offenders. In July 1994, the Home Secretary, Michael Howard, announced that the two boys originally sentenced to serve a minimum eight years for the murder of James Bulger were to be detained for a minimum of 15 years. This decision confirms a variance between practice in Britain and the rest of Europe, where there is a widespread view that such dates should be set by judges rather than politicians. In Britain, a European Court of Human Rights ruling in 1990 meant that a judge now set the target date for discretionary lifers, the final decision of release was made by a judge sitting with two parole panel members and the Home Secretary had no role in this. However, in July 1994, the European Court of Human Rights upheld the role of the Home Secretary in being able to change the target recommendation of the judge for mandatory life sentence prisoners and overturning subsequent parole board decisions that a person is ready for release (*The Guardian,* 23 July 1994).

The coincidence of the Bulger case with the debate about persistent young offenders confused two different issues, one being more associated with occasional heinous crimes and the other with the question of repeated offending. Both involve minuscule numbers of young people, probably no more than dozens in the entire UK in a generation.

There have been moves to target persistent young offenders at various times during the twentieth century. The main approaches fall into two distinct categories, the first being to attempt to meet their welfare needs and the second involving a punitive response to serious offenders. Research by Hagell and Newburn (1994) confirms the difficulty of identifying a sufficiently clear group of persistent offenders and therefore the problems associated with developing a strategy related to this group. Further, there is abundant evidence of the ineffectiveness of custodial, to say nothing of other purely punitive, methods of dealing with offenders (op. cit.).

Towards national standards in youth justice

While the probation service was the first to adopt national standards, SSI inspections led to the development of a similar approach in the personal social services. For example, an inspection of youth justice services in five social services departments (Devon, Hackney, Newcastle, Sandwell and Wigan) indicated that local strategies to implement the new legislation (Criminal Justice Act 1991) were well advanced, and services were underpinned by core statements of policy on youth crime and the provision of youth justice services, including the development of youth crime prevention policies. The extent to which youth justice policies were integrated with the wider policies for children and young people in social services departments varied: the inspectors drew attention to the fact that with one exception, the social services departments were 'less advanced than probation services in inspecting and promoting anti-discriminatory practice in the provision of youth justice services. Most had a departmental or local authority-wide equal opportunities policy but there were few examples of specific policies and practice guidance for youth justice services' (Social Services Inspectorate, 1994, p. 4).

These national standards cover policy frameworks, inter-agency arrangements, organisation and management, resourcing and operation of services, with particular regard to the detention of alleged young offenders, remands to local authority accommodation, pre-sentence reports and the supervision of offenders (op. cit., pp. 68–77).

Legal basis for youth justice services

Some of the legislation applying to children and young people in chapter 5 is also relevant in youth justice work. In addition, three Acts particularly apply: the Police and Criminal Evidence Act 1984, the Children and Young Persons Act 1933 and the Criminal Justice Act 1991. The Police and Criminal Evidence Act 1984 gives the police increased powers to stop suspected offenders and search and detain them, using reasonable force where necessary. Where a suspected young offender is detained, parents, or if they are unavailable or unwilling, social workers, are to attend as appropriate adults while the young person is being interviewed. Grave offences are dealt with under the Children and Young Persons Act 1933.

The Criminal Justice Act 1991 changed juvenile courts to youth courts and extended their jurisdiction to the 17-year-old group. The Children Act 1989 recognised the need to avoid prosecution. The Criminal Justice Act 1991 gave magistrates new powers to sentence, including unit files, community sentences and custody as well as post-custody supervision. It reduced the maximum period of detention in a young offenders' institution to 12 months and emphasised the value of joint working by giving chief probation officers and directors of social services joint responsibility for making arrangements to provide services to the youth court (Hagell and Newburn, 1994, p. 18). One aim of the Criminal Justice and Public Order Act 1994 is to enable the police to act to prevent, and break up, raves attended by young people and also to remove a person's right to silence.

Approaches to youth justice work

It is debatable whether the paradigm shift from the medico-treatment assumptions on which many professional social work responses to problem children and young people were based (see chapter 4) until the mid-1970s to a justice approach is more punitive or more empowering in its aspirations. This judgement partly depends on whether the advocates of justice are its right-wing supporters or liberal and radical campaigners for enhancing the rights of children and young people. What matters more is that the explanation for the successful diversion referred to above, of increasing numbers of young people from the youth justice system during the 1980s, lies partly in the clear articulation of the principles and practice of diversion at different levels of the system, or in different stages of the process, however conceptualised. One of the most significant developments involved the formalisation of co-ordinated approaches between many social services departments and other agencies in the planning and development of youth justice services.

Diversion from the criminal justice system

Diversion involves minimising the penetration of a young person into the criminal justice system. Diversion may occur at three main levels in the youth justice system: from charging by the police, from court and from custody. Thus, there are several main points where diversion may be achieved, such as: diversion from the criminal justice system; diversion from further contact with the system through cautioning; diversion from custody through a non-custodial sentence.

Diversion is associated with preventive work, in social work and in youth work. It has a long history, through the work of probation officers, the outdoor pursuits movement, boys' clubs, youth clubs (Jeffs, 1979) and voluntary child care organisations in the nineteenth century (Adams *et al.*, 1981, chapter 1). One example of a preventive approach to working with young people does not involve the personal social services at all. In order to try to prevent repetitions of the riot that occurred in July 1992 involving the police and young people in Burnley, Lancashire, the South West Burnley Youth Development Project, funded by the National Youth Agency, has been targeting teenagers – regular offenders ejected from schools and traditional youth clubs – and drawing them into activities to try to keep them out of trouble (*The Observer*, 24 July 1994, p. 10).

Of course, for social workers to engage in preventive work of this kind risks sucking young people into the youth justice system who otherwise would have not been associated with it. However, social workers are responsible for diverting children and young people from the criminal justice system wherever possible or, if they appear in court, preparing plans that divert them from custody. In the process, they often liaise with police when a child or young person is apprehended on suspicion of committing a criminal offence, act as the appropriate adult when a parent or guardian is not available and the police wish to interview the alleged young offender and, in appropriate cases, prepare a pre-sentence report (PSR) for the Youth Court. A section on pre-sentence reports focuses on 'offence analysis' and examines the possibility of further offending. Unless either agency already is involved with the family, a social worker prepares the PSR for a young person under 14 years of age, and a probation officer if the young person is aged 14 to 17. In cases where the Youth Court considers that the offence is too serious (i.e. it carries a sentence, for adults, of 14 years or more), children and young people may be committed to the Crown Court. Under the Criminal Justice and Public Order Act 1994, a persistent offender aged 15 to 17 can be committed to Crown Court and sentenced to Youth Custody of between 12 and 24 months. It should be noted that the tendency of government policy towards punishment in the community creates pressure on probation officers to police community sentences through revised national standards. Community service is designed to 'provide reparation to the community through challenging, social useful unpaid work', which may include manual labour. (Tissier, 1994, p. 25.)

Diversion through police cautioning

Cautioning rates continued to vary widely in the 1980s. Thorpe (1994) points out that the criminal statistics for England and Wales, in indicating that males under 17 cautioned by the police averaged 66% of all those cautioned and prosecuted, failed to point out local variations from the lowest rate (in Staffordshire), of 41% where the police prosecuted 59%, and the highest rate (in Northamptonshire), where the police cautioned 86% of those cautioned or prosecuted. Thorpe attributed the success of this initiative – more than 8 out of 10 apprehended juvenile offenders in Northamptonshire being diverted from the juvenile courts – partly to the activities of Juvenile Liaison Bureaux (JLB). JLB were introduced on a pilot basis in Corby and Wellingborough in Northamptonshire in 1980/81, and county-wide by the mid-1980s. (op. cit.).

In a longitudinal study of a sample of 367 juvenile cases through the pre-court decision-making process in one police force, Roger Evans (1994) found that less than 4% received three or more cautions and 16% received two or more, a third less than the estimated percentage of all juveniles dealt with in the youth courts.

The Home Secretary Michael Howard has turned away from the policy of diversion from court. Previously, policy maintained that an existing caution or conviction should not rule out a further caution. The Home Office moved towards a less liberal attitude to cautioning, in its circular giving guidance (Home Office, 1994). When the guidance was introduced the Home Secretary said 'from now on your first chance is your last chance. Criminals should know they will be punished. Giving cautions to serious offenders, or the same person time and again, send the wrong message to criminals and the public' (*The Guardian*, 16 March 1994).

Diversion from custody

Harris and Webb (1987), on the basis of research into supervision of young people in the youth justice system in the wake of the 1969 Children and Young Persons Act, theorise the practice of the control and welfare responses to young people at the *macro* (social and political purposes of supervision) level, at the *mezzo* (analysis of welfare organisations) level and at the *micro* (analysis of professional workers involved in supervision) level. By discussing the different conflicts, manipulations and re-interpretations as the different levels and players interact and both fulfil formal requirements while also subverting them, the authors demonstrate the limits of stability and competence of various aspects of the youth justice system. They also demonstrate the enduring power of its twin, and structurally opposed, elements of justice and welfare (op. cit.).

Whilst it is true that certain of the trends discernible in the 1969 Act were also discernible in the 1960s (Thorpe *et al.*, 1980), they have accelerated considerably since, and it was only in 1983 that the same safeguard – the care or control test – was extended to order to Section 7 (7) of the 1969 Act (Criminal Justice Act, 1982, Section 23), as applied to orders made under Section 1 (2) (F1) (Harris and Webb, 1987, p. 29).

Diversion from custody, while it was a desirable form of diversion in terms of the harmful impact of institutions on young offenders, did not increase in England and Wales during the 1970s. While the proportionate use of custody reduced in England and Wales, it actually increased in that period for juveniles. Between 1969 and 1979 the number of detention centre and borstal sentences passed on offenders aged 14–16 increased from 2750 to 6876 (Tutt, 1984, p. 7). The Criminal Justice Act 1982 did not reverse this trend. In 1982, 5080 offenders were serving borstal sentences, while in 1983 8244 were serving youth custody sentences (op. cit., p. 8).

Harris and Webb (1987) show how the shortcomings of the 1969 Children and Young Persons Act, among which was an unintended but huge increase in sentencing to custody reflecting increased punitive action by courts, and also a great disparity among the courts in sentencing policies, are reflected at the technical, the micro-political and the structural levels. At the technical level, serious difficulties arose because of the non-implementation of Sections 4 and 5 respectively of the Act which involved raising the age of criminal responsibility from 10 to 14 and that offenders aged 14–16 should be taken to court only when the police, after consulting the local authority, were convinced that this was necessary.

The Criminal Justice Act 1991 made significant changes in the ways young offenders are dealt with in the criminal justice system. The practice of social work with young offenders was affected also by the Children Act 1989, and social workers and probation officers were affected indirectly and directly by progress towards implementing all the National Standards for the Supervision of Offenders in the Community, jointly published by the Home Office, the Department of Health and the Welsh Office in 1992.

Issues in youth justice

Youth justice is beset by two interconnecting forces: political pressure to lower the age of criminal responsibility, and a trend towards harsher responses to youth crime

Pressure to lower the age of criminal responsibility

The age of criminal responsibility remains a contested area. In contrast with other countries, where it is higher – 15 in Denmark and Norway, 13 in France, 18 in Belgium and Luxembourg, 14 in

Germany – in Britain the trend is downward (*The Guardian*, 17 March 1995). The minimum age is 10, but from 10 to 14 the juveniles have to be proved to know they are committing a wrong. The issue has become unjustifiably complicated during the 1990s by the controversy over serious crimes committed by a tiny minority of juveniles. The overwhelming weight of professional and research commentary is on the side of the principle of diversion – minimising the contact a child or young person has with the criminal justice system, since most young people grow out of offending if tolerated without judicial intervention or labelling through criminal procedures (Rutherford, 1992).

Trend towards harsher responses to youth crime

Two aspects of this trend are identifiable. The first involves the direct imposition of harsher penalties. It was reported in the summer of 1995 that the government was considering proposals for the Ministry of Defence to privatise the military prison at Colchester, for use as a tough custodial institution for young offenders (*The Guardian*, 25 August 1995). Thorn Cross, Cheshire, due to open in Spring 1996, will cost £1.7 million (*NAPO News*, no.73, October 1995). This is despite evidence that tougher regimes have been found to be ineffective as a means of reforming offenders (Thornton, Curran, Grayson and Holloway, 1984).

The second aspect is a growing hostility towards measures viewed as too soft. Controversy arose in 1993 and 1994 over cases of young offenders being sent on so-called holidays as a reward for offending. The first case involved a young offender from an outdoor pursuit centre in Wales being sent abroad with a social worker on a holiday that involved diving. The second case was that of a teenage offender sent from Essex Social Services to a Centre Parcs holiday in Suffolk who committed offences while there in March 1994. The third case, which was loosely related, involved a young offender being allowed release from an institution to continue training as a young footballer. At the same time as the Department of Health called for a report from Essex Social Services Department in relation to the Centre Parcs holiday, police in Newcastle were questioning whether a young man nicknamed 'rat boy' should have been allowed home to visit his parents from a secure unit in Birmingham. This young man reportedly has a history of more than 30 abscondings and has been charged with almost 50 offences ranging from burglary to violence (*The Guardian*, 9 August 1994).

These incidents raise questions about how far diversionary policies and practices are supported by the mass media and reflect a 'welfare' consensus in youth justice policy, and how far they conflict with the view that young offenders should be punished and locked up as a deterrent to themselves and to others. The evidence from research indicates that custodial sentences do nothing but increase the likelihood of re-offending, and proportionately the effect is increased for longer sentences (Brody, 1976). While politicians and policy-makers across the political spectrum have generally accepted this, there is still a widespread expectation in the public, largely supported by the media, that more deterrent sentences are needed for persistent offenders, including the use of custody where appropriate. However, research suggests that there are very few frequent re-offenders, and even fewer whose frequent offending extends over a period of time (Hagell and Newburn, 1994). So, developing new institutions in which to incarcerate them is a waste of money. The danger is that any such new secure accommodation will be filled with young people who are not persistent offenders. Finally, there is a palpable conflict between the Children Act 1989, which requires that the welfare of the child should be paramount, and the Criminal Justice Act 1991, which requires that a number of factors – including the seriousness and relevance of the offence, the maturity of the offender, the suitability of the disposal and its proportionality with the offence – be taken into account when deciding how to deal with a young offender. At the same time, the Race Relations Act 1976 and the Sex Discrimination Act 1975 should be taken into account when a young person is dealt with in the youth justice system.

References and further reading

Adams, R., Allard, S., Baldwin, J. and Thomas, J. (1981) *A Measure of Diversion? Case studies in Intermediate Treatment*, Leicester: National Youth Bureau.

Belson, W. (1975) *Juvenile Theft: the Causal Factors,* London: Harper and Row.

Blag, H. and Smith, D. (1989) *Crime, Penal Policy and Social Work*, London: Longman.

Brayne, H. and Martin, G. (1993) *Law for Social Workers*, 3rd edn, Oxford: Blackstone.

Brody, S. (1976) *The Effectiveness of Sentencing: a Review of the Literature*, Home Office Research Study no.35, London: HMSO.

Children Act 1980, London: HMSO.

Children Act 1989, London: HMSO.

Children and Young Persons Act 1933, London: HMSO.

Children and Young Persons Act 1963, London: HMSO.

Children and Young Persons Act 1969, London: HMSO.

Criminal Justice Act 1948, London: HMSO.

Criminal Justice Act 1982, London: HMSO.

Criminal Justice Act 1988, London: HMSO.

Criminal Justice Act 1991, London: HMSO.

Evans, R. (1994) Out of their hands, *Community Care*, 16–22 June, 18–19.

Farrington, D. (1986) Age and crime, in Tonry, M. and Morris, N. (eds) *Crime and Justice,* vol.7, Chicago: University of Chicago Press.

Farrington, D. and Bennet, T. (1981) Police Cautioning of Juveniles in London, *British Journal of Criminology*, vol. 21, 123–135.

Hagell, A. and Newburn, T. (1994) *Persistent Young Offenders,* London: Policy Studies Institute.

Harris, R. and Timms, N. (1993) *Secure Accommodation in Child Care: between Hospital and Prison or Thereabouts?* London: Routledge and Kegan Paul.

Harris, R. and Webb, D. (1987) *Welfare, Power and Youth Justice: the Social Control of Delinquent Youths,* London: Tavistock.

Home Office (1965) *The Child, the Family and the Young Offender,* White Paper, Cmnd 2742, London: HMSO.

Home Office (1968) *Children in Trouble,* White Paper, Cmnd 3601, London: HMSO.

Home Office (1980) *Young Adult Offenders,* White Paper, London: HMSO.

Home Office (1988) *Punishment, Custody and the Community,* Green Paper, London: HMSO.

Home Office, Department of Health and Welsh Office (1992) *The National Standards for the Supervision of Offenders in the Community,* London: HMSO.

Home Office Departmental Committee on the Treatment of Young Offenders, 1925 Molony Committee Report, London: HMSO.

Home Office Circular 14/1985, The Cautioning of Offenders, London: Home Office.

House of Commons (1975) *Eleventh Report from the Expenditure Committee: Children and Young Persons Act, 1969* (Social Services Sub-Committee, Chairman, Renée Short) 2 vols, HC 534–1, 534–11, London: HMSO.

Jeffs, A. (1979) *Young People and the Youth Service,* London: Routledge and Kegan Paul.

Labour Party Study Group (1964) *Crime – a Challenge to Us All* (Longford Report), London: Labour Party.

Millham, S., Bullock, R. and Hosie, K. (1978) *Locking up Children: Secure Provision within the Child Care System,* Farnborough: Saxon House.

NACRO/ACPO (1995) *A Crisis in Custody,* London: NACRO.

Pearson, G. (1975) *The Deviant Imagination,* London: Macmillan.

Pearson, G. (1983) *Hooligan: a History of Respectable Fears*, London: Macmillan.

Police and Criminal Evidence Act 1984, London: HMSO.

Pratt, J. (1986) Diversion from the Juvenile Court, *British Journal of Criminology*, Vol.24, No.2, 271–276.

Prevention of Crime Act 1908, London: HMSO.

Probation of Offenders Act 1907, London: HMSO.

Race Relations Act 1976, London: HMSO.

Report of the Committee on Children and Young Persons (Ingleby Report), Cmnd 1191, London: HMSO.

Rutherford, A. (1986), *Growing out of Crime: Society and Young People in Trouble,* Harmondsworth: Penguin.

Rutherford, A. (1992) *Growing out of Crime: the New Era,* Winchester: Waterside Press.

Sex Discrimination Act 1976, London: HMSO.

Social Services Inspectorate (1994) *Responding to Youth Crime: Findings through Inspections of Youth Justice Services in Five Local Authorities Departments,* London: HMSO.

Stephens, M. and Becker, S. (eds) (1994) *Police Force, Police Service: Care and Control in Britain,* London: Macmillan.

Thompson, A. (1995) A share of responsibility, *Community Care*, no. 1080, 12–13.

Thornton, D., Curran, L., Grayson, D., and Holloway, V. (1984) *Tougher Regimes in Detention Centres*, Report of an evaluation by the Young Offenders Psychology Unit, Home Office, London: HMSO.

Thorpe, D. (1994) Police and juvenile offending, in Stephens, M. and Becker, S. (eds), *Police Force, Police Service: Care and Control in Britain*, 169–190, London: Macmillan.

Thorpe, D.H., Smith, D., Paley, J. and Green, C. (1980) *Out of Care: the Community Support of Young Offenders,* London: Longman.

Tissier, G. (1994) Social police? *Community Care*, no.1041, 3–9 November, 25.

Tutt, N. (1984) *Diversion – What is It?* Paper presented to a conference on crime prevention, Birmingham, 4–6 December 1983, Centre of Youth, Crime and Community, University of Lancaster, Northampton: Northamptonshire County Council.

West D.S. and Farrington, D. (1977) *The Delinquent Way of Life,* London: Heinemann.

PART FIVE

Future prospects

CHAPTER 11

Future of the personal social services

This chapter considers the future of the personal social services in a period when local government reorganisation is imminent. It discusses future prospects at the macro level and in terms of likely scenarios within unitary authorities; it also examines the issues of values, resources and the empowerment of service users and carers as key stakeholders in the personal social services.

At the outset, three contextual points are worth making. First, the complexity of the role of the personal social services has increased significantly since the previous major local government reorganisation a quarter of a century ago. Stephen Campbell, under-secretary for social services at the Association of County Councils, comments in the light of a review of the government's own guidance to the Local Government Commission of 1992 (*Policy Guidance to the Local Government Commission for England, 1992*):

> When you study these requirements you really have to recognise that social services comprise a complex, interactive, growing range of activities which demand a strategic capacity; the capacity to provide specialist services like child protection, intensive residential child care, adoption services, mental health services, and so on; the capacity to retain and train an appropriate workforce; the size to have just enough men and women in grey suits to manage complex services; and, above all, the separate identity which will absorb the understanding and culture of today's social services, nurture it and help it to develop in ways which reflect the overall demands of social policy (Campbell, 1994).

Second, the pace of change has quickened in the fourth quarter of the twentieth century. Since the late 1960s, the information revolution has brought about changes in the ways people communicate – interpersonally, through networking and within and between organisations. The struggle between the paradigm of empowerment and the consumerist ideology imposed by such legislation as the NHS and Community Care Act 1990 may have its roots in the community activism and consciousness raising of protests by people in the 1960s, but its implications are still being worked through in the 1990s. The tension between the individual and the state, the purchaser/provider and the recipient of services remains somewhat uncertain; depending on the standpoint of the commentator it induces either pessimism or a feeling that service users still have much to work for.

Third, the continuance in power of the Conservative government, from 1979 at least to the end of 1995 when this book was being written, has contributed significantly to the steady erosion of the provision of universalistic welfare by the state. This is most evident in the personal social services, as illustrated in the increasing prominence of private provision for older people, especially those requiring full-time residential nursing. Service provision has been fragmented through the proliferation of numerous contractual arrangements made by purchasing social work and social services departments that formerly provided services themselves, with a range of voluntary and private agencies. The superimposition on the personal social services of commercial values achieved most notably by the NHS and Community Care Act 1990 marked a key point in a process of change whose ripples seem likely to spread well into the next century.

The end of the twentieth century may be viewed as coinciding with the apocalyptic collapse of the welfare state, the blossoming of consumerism in the managed markets of health and social care, or as a mid-point in the slow growth of empowered citizens' services, in the post-welfare state era. Two diverse tendencies in Britain – towards the increasing complexity of functions of individual agencies and a greater interdependence of and collaboration between providing authorities – are paralleled by longstanding trends in other countries, notably the USA, and look set to continue (Schulberg and Baker, 1975, p. 19). Local authorities, in the language of the Major government, by the 1996 local government reorganisation have become enabling authorities, purchasing the overwhelming bulk of health and social care services from a range of providers in the public, voluntary and private sectors.

Changing context of politics and social policy

The future of the personal social services will be shaped to a large extent by the government in power, in the light of the NHS and Community Care Act 1990 and the local government reorganisation of 1996. It is well-nigh impossible to predict what will be the medium-term, let alone the long-term, implications of these changes. A Labour government may bring modest reversals in the trend towards marketisation in the health and social care sector. A continuing Conservative government could undermine further the position of professions such as social work, regarded by some as too imbued with the 'ologies' and anti-oppressive practice. An extreme right-wing scenario could involve the virtual elimination of UK-wide arrangements to safeguard the interests of vulnerable and poor people requiring more than the barest minimum of financial or social security from the state, and the return to a revived version of the nineteenth century Poor Law, administered and dictated by the business fundholders of the locally managed markets of health and social services.

The impact of marketisation extends well beyond health and social care. In one obvious sense, the significant unit of local provision into the twenty-first century is likely to be the unitary local authority, working in partnership with health authorities. This means that, increasingly, health and social services will collaborate with housing, leisure, environmental health, education and so on. In some instances, actual mergers of housing and social services, housing and environmental health, or housing and leisure services are envisaged, or have already happened. This mixing, merging and collaboration involving different departments makes more complex the task of predicting future trends. But some workforce changes are already apparent, notably the increasing tendency towards the casualisation of the workforce in probation and social services, as time-limited contracts are introduced more widely and temporary and part-time staff are employed in posts formerly occupied by permanent full-time workers. Reed Care, a leading supplier of social work staff in the UK, reported in mid-1995 that the demand for temporary staff had increased by more than 30% over the previous three years (Reed Care, 1995).

Le Grand and Bartlett (1993, p. 218) conclude their case studies of social housing, school education, GP fundholding and care management in community care with the comment that those specific areas 'seem to be closer to meeting the market structure and information conditions for quasi-market success than community care, at the level of the social services department, and health authority purchasing. However, even here there are problems; and there is cause for concern in education, fundholding and social housing with respect to the other conditions, particularly those of transactions costs and cream-skimming.' Market structuring refers to the condition that there should be many providers and purchasing agents, to avoid monopolies; information refers to the necessity for providers to have sufficiently accurate and independent information to enable them to price their services; transactions costs refer to the requirement that the institutional and bureaucratic framework imposes minimum costs consistent with the inevitable uncertainties of market operations; cream-skimming refers to the risk that providers will focus their efforts on block contracts in the most lucrative areas and neglect, for example, service users who present problems, require risk management and tempt providers to screen them out in a rationing process.

Local government reorganisation

The publication of a Consultation Paper under Michael Heseltine as Secretary of State for the Department of the Environment, entitled *The Structure of Local Government in England* (Department of the Environment, 1991) put structural changes in local government onto the political and administrative agenda and led directly to the Local Government Act 1992. This set in motion a process of local government review by a body of that name, charged with implementing the general concepts of unitary and enabling local authorities. Wilson and Game (1994, p. 299) argue that the detailed working out of these concepts in practice was somewhat lacking and that there is, perhaps, a tendency in Britain for structural solutions to be sought rather too readily to the problems of achieving effective local government (op. cit., p. 300).

In 1996, on the twenty-fifth anniversary of the Seebohm reforms, the local government reorganisation takes effect. It was motivated first by the longstanding concern with finding the ideal size of local authority to deliver services; second, it was designed to capitalise on the assumed benefits of the unitary formula – delivering services as far as possible within a relatively restricted locality; third, and less explicitly, some government interests used local government reorganisation as a stick with which to beat the large Labour-controlled authorities and restrict their power by cutting them down to size. The shire counties, largely demolished in the reorganisation, fell victim to the belief that small and unitary is better than large and multiple. The reality was that the greater part of England, and notably London, was not touched directly by the reorganisation. Admittedly, though, in England, Wales and Scotland the average size of departments was set to fall in the reorganisation, and their numbers to increase by some 50% (Warner, 1994, p. 6).

The local government reorganisation of 1996 extends to county councils, Scotland and Wales the principle of providing the personal social services within unitary local authorities. In Scotland and Wales, the reorganisation ran into several issues early on, including the longstanding antagonism towards what many perceived as this imposition from England. Additionally, as in parts of England, there was local resistance to divisions that increased the number, but not necessarily the effectiveness, of authorities. Thus, doubt was cast on the ability of smaller unitary authorities to deliver a full range of community care services to meet the variety of needs in a particular area.

Two linked preoccupations of those concerned with successive local authority reorganisations in Britain are the size of authorities and the benefts of merging departments. Arguments for and against the relatively small unitary authority revolve around whether the localism of smallness is felt to improve functioning sufficiently to overcome the disadvantages of not achieving sufficient economies of scale. In some cases, mergers of departments have improved functioning, whereas in others various levels of collaboration and co-operation have achieved significant benefits. In some localities, a high degree of boundary-crossing between the functions of health and social services has been achieved. In some of the smaller of just more than twenty-two Welsh unitary authorities that replace the eight existing counties, on the other hand, there are fears that specialist services, such as those to people with sensory impairments, will be casualties of early cost-cutting. In Scotland, the reorganisation replaces the existing two-tier system of regional and district councils with 32 unitary authorities, and there are fears of increasing difficulties of collaboration to negotiate and operate contracts with greater numbers of parties to them.

It is unlikely that within the next decade there will be another major overhaul of the unitary authorities put in place by local government reorganisation in 1996. Thus, a move towards the joint health and social services boards of Northern Ireland is unlikely on the UK mainland. However, as indicated above, in many parts of the country new local arrangements for organising and delivering social services have already led to the reconfiguration of the former social services departments, in new arrangements involving other local authority departments. Given the shift in the consensual basis for the personal social services and the fundamental restructuring of service delivery around the creation of internal markets within health and social care, is it possible to make predictions about what the likely shape of the social services will be in the early years of the next millennium? On the assumption that the principal uncertainty is the political complexion of the next government, the rest of this chapter considers some of the main options at the macro level and some major issues affecting policy and practice at local authority level.

Four options at the macro level

I shall simplify the complexities of the debates around the different possibilities by not attempting to predict the disposition of the major political parties after the next General Election, and considering four options: the free market at one extreme, managed market (liberal pluralism), socialist centralism and socialist democracy (radical pluralism). Each of the four options struggles with four basic purposes in tension with each other: the pursuit of democracy, economic prosperity, social justice/equality and liberty/individual freedom, or, in today's terminology, empowerment.

Conservatism

Free market position

The free market position approximates to a Thatcherite stance.

Just as Marxism evolved and did not represent a single set of beliefs, involving neo-Marxist critiques (Edgell and Duke, 1991, pp. 30–31) and revisionist accounts, Thatcherism also represented in the period since 1979 a break from the past but also an evolving set of responses during the 1980s to particular economic and political circumstances. Edgell and Duke (1991, pp. 215–216) identify three overlapping periods of Thatcherism, under the general headings of recession, recovery and regression, although Thatcherism involved a continuing fight against inflation and to control public spending throughout the period. In the first phase from the late 1970s to the mid-1980s, the emphasis was on cutting public expenditure and defeating trade unionism, notably in the confrontation with the miners in 1984–1985. During the second phase, when the economy recovered somewhat from the mid- to the late 1980s, the prioritising of public spending control continued and there was an increased emphasis on unemployment policies. In the final phase, from the late 1980s, rising interest rates and declining revenues from North Sea Oil threatened the continued economic recovery as expressed in both profits and employment. The dominant themes in Thatcherism throughout the period were support for capital and the market and opposition to labour and the state.

Walker (1989) views the principal strategy of the incoming Conservative government from 1979 as residualising the role of the personal social services in the provision of community care services, through reducing the contribution of local authorities as service providers and encouraging the growth of voluntary private and informal provision. Thus in 1980, Patrick Jenkin, then Secretary of State for Social Services, put forward a residual role for the social services as 'a long stop for the very special needs going beyond the range of voluntary services' (speech to the conference of the Association of Directors of Social Services, 19 September, quoted in Walker, 1989, p. 213). In 1981, the White Paper on services for older people reflected the shift in emphasis: care in the community must increasingly mean care *by* the community (DHSS, 1981).

A free market economy relies strongly on provision by the voluntary and private sectors. In Britain and the USA, the free market version is in force. If this approach were pursued to its logical extreme in the future, the entire provision of personal social services would be handed over to the free market, at the cost of the delivery of social justice, for example, to underprivileged and oppressed groups, including children needing protection, older and disabled people, to say nothing of discriminated-against groups such as people with HIV/AIDS, gay people wishing to adopt children and people from some ethnic minorities, notably black people. The arguments against this approach can be made on two grounds: first, that it is unacceptable in terms of anti-oppressive values for a market economy to support personal social services that do not promote social justice but actually increase social injustice; second, it can be criticised at the technical level. As Mishra (1986, p. 167), puts it, 'at a purely technical level, the monetary medicine applied by these pro-market regimes has been so strong as to endanger the patient's life itself. Inflation has been tamed and wage demands lowered at an enormously high cost in the form of unemployment and bankruptcies. In short, the neo-conservative solution has little to recommend (it) either as a value-orientation, or even as a short-term technical fix.'

Civil capitalism

It would be difficult to find an example of 'pure' free market thinking in the 1990s that related in a detailed way to the realities of the personal social services. What Green (1993) calls 'civil capitalism' approximates to a free market position and is an attempt to challenge what he calls 'hard-boiled economic rationalism'. He advocates competitive markets in economic and health and social care sectors that encourage the independence of the individual, a notion of citizenship based on a commitment to civic duty and of shared personal responsibility for mutual well-being of people in society. He argues that the welfare state suppressed not only the incentives provided by the competitive market place, but also institutions in the voluntary and private sectors that provided an outlet for people to develop notions of altruism, service and achievement. His prescription is concerned with re-energising 'civil society'. He draws on the history of the friendly societies and the need to revitalise the traditions of self-help and mutual help with which they have been associated for several hundred years in Britain.

Green's argument is that the full use of what he calls 'human capital' is the basis of the free market, whereas Thatcherism has imposed more central control rather than widening the scope for human creativity in a genuinely free market. Green also sees a danger of the state relief of poverty as people growing used to living on income support. So at the individual level, Green wants to encourage self-help and to empower the citizen through nurturing independence. For example, he advocates an approach to personal independence planning as part of the way to counter unemployment. He quotes the scheme in the USA called 'America Works', in which employers take welfare recipients for a trial period in the hope that although some of them start on a low wage, they will get the chance to demonstrate their value and gain further training or promotion. Thus the focus is on the personal skills of the individual and the overcoming of discrimination and a lack of self-esteem through actually working rather than simply being on benefit (op. cit., pp. 150–151).

Green emphasises that at the collective level 'as state welfare has grown so it has squeezed out voluntary associations and diminished the spirit of personal responsibility on which a vibrant society rests' (op. cit., p. 147). To counter these tendencies, he proposes three kinds of policies: those aimed at economic growth, those aimed at the removal of public policy obstacles to individual, or family, advancement, especially high taxes, and lastly an emphasis on personal independence (op. cit., p. 149).

Socialist centralism

This socialist option is based on central provision by the state. Mishra argues that this contains some problems as well. At its heart, the centralist vision of Marxist socialism promotes the view of the state, the collective well-being of society, over that of the individual. This runs against the liberal democratic nature of the left-centre of British politics, with its emphasis on individual liberty and the rule of law. So the socialist alternative needs not only to demonstrate the value of collectivism and distributive egalitarianism, but also that it can deliver individual liberal values. So far, Marxist states have not demonstrated that they can deliver economic and social goods effectively without a high degree of central social control and even coercion of people. One of the principal attractions for central and eastern European states that have thrown off communism is that they look to capitalism as a source of enhanced democracy and individual freedom.

Taylor-Gooby and Dale (1981, p. 27) present a Marxist view that they see as more robust than the analysis by George and Wilding (1976), which is 'a Marxist "ideology" of state welfare as a union of particular values of liberty, equality and fraternity with a conflict theory of contemporary social formations: an interpretation compounded by the choice of peripheral proponents of Marxism as paradigms'. They criticise roundly the limitation of the empiricist social administration tradition which they say is nine-tenths preoccupied with charting facts about the shortcomings of state welfare (Taylor-Gooby and Dale, 1981, pp. 24–25). They see the failures of empiricist social administration as reflecting the debarring of the perspective from addressing 'some major ideological issues of democratic welfare capitalism' (op. cit., p. 25). They argue that the social administration school 'has tended to interpret Marxist social theory in such a way as to destroy the link between the intellectual and the material, to present conclusions without foundations' (op. cit., p. 27). The authors conclude: 'we have argued that defence of the welfare state requires its transformation in the context of a programme of fundamental social change towards socialism.... Socialism ... involves common ownership of the means of production. … The ideal conception of communism suggests a vision of freedom. We do not know if this is possible. We do know that the notion of socialism as democracy plus a planned economy, represents a possibility of the realisation of greater freedom than the welfare state' (op. cit., pp. 266–268).

Despite the stridency of this view, it has to be acknowledged that the political changes in Europe and the former USSR since the early 1980s have made social policies based on socialist centralism an even more contested option than before.

Managed market

Liberal pluralism would involve a return to the welfare state as originally conceived and executed, combining a managed market economy with a pluralistic and a well-developed system of social welfare. This position is reliant on the existence of a corporate welfare state. Its advocates see the mixed market that underpins it as a more attractive option than the socialist welfare state, in that it will lead to a more egalitarian society. There is no evidence that a corporatist welfare state is any more likely to increase equality, in terms of the distribution of income and wealth, than is the socialist state. What it does offer is the possibility of introducing some operational consensus between policy-makers and providers about minimum state-protected levels of services that are acceptable in order to meet agreed standards of social justice in the community. The Borrie Report (chapter 1) represents one possible version of a managed market position (Borrie and Atkinson, 1994).

The incoming Conservative government of May 1979 was committed to privatising a good deal of public sector provision, but perhaps because many people remained sensitive to what they saw as the risks associated with dismantling the welfare state, in the health and social care sector a compromise strategy was devised. This amounted to reducing the dominance of the public sector by residualising the role of local authorities in community care, thus reducing to a marginal level their role as service providers, and ensuring that the main provision was through the voluntary, private and informal sectors.

Walker (1989, pp. 215–216) argues that the government has implemented the policy of residualisation through three processes – fragmentation, marketisation and decentralisation of administration – while maintaining centralisation of control over resources. Fragmentation involved dispersing to many providers in public, private, voluntary and informal sectors the provision of services, in the guise of promoting the so-called mixed economy of welfare, which, rather than a free market, is a market managed by government. Marketisation involved the implementation of the Local

Government Act 1988, which gave the Secretary of State for the Environment powers to extend the list of services which have to be contracted out. The implementation of community care was accompanied by the government directing that 85% of services would be provided by other than the public sector authorities by 1994. The third element involved the contradictory decentralisation of the administration and operations of the social services, and simultaneous centralisation of control over resources, as 'one manifestation of the general neo-liberal strategy of rolling back the frontiers of the state while centralising state control' (op. cit., p. 216).

Knapp (1989, p. 230) demonstrates the complexity of the emerging mixed economy of welfare and examines the four models of contracting out: competitive tendering, vendor reimbursement, delegate agencies and grants (op. cit., p. 234). Knapp has evaluated the claims of supporters for contracting out that it increases choice, encourages non-public agencies to experiment and innovate and encourages more cost-effective services by voluntary and private providers than public agencies. As far as choice is concerned, he observes that the regulation of quality inherent in contracting out actually may narrow and reduce choice. While contracting out can encourage innovation, there are also dangers that it will reduce innovation. As far as cost-effectiveness is concerned, most research indicates that efficiency differences are bigger within sectors than between them. 'If a government department's only objective is to improve efficiency it could have a greater impact if it puts its *own* house in order rather than in engaging in contracting out' (op. cit., p. 238).

Socialist democracy

Associative democracy

Contemporary thinking in a broadly socialist democratic tradition can be illustrated by drawing on Hirst's ideas about associative democracy. Hirst (1994, p. 9) proposes associative democracy in response to threats he identifies to the stability of Western societies, not in internal class war nor in war with external enemy states, but in 'diffuse social problems and sources of unrest.' His argument is that centralised bureaucracies cope rather badly with the demands for flexibility of provision for the needs of a growing underclass of people, in terms of freedom of movement, effective work and welfare at local level. Moreover, unless such provision 'targets *and* empowers the members of this "class", then the way is open to an escalating conflict between crime and deviancy and disabling authoritarian measures which aim at the protection of the majority' (op. cit., p. 10). Hirst views associative democracy as the key to empowerment in this context: 'Associationalism makes accountable representative democracy possible again by limiting the scope of state administration, without diminishing social provision. It enables market-based societies to deliver the substantive goals desired by citizens, by embedding the market system in a social network of coordinative and regulatory institutions' (op. cit., p. 12). Thus, Hirst advocates voluntary, self-governing associations progressively to become the primary means of government, linked with the devolution of power to the lowest level consistent with effective government and with the government continually seeking consent and co-operation from the governed. 'Associationalism makes a central normative claim, that individual liberty and human welfare are both best served when as many of the affairs of society as possible are managed by voluntary and democratically self-governing associations' (op. cit., p. 19). Hirst's prescription is based on a mixture of the principles of economic, industrial and social co-operation in self-regulating communities, advocated by Robert Owen (in the social experiment of New Lanark), Pierre-Joseph Proudhon (a decentralised, federated state, based on local artisan and co-operative production in a mutualist economy) and George Jacob Holyoake in the nineteenth century.

The strength of the concept of associative democracy lies in its attempt to address the realities of the interpenetration of share owning with former nationalised industries and their workforces, including market-based field of welfare. Its weakness may lie in the pragmatic concern that it would have to appeal to one of the major political parties in Britain to have a chance of becoming a part of the political and policy agenda. Also, it is not clear in practical terms how it would address the social inequalities whose redressing is part of the role of the personal social services, according to a socialist agenda.

Issues affecting policy and practice at local authority level

Inevitably, the abstract nature of the subject matter of the preceding section led to no neat conclusion making connections with everyday realities. This final section considers the impact of the changes currently in train on the various stakeholders in the personal social services. Even here, some imponderables are noted as the discussion proceeds, and set to one side.

Impact on authorities

The full impact of marketisation, taken in conjunction with changes such as the reorganisation of local government, will be unpredictable for some time. In fact, Tom Hopkins has observed that authorities are riding a roller coaster of changes, and while at times the movement is slow and uphill, at other times the roller coaster moves ever faster and in any case is impossible to alight from by choice (personal discussion with the author). This helpful analogy gives some idea of how it feels to be an employee of, for example, a social services department in the 1990s. But a further feature to be added is the uncertainty of which services will be provided by which authority in the future. For example, there is doubt about whether health or social services will in the longer term be the lead body for community care. This uncertainty reflects a degree of ambiguity in the respective roles of health and social services in different parts of community care. One possibility is that the fact that health authorities are less disrupted by local government reorganisation than local authority social work and social services departments will lead the government to shift the lead responsibility for part or all of community care from the latter to the former.

In any event, local authorities will need to develop stronger collaborative arrangements than at present for working together and with health authorities. For their part, NHS purchasing authorities, each with an average of about five NHS trusts within it, will have to adjust to working with a larger number of social services departments than before. The typical social services department will need to collaborate with housing departments to incorporate housing issues into community care assessments and planning. Norman Warner (1994, p. 6) notes that as Director of Kent Social Services Department he worked with no fewer than 14 different housing authorities. Similar collaborations with environmental health and education are very likely.

Impact on staff

The creation of managed markets in health and social care marks a process, whose endpoint is impossible to predict. The shape of the purchasing and providing authorities seems likely to change further. In part, this will be determined by any future repositioning of responsibilities allocated to lead authorities for particular services. For example, the creation of managed markets in community care has already meant that resources tend to follow service users into different settings where their care needs are being addressed. Where this happens on a large scale – for example in the relocation of people leaving hospital care to their former place of residence – it has implications for the contraction of some services purchased and provided in one area and their expansion in another. In Strathclyde, for instance, Central Scotland Healthcare, with a workforce of some 3500 staff and one of the largest NHS trusts in

Scotland, may need to shed up to a fifth of its staff over the next three to five years. They may follow the services to the new areas where service users are living, but not all staff will be able or willing to relocate in this way.

The implications of these changes for senior management are dramatic. Senior and middle managers' responsibilities are likely to change, the latter becoming more involved in policy and resource allocation (Mitchell, 1995). There will be a continuing need for the redesign of the workforce of authorities, agencies and groups in all sectors of health and local authorities providing human services in general and personal social services in particular. The point made by Walton 20 years ago in the wake of the Seebohm reforms still has relevance. He notes how the growing size and complexity of social work services increased the trend towards forward planning and elaborated formal hierarchies. He identifies a tension between the possible 'pattern of male rationalistic domination' over these organisations with the consequent 'danger of losing some essential qualities, in offering services to individuals in need' (Walton, 1975, p. 262).

Educators in universities and trainers in authorities and agencies will need to adapt their programmes and courses to meet the changing requirements of staff, particularly the need for more flexible learning, with the learner having greater power to choose where, how quickly, at what level and in what areas, professional and personal development is needed (Adams and Hopkins, 1994). This is corroborated by the positive experiences noted by staff from the *Making Open Learning Work Project* of the National Institute of Social Work (NISW), (1995, p. 5), in monitoring the use of open learning packages to support the Health and Social Services Management Programme (HSSM) – a workplace-based management development (Health and Social Services Management Programme, 1994).

The ideological shift from what could be called a public sector to a commercial style of working will continue to work its way through not only senior managements, but all other parts of health and local authorities. In future it will affect the education and training of staff at vocational, professional and managerial levels. The trend towards the adoption of operational standards in caring at N/SVQ levels 2 to 4 and in social work through the review of the Diploma in Social Work may prevent the abandonment of practice values such as respect for persons, confidentiality, promotion of people's rights, anti-discriminatory practice and the empowerment of service users and informal carers. Some pessimistic commentators argue that some or all of these may be lost, particularly in settings where the organisation, agency or body adopts a resource-driven rather than a needs-led or user-led approach.

At the level of direct work with service users, staff in some aspects of the personal social services – notably sensory impairment – are likely to encounter tensions between trends towards specialisation and the maintenance of generic roles. As noted above, in small, unitary authorities such specialist staff may be more vulnerable to redundancy, although it is also possible that joint, or consortium-based, commissioning by two or more authorities may enable specialist services to be developed.

The contract culture of quasi-markets has generated a specialist lexicon of meanings for concepts previously taken for granted, such as partnership. The partnership between two parties to a contract in the 1990s contract culture is likely to be more formal, output-directed and time-limited than an open-ended unwritten agreement between two collaborating parties. The introduction of the contract culture implies formalisation throughout the relations between local authority and other funders and the voluntary agencies. Many informal practices have been revised or have simply disappeared. The legal, formal and technical language and procedures of contracts makes explicit the expectations of the parties to them, but also generates their own implicit concepts and assumptions. To tease these out and work through them successfully requires excellent networks and stable informal relationships, both of which are at a premium in a time of rapid changes (Jarman, 1994, p. 4). The commissioners of contracts may emphasise outputs at the expense of outcomes, the former detailing the activities to be provided, without considering the outcomes in terms of whether any differences are produced for service users (Jarman, personal communication to author). In areas of new work, there may be tendencies towards more funders of particular initiatives or projects, perhaps where the field of work is new or responsibility shared, and towards more short-term projects. These changes may lead to higher management costs and have considerable impact on uncertainties and possible discontinuities of service for providers. They create a formidable and complex agenda. Voluntary organisations increasingly need to balance the requirements of the new contract culture against influences from their stakeholders: principally but not solely the donating public, professionals and service users.

The future role of voluntary organisations in the personal social services is likely to change, and probably to increase. Some, but by no means all, seek charitable status, which has implications for their legal standing, role and finances. About 4000 new charities are registered every year. Many do not survive long, and a feature of the field is the high turnover of new voluntary organisations. The law relating to charities is closely linked with the regulations of the Charity Commission. Over and above this, as chapters 4, 5 and 8 indicated in the family and child care areas, voluntary child care organisations are bound by a complex and ever-expanding web of child care law for children and families as service users, in areas such as the Children Act, family law, the registered homes and adoption legislation. The concerns of some of the larger and more influential voluntary child care organisations – notably Barnardo's, the Children's Society, National Children's Homes and Save the Children Fund, not just with providing a service but with acting as influencers of welfare policy, has implications for their status as charities. Charities, as such, are not permitted to act in an overtly political role; however, the definition of 'political' may be somewhat blurred. An example is the report *Liquid Gold*, by Action for Children, Barnardo's, Children's Society, NSPCC and Save the Children Fund, which highlighted the consequences for poor families of disconnections by the water companies. The impact of such publicity may be quite dramatic. Subsequent to the publication of the above report, Yorkshire Water, for example, changed its policy.

Impact on the voluntary and private sectors

Marketisation in the personal social services may lead in the longer term to fewer and larger block grants. But in the immediate future, there is a trend towards proliferation of small groups and organis-ations, such as in the independent – voluntary and private – sector claiming to represent people's interests, through research, training, political lobbying and a certain amount of direct service provision. But there is a tendency still for many such bodies in the indepen-dent sector not to involve empowered service users speaking for themselves, but to be part of the perpetuation of elites and rela-tively privileged professionals – such as the rapidly expanding workforce of former statutory sector employees now turned con-sultants – continuing their debates about what people need and what should happen, in their ever-proliferating journals, confer-ences, fora and study groups. All this is one remove from provid-ing means by which dispossessed and oppressed people can voice their demands and needs directly, rather than having them filtered through professionals. For example, in one Scottish authority, a single forum for interests involving older people is the sole body to which authorities turn in their routine consultations with the huge, diverse and fragmented field of service users and carers. Thus, managed markets may provide better opportunities for current and potential service providers to contribute on the supply side, whilst the contribution of the potential and current service user on the demand side seems likely to be patchy in some areas and non-existent in others.

In many ways, the structures that allocate resources to education and training, for example, in the personal social services – notably those of CCETSW in its regulation of practice teaching in Diploma in Social Work programmes – remain biased away from the voluntary and private sectors, towards the statutory sector. In support of this, there is not much evidence yet of private providers' commitment to professional or vocational education and training, as opposed to using its products. Yet, though this is a negative feature of the fragmentation of provision of services, it does provide opportunities for some of the struggles of the 1960s and early 1970s, which took place under the aegis of community work and neighbourhood work in many localities, to be revitalised under the banner of empowering service users and informal carers, to say nothing of the situation of the volunteer in general. The advent of the empowerment paradigm has provided the rationale for a discourse encompassing the dialectic between the individual service user and/or carer and the state – mediated through the purchasers and providers of local services – which is not hampered by the politics, particularly the Marxist politics, of 20 years earlier (Adams, 1996, chapter 1). The emergence of citizen empowerment is timely, in that it transcends party politics. Anti-discriminatory policies and practices and user empowerment movements are not depoliticised, but their politics transcends the traditional polarised political divisions between Right and Left. There is still likely to be a struggle between consumerist and empowerment rhetoric and *genuine* citizen empowerment, for example. The multiplication of groups and individuals involved in providing, and receiving, personal social services does not necessarily mean that the service user has a more meaningful say in the nature and resourcing of services. But, ironically, Thatcherite and Majorite policies such as charters for consumers have put the issue of local democracy and empowerment higher on the agenda of local authorities than it has been for 20 years.

Redefining professional boundaries

The changing roles of health and local authorities, working in partnership with bodies in the voluntary and private sectors, imply a level of change that impacts on the roles of staff. The growing necessity for collaboration between managers and professionals at the interface with service users and carers increases the need to scrutinise and, on occasions, redefine professional boundaries in line with new responsibilities. This does not mean abolishing professions. Thus, for instance, the oft-quoted question from the title of Brewer and Lait's (1980) book, *Can Social Work Survive?*, is pure rhetoric, since, if nothing else, the demands for professional intervention in areas such as mental health and child protection would ensure that if the social work profession were abolished overnight, it would have to be re-created the following morning.

However, there are increasing pressures on social workers, as on other professionals, to develop their multidisciplinary practice and, like occupational therapists, to cross boundaries into other organisational and professional territories.

Two contrasting trends are discernible: on one hand towards the emergence of discrete new professional areas, and on the other hand towards the dissolution of single professional interests in new holistic or corporate entities, crossing disciplinary, professional and organisational boundaries, and in effect reconfiguring the human services. Which of these trends will win out? The answer may be that almost certainly they both will, in different ways. Jenny Weinstein of the Central Council for Education and Training in Social Work (CCETSW) argues the case for joint professional training of police and social workers in areas such as child protection, as a means of enhancing performance and mutual understanding (Weinstein, 1994). But she does not, and would not be justified to, argue for the merging of the two professions. Joint working, it would seem, far from doing away with professional differences, can actually enable professionals to sharpen their perception of areas discrete to each profession, areas of collaboration and that very small area ripe for merger.

Service users and carers: consumers or empowered citizens?

Reforms are likely to continue in local government, intended to make local authorities more responsive and accessible to local people as consumers of services. To date, these have varied enormously in depth and scope. 'Some have involved such radical changes as carrying out internal decentralisation schemes. Programmes of consumer reform include, at the less significant end, innovations like a new letterhead or the introduction of jingles to entertain callers waiting on the telephone. Others entail improving the accessibility of the authority and its staff to consumers. Some authorities, for instance Manchester and Leicester City Councils, provide complaints or information centres where citizens can go to seek advice or register complaints' (Elcock, 1993, p. 168). Other local authorities carry out consumer research to find out what people think of local services.

What Stewart (1986) called the public service orientation involves different combinations of market-based and collectivist approaches to local government. Elcock (1993) suggests that public service orientations encourage three main sorts of change in the future management of local services. First, councillors may give directions to local authority staff. Councillors adopt a role less involved in the detail of administering the local authority's services and more involved in processes of strategic planning, while establishing a more consumer-oriented organisational culture. Second, this involves strengthening the role of what Lipsky (1980) calls 'street level bureaucrats'. These are the more junior staff who have face-to-face contact with members of the public.

Decentralisation initiatives, community fora, participation exercises and general efforts to improve the accessibility of staff and services for citizens, all force local authority staff to have more frequent contacts and to relate more sympathetically with members of the public. Clients must be offered more choice, through real or simulated markets. ... Decentralisation and devolution of powers also increase the area of discretion which must be available to the street-level bureaucrats so that they can respond effectively to the needs, problems and wishes with which their customers present them, thus in turn weakening the supervisory roles of middle and senior staff. This process of rendering the middle managers redundant is being accelerated by the introduction of information and communications technologies in decentralised offices. Information is available both to street-level bureaucrats and their clients at the touch of a button, instead of having to be supplied by staff at headquarters. The result can be the 'polo effect': the creation of an organisation with a hole at the centre (Booth and Pitt, 1984).

Third, this involves local authorities being run by general managers, charged with responsibility for changing the culture of the organisation. Michael proposed that this could be achieved by such means as appointing a council manager, or directly electing a chief executive or mayor (Department of the Environment, 1991). Elcock (1993, p. 170) notes trends towards: the transfer of powers from the centre to decentralised offices; greater responsiveness to local needs by providing differentiated services; increasing diversity of networking, co-operating and collaborating in the mixed economy of welfare; the development of new skills, structures and attitudes necessitated by the enabling role of local authorities.

Future trends include: the likelihood of continuing increased demand for services from users, the growing strength of managerialism, the extension of the contract culture to work areas, like child care, hitherto less effected; continuing problems of joint working with areas such as health and housing; growing shortages, and rationing, of resources; a tendency towards employing fewer staff with advanced or even basic social work qualifications; and an emphasis on quality control or the maintenance of standards rather than quality maximisation (Adams, 1977).

There is a move towards social services departments stimulating organisations in the voluntary sector that can provide services as co-operative and user-managed ventures. It remains to be seen whether the trend to externalising the management of facilities such as bereavement counselling, residential and day centres for older people will extend far beyond this significant but restricted range. Two motives that will stimulate this movement are the need to keep within government spending requirements and a general consensus about the positive contribution that voluntary organisations can make.

Examples of collaboration between health and social services include the local authority and health authority producing a joint community care charter, a joint strategy for mental health services, using the Care Programme Approach and allocating the specific grant for mental illness work.

The future extension of joint funded work between social services and commissioning health agencies may build on current practice. For instance, in one London borough an annual grant is given to one voluntary organisation controlled by severely disabled people, which acts as a broker to enable other severely disabled people to purchase services and live independently; and a London borough finances a joint forum for black people, voluntary organisations and elected councillors; this enables people to meet and discuss issues such as racial harassment and have direct access to decision-makers.

One of the main organisational problems is pressure on budgets. This has led to some authorities, perhaps as much as 30% over SSA target in the early 1990s, losing up to £6 million or 20% of their operational budgets over the three subsequent years.

The relationship of voluntary organisations with the statutory sector in future will no doubt be predicated on the uniqueness and quality of the specialist services they provide, rather than them simply performing tasks that rightly should be carried out by the local authority on behalf of the state. At the same time, it may be difficult for a small voluntary body, totally funded by a block grant from a local authority, to become anything other than a dependent provider of a specialist service. While, by definition, no voluntary organisation would retain any funding if it became totally autonomous from the local authority, the desired relationship is probably one of interdependence rather than dependence (Jarman, 1994, p. 9).

There is a need for more research into the issues raised by collaboration within and between statutory, voluntary, private and informal sectors across the human services. Areas such as continuing health care, with increasing numbers of people needing long-term, possibly indefinite, health and social care for a range of chronic conditions, illnesses and impairments, involve complex relationships between local and health authorities and housing departments in particular, where direct action by one party affects all the others. In such circumstances, there is a need to clarify and manage separate accountabilities, as well as responsibilities that may overlap or conflict.

But problems of collaboration, like budgetary constraints, are 'only' technical issues. Over and above this, first line managers and practitioners have to work through the consequences of these constraints and reconfigurations of service purchasers and providers in the new marketplace for services. The knock-on consequences of the maturing of the contract culture will take some years to work through. The immediate impact is likely to be felt in increased confusion and uncertainty about expectations, roles and relationships. The shift in organisational, professional, service and user values represented in Fig. 3.1 (chapter 3) produces more fundamental difficulties for stakeholders in the personal social services than simply role conflicts and accountabilities; it amounts to an ideological crisis over the growth of the commercial culture within the human services.

Campbell (1994, p. 7) asserts that 'there is only one starting point when considering the local government review in relation to the personal social services, and that is the interests of service users and others who need services.' Titmuss's words in 1965 have an ironic resonance in the mid-1990s: 'We have moved a long way from the notion that the main job of local government was to *govern* local areas; one of its main tasks today is to provide accessible social services to meet local needs and to develop a greater degree of community participation in the provision of such services. If that overworked term "Community Care" has any meaning at all then it must have something to do with the provision of services which are essentially social, essentially personal and primarily local' (Titmuss, 1979, p. 90). The fundamental component shared by all the options considered above, as Bill Jordan indicates (Jordan, 1994, pp. 26–27) is power. It is worth making the fairly obvious, but often unacknowledged, point that unless and until power imbalances between different stakeholders – notably purchasers, providers and users of services – are redressed and the grossest inequalities eliminated, genuine empowerment is not likely to be achieved by service users or carers (Adams, 1996). The empowerment of service users may take place only at other people's expense – if professionals, managers and politicians, for example, begin to give up some real power.

References and further reading

Adams, R. (1996) *Social Work and Empowerment*, London: Macmillan.

Adams, R. (1997) *Quality Social Work*, London: Macmillan.

Adams, R. and Hopkins, T. (1994) Barriers to the implementation of open learning initiatives in social work, Paper presented at Using Open Learning in Health and Social Care conference, April 1995, Open Learning Foundation and University of Humberside, Hull.

Bamford, T. (1990) *The Future of Social Work*, London: Macmillan.

Booth, S. and Pitt, D. (1984) *Continuity and Discontinuity: IT as a Force for Organisational Change,* in Pitt, D. and Smith, B.C. (eds), *The Computer Revolution in Public Administration,* Brighton: Wheatsheaf Books.

Borrie, G. and Atkinson, A.B. (1994) *Social Justice: Strategies for National Renewal*, Report of the Commission on Social Justice (Borrie Report), London: Vintage.

Brewer, C. and Lait, J. (1980) *Can Social Work Survive?*, London: Temple-Smith.

Campbell, S. (1994) A game of consequences, *Community Care*, 29 September–5 October, 7

Department of Health and Office of Population Censuses and Surveys (1992) *The Government's Expenditure Plans 1992–1993*, Departmental report, SM1913, London: HMSO.

Department of the Environment (1991) *The Structure of Local Government in England*, London: DoE.

DHSS (1981) *Growing Older*, Cmnd 8173, London: HMSO.

Edgell and Duke (1991) *A Measure of Thatcherism: A sociology of Britain*, London: HarperCollins Academic.

Elcock, H. (1993) Local government, in Farnham, D. and Horton, S. (eds), *Managing the New Public Services*, 150–171, London: Macmillan.

George, V. and Miller, S. (eds) (1994) *Social Policy towards 2000: Squaring the Welfare Circle*, London: Routledge.

George, V. and Wilding, P. (1976) *Ideology and Social Policy*, London: Routledge and Kegan Paul.

Glennerster, H. (1992) *Paying for Welfare: the 1990s*, Hemel Hempstead: Harvester Wheatsheaf.

Green, D.G. (1993) *Re-inventing Civil Society: the Re-discovery of Welfare without Politics*, London: IEA Health and Welfare Unit.

Hayek, F. (1960) *The Constitution of Liberty*, London: Routledge and Kegan Paul.

Health and Social Services Management Programme (HSSM) (1994), Milton Keynes: Open University.

Hirst, P. (1994) *Associative Democracy: New Forms of Economic and Social Governance*, Oxford: Polity Press.

Home Office, NACRO and Mental Health Foundation (1994) *The NACRO Diversion Initiative for Mentally Disturbed Offenders: an account and an evaluation*, London: Home Office.

Jarman, M. (1994) *Together towards 2000: a Perspective from the Voluntary Sector*, Paper presented to NCVCCO/ADSS North West Conference 24 November.

Jones, K., Brown, J., Cunningham, W.J., Roberts, J. and Williams, P. (1975) *Opening the Door;* a study of new policies for the mentally handicapped, London: Routledge and Kegan Paul.

Jordan, B. (1994) The poverty trap, *Community Care*, no.1027, 28 July–3 August, 26–7

Knapp M. (1989) Private and voluntary welfare, in McCarthy, M. (ed.) *The New Politics of Welfare: an Agenda for the 1990s?*, 225–252, London: Macmillan.

Le Grand, J. and Bartlett, W. (eds) (1993) Quasi-markets and social policy: the way forward, in Le Grand, J. and Bartlett, W. (eds), *Quasi-Markets and Social Policy*, 202–220, London: Macmillan.

Lipsky, M. (1980) *Street Level Bureacracy*, London: Russell Sage.

Local Government Act 1988, London: HMSO.

Local Government Act 1992, London: HMSO.

McCarthy, M. (ed.) (1989) *The New Politics of Welfare: an Agenda for the 1990s?*, London: Macmillan.

Mishra, R. (1986) *The Welfare State in Crisis: Social Thought and Social Change*, Brighton: Harvester Press.

Mitchell, D. (1995) Staying Ahead, *Community Care*, 26 January–1 February.

NHS and Community Care Act 1990, London: HMSO.

Owen, R. (1972) *A New View of Society*, (reprint of 1814 edition), London: Macmillan.

Policy Guidance to the Local Government Commission for England (1992).

Reed Care (1995) Responding to changing trends, *NISW Noticeboard*, Autumn, 4.

Rowntree, S. (1901) *Poverty: A study of town life*, London: Macmillan.

Schulberg, H.C. and Baker, F. (eds) (1975) *Developments in Human Services,* vol.II, New York: Behavioural Publications.

Stewart, J.D. (1986) *The New Management of Local Government*, London: Allen and Unwin.

Taylor-Gooby, P. and Dale, J. (1981) *Social Theory and Social Welfare*, London: Edward Arnold.

Titmuss, R.M. (1979) Social work and social service: a challenge for local government, in Titmuss, R.M. (ed.) *Commitment to Welfare*, London: Allen and Unwin.

Townsend, P. (1962) *The Last Refuge – A survey of residential institutions and homes for the aged in England and Wales*, London: Routledge and Kegan Paul.

Walker, A. (1989) Community care, in McCarthy, M. (ed.) *The New Politics of Welfare: an Agenda for the 1990s?*, 203–224, London: Macmillan.

Walton, R.G. (1975) *Women in Social Work*, London: Routledge and Kegan Paul.

Warner, N. (1994) Tilting at windmills, *Community Care,* 29 September–5 October, 6.

Weinstein, J. (1994) *Sewing the Seams for a Seamless Service,* London: CCETSW.

West, D. (1994), *Purchasing and Contracting Skills,* Improving Social Work Education and Training no.18, London: CCETSW.

Wilson, D. and Game, C. (1994) *Local Government in the United Kingdom*, London: Macmillan.

LIST OF DOCUMENTS

Document 1
PROMOTING WOMEN

Introduction

Women are the main users and providers of social services but they have little say in how these services are organised or managed. Whilst eighty-six percent of all staff working in social services departments are women, seventy-nine percent of their senior managers are men.

It is increasingly recognised that this situation is not only inequitable but also very wasteful of scarce resources. The greatest asset available to social services agencies is the skill and experience of their staff. If women are denied opportunities to use their abilities to the full then the quality of service offered to users will suffer. The need to cherish human resources becomes even more acute at a time when social services departments are having to respond to the challenges of major legislative changes.

Some progress is being made. In 1990 eighteen percent of all senior managers in social services departments in England and Wales were women. By 1992 this had increased to twenty-one percent. But progress is uneven. Thirty-three authorities still have no women in their senior management team and, with the exception of a few London boroughs, women at this level are still very much a minority

From: Department of Health/Social Services Inspectorate (1992) *Promoting Women: Management Development and Training for Women in Social Services Departments*, p. 1, London: HMSO.

Document 2
WAGNER REPORT

Chapter 8 Staffing issues

1. It is vital that staff with the right personal qualities and skills are recruited and selected; that they are adequately paid, and have conditions of service and training opportunities which match the job. The fact that residential work is able to attract people of different ages, from various walks of life and ethnic backgrounds, possessing a rich assortment of personal qualities, skills, interests and experiences is its strongest asset, which needs to be built on. Also, as residential provision becomes more closely integrated into local services networks, we should expect staffing patterns to reflect the social and multi-cultural characteristics of neighbourhoods and communities.

Numbers of staff

2. How many staff are there? The simple answer is that no-one really knows. This was brought to our attention by the Local Government Training Board, which for its most recent survey of manpower, training and professional qualifications (1986) has had great difficulty in obtaining accurate data on which to calculate staffing numbers. A similar problem confronted a workforce planning group, established in the wake of the LGTB to identify the elements of a comprehensive workforce planning and training strategy for the personal social services as a whole (*Workforce Planning and Training Need. An Interim Report by Working Group on Workforce Planning in the Personal Services 1987*. Chair: Professor Adrian Webb. Copies of report available from CCETSW). Thus the staffing estimates in Table 1 are presented only to give an idea of the broad shape of the residential workforce. It can be seen that there are roughly similar numbers of direct service and domestic and other manual staff, who form by far the largest proportion of the workforce. As most of the direct service staff are considered as manual workers i.e. as care assistants, we

Table 1 Numbers of staff working in statutory, private and voluntary sectors (Great Britain)

	Statutory	Private	Voluntary	Total
Direct service staff (care assistants,* child care workers etc.)	62,900	27,000	20,000	109,000
Management and supervisory	19,500	10,000	3,500	33,000
Domestic and ancillary staff	61,000	21,000	13,500	96,000
Total	143,400	58,000	37,000	238,000

Source: Working Group on Workforce Planning in the Personal Social Services 1987, Appendix Tables 1.3, 1.5 and 1.6.
*Excluding Scotland.

can also see just how far residential services depend on a vast army of low paid, un-trained people; the majority of whom are women, many working part time. Insofar as it is the children's services that have been contracting, with the major expansion taking place in private sector, provision for the elderly, this position is unlikely to change substantially in the foreseeable future.

3. Examination of workforce patterns demonstrates the need for a continuing forum for debate on these issues. Some are of concern to the Central Council for Education and Training in Social Work (CCETSW), some to employers or trade unions, but there is no overall body which is formally charged with workforce planning. A group representing the main interested parties could carry out this task, without which there is the continued risk of unintended and unmonitored consequences of decisions.

From: National Institute for Social Work (1988) *Residential Care: a Positive Choice*, pp. 70–71, London: HMSO.

Document 3
REPORT OF SSI CHIEF INSPECTOR 1993–94.

Key issues in the personal social services

Summary: the changing social environment – implementing legislation – public concerns – resources – local government reorganisation – deregulation

1.1 The changing social environment

PSS are being delivered in a social and demographic environment which has undergone substantial changes over the last two decades. The main trends in Great Britain influencing the planning and provision of services include:

- An increasing number of elderly people: by 1996, the number of people aged 75 and over will have increased by more than 60% compared with the number in 1971.

- More people are living alone: the number of people living alone increased from 6.3% in 1971 to 11.1% in 1992.

- Divorce rates are up while marriage rates are down: between 1971 and 1991, the number of marriages decreased by 24% but the number of divorces more than doubled.

- The number of lone parent families is increasing: the number of such families more than doubled between 1971 and 1991 and the rate of increase accelerated in the late eighties. In the five years to 1991 the number of single lone parents increased by 24% and the number of dependent children in such families increased from 1.7 million to 2.2 million – 18% of all dependent children.

- According to mid-1980s estimates, 14% of adults and 3% of children had one or more disabilities, ranging from the relatively slight to the very severe. Estimates of the most severely disabled who are likely to need social services help, were 1.3% of adults and 0.5% of children.

- The number of disabled people can be expected to rise since the prevalence of disability increases with age and rises steeply after the age of 70.

- About 4% of the population aged 16 and over – 1.8 million people in all – were estimated to be caring for a sick, disabled or elderly person living with them.

1.2 Implementing legalisation and guidance

The main focus of PSS activity in 1993/4 continued to be the implementation of the

Children Act 1989 and the National Health Service and Community Care Act 1990, this being the first full year of operation of the new community care arrangements. Both pieces of legislation have required a major change in the organisation, practice and business of managing and providing PSS.

This has placed services users and their carers at the heart of service delivery, providing them with opportunities to participate in the planning of services and where possible to exercise choice about the care they receive at local level. It has encouraged people to expect a high standard of individually appropriate services and the right to register dissatisfaction and seek improvements through complaints procedures.

Significant progress has been made by many local authorities in separating the commissioning and purchasing of care from the provision of services. This has involved joint working between health and social services at strategic and operational levels and collaboration with the widest possible range of agencies in the independent and other statutory services. It has required the implementation of new assessment and care management procedures and a crucial transition from service-led to needs-led delivery of services.

Local authorities have continued to develop the role of their own inspection units through inspection of their SSD's own residential homes, seeking views from users and carers about home life and making units more accessible and accountable. The Registered Homes (Amendment) Act 1991 which took effect on 1 April 1993 extended their registration responsibilities to small independent sector homes, having less than four residents.

Overall, SSDs have achieved remarkable progress and some considerable success in establishing these fundamentally new ways of working, but SSI inspection and monitoring have also revealed failures to meet some statutory obligations and deficiencies in services that need to be addressed urgently.

1.3 Public concerns

A number of issues of public concern arose during the year. There was considerable debate about mental health services, particularly for those severely mental ill people who may constitute a risk to themselves or to others. Relevant here was the tragic case of the death of Jonathan Zito, killed by Christopher Clunis who was suffering from schizophrenia and a casualty of a breakdown in after care services following his discharge from hospital into the community. There were distressing revelations of child abuse and neglect and the deaths of a number of children, some of which called into question the adequacy of child protection systems. Instances of abuse of older people were also a matter of public concern. In the area of juvenile justice there was a desire to take a firmer and more rigorous line, but also a recognition of the need to maintain a balance between 'control' and 'care' in the provision of secure accommodation and other services for young offenders.

1.4 Resources

Spending on the PSS has increased over recent years. Annual growth in expenditure since 1986/87 averaged 5.6% in real terms, but the rate of increase has accelerated since 1990/91 with the need to provide resources for major legislative initiatives, particularly the Children Act 1989 and the community care reforms. From 1990/91 to 1994/95 total resources available for PSS will have increased from £3.6 billion to £6.4 billion, representing real terms growth of 48%.

In 1993/94 PSS standard spending (the Government's view of the resources required to deliver adequate services) was £5,020 million. In addition the Special Transitional Grant (STG), ringfenced to allow local authorities to meet their new community care responsibilities, amounted to £565.4 million. Total PSS expenditure budgeted by authorities was £5,740 million. Local authorities generally have discretion to decide the allocation of resources between services in the light of local priorities as well as legislative responsibilities.

The local government settlement for 1994/5 provided for an increase in standard spending to £5,667 million, including £538.6 million carried forward in standard spending from the 1993/4 STG (of which £398.6 million came from the Department of Social Security budget plus £140 million additional funding). The additional total for the 1994/5 STG will be £735.9 million, ringfenced again for community care responsibilities.

1.5 Local government reorganisation

The Local Government Commission has been established to review the need for change in county areas. Such changes are likely to have important implications for the organisation and delivery of social services.

The Chief Inspector is included in those consulted by the Commission on its draft proposals. In commenting on proposals, he is bearing in mind the need for the SSD of each new authority:

- to have strong professional management to secure high quality services for very vulnerable people;

- to contain a range of specialist skill and knowledge reflecting the wide variety of individual and family needs to be addressed;

- to have the ability to engage effectively in strategic planning of services with other key agencies, notably the NHS;

- to have effective collaborative machinery particularly in areas of child protection and the maintenance of local registers of children who are disabled;

- to be able to fulfil its regulatory and other statutory responsibilities.

1.6 Deregulation

Under the Government-wide Deregulation Initiative all Departments are currently looking critically at all legislation that affects businesses, to reduce the regulatory burden where possible and to look for scope for improvement in the way that regulation is applied and enforced. In 1993, DH with the involvement of SSI began its consideration of the impact of social services legislation on private and voluntary organisations involved in the provision of care.

From: Social Services Inspectorate (1994) *Putting People First*, the Third Annual Report of the Chief Inspector, Social Services Inspectorate, 1993/94, pp. 6–9, London: HMSO.

Document 4
JASMINE BECKFORD INQUIRY REPORT

On 28 March 1985 we were appointed by the council of the London Borough of Brent, and subsequently in conjunction with the Brent Health Authority, to inquire into and report on the events leading up to, and the circumstances surrounding the death of Jasmine Christina Beckford who was born on 21 December 1979 and died on 5 July 1984.

Terms of reference

Our terms of reference were as follows:

(a) To investigate all the circumstances surrounding the death of Jasmine Beckford, a child who was in the care of Brent Council.

(b) To determine what action had been taken by the Directorate of Social Services in the period preceding the circumstances (events) and what support had been given to the family, and the adequacy thereof.

(c) To determine whether any immediate steps should be taken arising from the Inquiry, and to advise what action relating to staffing issues should be taken and/or followed if necessary, and to recommend accordingly.

(d) To inquire into the co-ordination of services to the family by the relevant Local Authority and Health Services and any other persons or agencies involved and the liaison between them and to make appropriate recommendations.

We have interpreted our terms of reference not merely in the letter but in their spirit. Although, for example, we were not specifically called upon to examine the twin issues of trans-racial fostering and of employment of a white social worker with the Beckford family, which was Afro-Caribbean in ethnic origin, we could hardly fail to notice the importance attached to these aspects of our Inquiry by the inclusion of Mr. Russell Profitt (who is Principal Race Relations Adviser to the London Borough of Brent) as our adviser. (We mention this aspect of the Beckford case later in this chapter.) Other topics did not, on the face of them appear to concern us, but we were soon made aware of their relevance. It could not have been anticipated that the proceedings before the Willesden magistrates would be so central to the issues we had to examine. Again, on 4 July 1985 the Department of Health and Social Security issued a consultative paper on Child Abuse Inquiries. Our experience of conducting the inquiry in public, during which many of the thorny procedural matters relating to child abuse inquiries were exposed, provided a unique opportunity to add our thoughts to an important aspect of our task.

Furthermore we were conscious throughout our work that an Interdepartmental Working Party, serviced by the Department of Health and Social Security, was undertaking a thorough review of Child Care Law. (It reported on 4 October 1985.) Here again we considered that we had something to offer in the course of the continuing debate about the protection of children in care. We were also alive to the recent creation of a Social Services Inspectorate within the Department, which prompted us to look rather more closely into the structure of the local authority child protection service than would otherwise have been the case. These examples are not exhaustive. We cite them merely to indicate the reasons why we have interpreted our remit in a more extensive and expansive way than a strict reading of our terms of reference would indicate. In any event, as we shall indicate in our chapter on inquiries (Chapter 3), a major justification for such a large expenditure of public funds is the seizing of an opportunity to go beyond an examination of the events that surround the fatality of a particular child in care, and to examine some of the broader issues that provide the framework, both statutory and in practical application, of the law of child care. Part IV of this report reflects what some critics might describe unkindly as a half-baked exegesis on the management of the child abuse system. We hope the description is inapt.

The circumstances leading to the Inquiry

Jasmine Beckford died at the age of $4\frac{1}{2}$, in Kensal Rise, North-West London, at the home of Mr. Morris Beckford (her step-father) and Miss Beverley Lorrington (her mother) of cerebral contusions and subdural hæmorrhage as a direct result of severe manual blows inflicted on the child's head shortly before death. At the time of her death, and for some months (if not years) before, Jasmine was a very thin little girl, emaciated as a result of chronic undernourishment. When she was discharged from hospital after being taken into care she weighed 18lbs 14ozs. Seven months later, when she was reunited with her parents after being fostered, she weighed 25lbs 5 ozs. She died, 27 months later, weighing 23lbs. Apart from her stunted development, she had been subjected to parental battering over a protracted period, multiple old scars appearing both to the pathologist who conducted the post-mortem and to the consultant orthopædic surgeon who gave evidence to us, as being consistent with repeated episodes of physical abuse, to say nothing of the psychological battering she must have undergone.

Morris Beckford was convicted of Jasmine's manslaughter at the Central Criminal Court on 28 March 1985, and was sentenced by the Common Serjeant, Judge Pigot QC, to 10 years' imprisonment. Earlier in the trial Beverley Lorrington changed her plea to guilty of child neglect; she was sentenced to 18 months' imprisonment. (For the full list of charges and verdicts, see Appendix D:1.)

From 17 August 1981 until her death, Jasmine and her sister, Louise (then two and a half months old) were the subject of Care Orders in favour of the London Borough of Brent, for the earlier part of which they had been boarded-out with foster parents, and subsequent to April 1982 had been physically in the care and control of their parents, Morris Beckford and Beverley Lorrington. Those bare facts and circumstances leading up to Jasmine's violent and unnatural death, which were not publicised until the newspaper reports of her parents' criminal trial, aroused a considerable volume of public disquiet as reflected in the extensive treatment accorded to the case by both national and local press and by radio and television.

Throughout our Inquiry we have been acutely aware of the time it has taken to set up the Panel of Inquiry, for us to conduct a thorough investigation of the events and to ensure a fair hearing to all those whose involvement has inevitably come under the public searchlight, and of the need to report expeditiously. We have thought it helpful to remind all those entrusted with the task of deciding when and how to hold a child abuse inquiry, of the first such inquiry in modern times – namely, the inquiry conducted in 1945 by Sir Walter Monckton (later Viscount

Monckton of Brenchley) into the circumstances which led to the boarding-out of Dennis and Terence O'Neill, and the steps taken to supervise their welfare.

Dennis O'Neill was boarded out at Bank Farm, Minsterley, Shropshire on 28 June 1944 by Newport Borough Council, to whom he had been committed on 30 May 1940 as a 'fit person' within the meaning of sections 76 and 96 of the Children and Young Persons Act 1933 (Dennis O'Neill was joined by his brother, Terence, on 5 July 1944). Dennis O'Neill died, shortly before his 13th birthday, on 9 January 1945 as a result of acute cardiac failure following violence applied to the front of the chest and back, while – be it noted – in a state of undernourishment due to neglect. The foster-parents, Mr. and Mrs. Gough, were charged with his manslaughter. On 19 March 1945 at Stafford Assizes, Reginald Gough was found guilty of manslaughter and sentenced to 6 years' penal servitude (by that time indistinguishable in practice from ordinary imprisonment): Esther Gough was found not guilty of manslaughter, but guilty of child neglect, and sentenced to 6 months' imprisonment, sentences which bear comparison with the severer penalties inflicted on Morris Beckford and Beverley Lorrington. The two relevant authorities, Newport Borough Council and Shropshire County Council asked the Home Secretary to order a public inquiry. This he did on 28 March 1945. Nowadays the relevant local authority is normally expected to set up the requisite inquiry. **Where (as here) the inquiry is, exceptionally, one of enormous public interest and likely to involve such large financial cost that it is unreasonable for local government to bear, we think that the Secretary of State should initiate the inquiry under his statutory powers given in section 98, Children Act 1975. And we so recommend.**

Sir Walter Monckton's one-man inquiry sat for four days in mid-April 1945, when 22 witnesses were called and 7 parties were legally represented. Sir Walter reported on 8 May 1945, four months after Dennis O'Neill's death which had attracted widespread attention both in and out of Parliament, and led to (*sic*) the setting up of the Curtis Committee on the Care of Children (HMSO, Cmnd. 6922) on 25 March 1945; it reported in September 1946 (The Children Act 1948 was the direct legislative response).

In the other famous modern inquiry, into the death of Maria Colwell, the dates are not uninformative. Maria died on 7 January 1973; her step-father was convicted of murder on 16 April 1973, but his conviction was reduced to manslaughter by the Court of Appeal on 19 July 1973 and a sentence of 8 years' imprisonment substituted. On 17 July 1973 the Secretary of State appointed an inquiry. The Inquiry sat in public for 41 days between October and December 1973, hearing 70 witnesses with 7 parties represented and reported (with a partial dissent from Miss Olive Stevenson) in April/May 1974.

We allude in a later chapter to the methods of conducting child abuse inquiries which we think could materially expedite the time taken in reporting to the initiating authorities. But one matter that is to be elicited from both the O'Neill and Colwell Inquiries immediately strikes us. The criminal proceedings in respect of a child in care or under supervision of a local authority (where it is apparent that an inquiry will inevitably follow the criminal process, if any) could, and should be given the highest priority in criminal investigation by the police, in the prosecution by the relevant prosecutor (which in future will be the national independent prosecuting service) and in the Crown Court's calendar of criminal business. While we have not felt it necessary to examine why it took so long for Morris Beckford and Beverley Lorrington to be brought to trial, we can see no reason why it took nearly nine months. (About the same delay occurred in the recent cases of Tyra Henry, a child who was killed while in care of Lambeth Borough Council, and of Reuben Carthy who was killed by his mother in Nottingham, both taking more than six months to come to trial.) The arrests were made instantaneously: there were damning admissions from Morris Beckford at his first interrogation; and the prosecution evidence was limited both in scope and volume; the trial lasted only three days. The delay appears to us to have been inexcusable. Whatever may be the explanation for this inordinate delay in the criminal process, **we strongly recommend that in future in all child abuse prosecutions involving children in the care of a local authority, where the public is almost certain to express disquiet about the handling of the case by social services and other relevant agencies, suggestive of fault by social workers and other professional people, the criminal trial should, other than for exceptional reasons, take place within 3–4 months of the homicidal event, and certainly not beyond six months.** In both the *O'Neill* and *Colwell* cases, the trial took place inside 3–4 months. The Home Secretary has recently acquired the statutory power under the Prosecution of Offenders Act 1985 to place time limits within which criminal trials must take place. Child abuse cases represent a classic instance of the type of prosecution where the exercise of this power would have been entirely appropriate.

From: Blom Cooper, L. (1985) *A Child in Trust: the Report of the Panel of Inquiry into the Circumstances of the Death of Jasmine Beckford*, pp. 1–4, Wembley: Brent Borough Council.

Document 5a
TAKING CHILDREN SERIOUSLY

The rights of children and young people to make complaints

Children and young people use a wide variety of statutory services – education, health, social services etc. – and others run by voluntary and private bodies. More than 200,000 children in the UK spend significant periods of their lives in a variety of institutions away from their 'natural' home: boarding schools, children's homes, secure units, hospitals, young offender institutions etc.

Over the last few years there has been an increasing recognition of the need for children to have ready access to well-publicised complaints procedures with an independent element (cases of serious abuse of children in both boarding schools and children's homes have provided the main impetus for reform). There are also now various voluntary sector advocacy schemes for children, and the proposed IRCHIN/A Voice for the Child in Care national service.

While preparing this report we sent a questionnaire to a wide range of statutory and non-statutory bodies which operate complaints procedures. We received replies from 30 bodies (see list at end of appendix). In general, whether complaints procedures relate to a particular service, e.g. the health service, or consumer complaints about gas or water supplies, or to particular issues, e.g. to those within the scope of the Equal Opportunities Commission and Commission for Racial Equality, children have the same access to them as adults.

The survey found that very few complaints are received from children (in the case of some procedures, no complaints had been received from under-18s since they were initiated). In some cases this is because the relevant services are available to very few children and young people. But in many cases it is clear that little attempt has been made to inform children and young people about the procedures, to make them readily accessible, or to reassure children and young people about the consequences of making complaints.

From: Rosenbaum, M. and Newell, P. (1991) *Taking Children Seriously: a Proposal for a Children's Rights Commissioner*, p. 50, London: Calouste Gulbenkian Foundation.

Document 5b
TAKING CHILDREN SERIOUSLY

(ii) Individual complaints

It would be unrealistic and in the current context unhelpful to children and young people and wasteful of resources to give the Commissioner the role of investigating individual complaints from the UK's 13.2 million children and young people under 18. To try to fulfil this role without large resources and a substantial network of local offices and advocacy schemes would mean offering children a remote and inaccessible centralised system. It is clear that children are unlikely to use procedures that are not local and readily accessible. It could also duplicate or conflict with the procedures and sources of help already available to children and young people, some of which are recent and very welcome developments. For example, IRCHIM (Independent Representation for Children in Need) and A Voice for the Child in Care have agreed to establish a national service to provide children in need with independent advice, advocacy and representation.

At a later stage it may be possible if the resources are available and in the light of the Commissioner's work so far to add to his/her role – or create separately – a carefully designed local or regional system to receive and investigate children's complaints across a defined range of services, together with a network of advocates to support children in making complaints. Such a system could benefit from the work the Commissioner had already done on improving existing complaints procedures. In the special case of the 80,000 or so children in care there may be a more urgent case for providing an independent body to receive complaints which are not satisfactorily resolved at a local level. Unlike other children in England and Wales, children in care will not have the right to seek to challenge their parenting by local authorities in court – others will have this right under section 8 of the Children Act 1989. And the Secretary of State's powers to intervene under section 84 of the Act are limited. This need could be met by establishing a new office or by providing the Commissioners for Local Administration with the resources and any necessary additional powers to fulfil the role.

In exceptional cases however the wide powers of the Commissioner to initiate investigations could enable him/her to investigate an individual case (the Commissioner's powers here would be as for other investigations). We would expect this to be limited to cases which raise important questions of principle which the Commissioner cannot tackle in other ways. Another possibility which could be examined is that the Commissioner should be able to refer particular cases to the Commissioners for Local Administration for investigation, when there is no other appropriate procedure, even where they currently fall outside the Local Commissioners' remit.

From: Rosenbaum, M. and Newell, P. (1991) *Taking Children Seriously: a Proposal for a Children's Rights Commissioner*, p. 25, London: Calouste Gulbenkian Foundation.

Document 6
PINDOWN INQUIRY REPORT

12.7 At the beginning of 1988, nearly two years after Glynis Mellors' Report, a set of 'rules' of Pindown was written down on the front cover of the 'Pindown – Other House' log book at The Birches (see appendix F, document 5 and Chapter 9, paragraph 9.15). The 'rules' are in the handwriting of Louise Doherty, a residential worker, who was acting on the instructions of Peter Nicol-Harper, who was in charge of The Birches. Four years after it commenced Pindown in its traditional form is documented again: the removal of clothes and personal possessions on admission; baths; wearing of night wear underwear and dressing gown and 'no footwear of any description'; meals in the room; knocking on the door for permission to 'impart information' or go to the bathroom; no communication with other residents; no television, music, magazines, cigarettes or telephone calls; visits from social workers or parents are permitted 'by arrangement with team leader'; during the day any school work set should be completed and 'all books and writing materials should be removed after 4 o'clock; and rising at 7 a.m., bed 7 p.m. after having a bath'. The 'rules' are headed by the instruction 'it is essential that each child is made aware of these rules at the time of their admission'. (...)

Basic philosophies

12.10 Tony Latham then described the 'basic philosophies' of the special unit: 'The isolation of a young person to a room away from the main care of the building, where loss of privileges are asserted. The young person is supervised 24 hours a day under a contract basis whereby issues, problems and relationships can be confronted. Care is presented as totally negative experience initially ensuring that the participant can clearly identify their problems, come to terms with them through counselling and time out sessions with appointed staff, and is encouraged to work through a problem by not being allowed to take the easy way out. To ensure that work with the children on these lines is planned and clearly structured, it needs to include family contact, participation and agreement to the sanctions employed (where applicable) and the opportunity for the child to learn how privileges are earned and co-operation brings rewards.'

12.11 In respect of the unit's use, Tony Latham wrote that the *'special unit should seldom be used. It should be a last resort and not be used liberally to exert heavy handed discipline or sanctions to children. Family Centre staff have worked with its philosophies and have seen what rewards and changes it brings in children when all else fails. Area Office Social Workers generally do not agree with its operation but are unable to offer alternatives, save secure units'* (emphasis added).

12.12 The actual use of Pindown, in our view, wandered far from its so-called 'philosophy'. Whilst a very few children who were in Pindown for a very short time were said to have benefited from it, almost all who were in Pindown over the years suffered in varying degrees the despair and the potentially damaging effects of isolation, the humiliation of having to wear night clothes, knock on the door in order to 'impart information' as it was termed, and of having all their personal possessions removed; and the intense frustration and boredom from the lack of communication, companionship with others and recreation. To many Pindown must undoubtedly have appeared as 'heavy handed discipline'. It is insignificant, in our view, that at the beginning of November 1983 when one of the first children was transferred from The Birches to 245 Hartshill Road to go into Pindown, the entry on the log book stated: 'R is at the secure unit at Hartshill'. Later on the 9 November 1983 John Aston recorded in the Hartshill log book: *'Tony please note.*... to keep the impression of a special/secure (sic) unit going means no allowance of preveleges (sic) as it would defeat our "face" to other members of The Birches'. When Peter Nicol-Harper, who was an experienced practitioner of Pindown and who had tried to introduce a 'positive' form of it in early 1988 at The Birches, gave evidence he expressed the view that the Pindown unit had been used, at least on some occasions, as secure accommodation.

12.13 There are many references in the records to children being 'detained in the special unit' and to 'solitary confinement'. One particular example, noted in an earlier chapter, is not, in our view, unrepresentative. A boy, just fifteen years old, had 'absconded' from school and was put in the unit in early 1985 in 245 Hartshill Road. A log book entry states: *'another week of solitary confinement for* (P.E.) has had some rather peculiar effects. He is talking to himself a great deal and we had tears several times during the course of the week. Sleeping in staff also report incidents of (P.E.) talking in his sleep' (emphasis added).

Definition

12.14 Pindown is referred to in many different ways in the documentation we received. The following is a list of some of the descriptions: 'Basic Pindown'; 'Total Pindown'; 'Heavy Pindown'; 'Strict Pindown'; 'Negative Pindown'; 'Nasty Pindown'; 'B-Plan Pindown'; 'Stage 2 Pindown'; 'Semi-Pindown'; 'Partial Pindown'; 'Relaxed Pindown'; 'Sympathetic Pindown'; 'Positive Pindown'; 'Therapeutic Pindown'; and 'Maisie'.

12.15 With some exceptions, the names in the main give a clue as to the approach used in the practice of Pindown. What, however, are the minimum criteria which qualify the practice as Pindown? It is almost impossible to be absolutely precise but we decided that four features were usually present: firstly, isolation for part of the time in a part of a children's home cordoned off as a 'special' or Pindown unit; secondly, removal of ordinary clothing for part of the time and the enforced wearing of shorts or night clothes; thirdly, being told of having to earn 'privileges'; and fourthly, being allowed to attend school or a 'school room' in the unit, and changing back into shorts or night clothes after returning from school.

12.16 'Full' or 'Total' Pindown, in our view, must have the following features: firstly, persistent isolation in a part of a children's home cordoned off as a special or Pindown unit; secondly, removal of ordinary clothing for lengthy periods and the enforced wearing of shorts or night clothes; thirdly, persistent loss of all 'privileges'; fourthly, having to knock on the door to 'impart information', for example, a wish to visit the bathroom; and fifthly, non-attendance at school, no writing or reading materials, no television, radio, cigarettes or visits.

12.17 The place in which Pindown was practised was variously called, 'the special unit'; 'the Intensive Training Unit'; 'the structured unit'; the 'sculptured unit'; the 'secure unit'; the 'time out area'; or 'the crash pad'.

12.18 As noted in chapter 1, the origin of the word 'Pindown' was said to be the use by Tony Latham of the words, 'we must pin down the problem' whilst he gestured with his forefinger pointing towards the floor. The children began to speak of 'being in Pindown'.

From: Levy, A. and Kahan, B. (1991) *The Pindown Experience and the Protection of Children: the Report of the Staffordshire Child Care Inquiry 1990*, pp. 118–121, Stafford: Staffordshire County Council.

Document 7
A HUNDRED THOUSAND FORGOTTEN CHILDREN

Following the publication of a letter from me to *The Guardian* newspaper (21st January 1976) I received enquiries from many people involved in child care. I was also asked by the Secretary of the Personal Social Services Council to make some observations concerning the kind of issues which might be considered as central to any enquiry. I prepared a paper 'Observations on Child Care in Britain' and this was circulated to various interested organisations. Although that paper dealt with the declining standards of child care social work and with some sad or even dangerous situations which had become known to me, it did not draw upon statistics since it was in the main concerned with attitudes and motives, and was a summary of my own recent experiences and impressions.

The present report, which should be seen as supplementary and supporting the earlier one, is concerned with the statistics of children, who are in the care of local authorities and voluntary societies in England and Wales. It seems to me that it would be a typically bureaucratic understatement to say that what the figures reveal gives cause for concern. If we remember that the figures represent children, and that each unit represents part of the life experience of some child, then, the situation as we have it, and the trend revealed, are depressing, if not tragic. Apart from all other issues raised in this paper the news media seem to have overlooked the shocking fact that we have now shot past the 100,000 mark for the numbers of children in care. (Local Authority and voluntary societies.) One Hundred Thousand children in care, and so far as we can tell still going up, yet hardly a ripple of concern. In 1972 the total was 95,500. Even that was high by comparison with earlier years. But on 31st March 1975 there was a recorded 105,193 children in care.

From: Redgrave, K.B. (1976) *A Hundred Thousand Forgotten Children: a Report to the Personal Social Services Council*, duplicated report, p. 1.

Document 8
CHILDREN IN THE PUBLIC CARE

1.17 Local authorities use a wide range of services for children in their care. They have looked traditionally to boarding out with foster parents and living in residential homes as the principal means of providing that 'special' relationship for children in care. Cycles of fashion have led to alternating periods of dominance by foster care and residential home care. Both now operate in the context of values that place a premium upon keeping the natural family together and restoring it where possible if separation becomes necessary.

1.18 The current preference for fostering derives from:

- a cluster of values about the family as the natural unit for bringing up children;

- research evidence in the past of children remaining in residential homes who would have benefited from and needed family life;

- the influence of reports by the Audit Inspectorate (5) and Audit Commission (6) which suggested that, if fostering was preferable for the child, it was also much less costly for the authority.

1.19 This preference has been expressed in such a way that the numbers of children boarded out have remained remarkably steady in the face of the large reduction in the overall number of children in care: 33,000 in 1978, reaching 37,000 in 1982, falling back to 34,500 in 1990. In the same period, the numbers in residential care have declined by 60% (...)

Chapter 2 Residential Child Care

The providers

2.1 Residential care is difficult to define. For the purposes of this review I have taken it to mean continuous residence in permanently staffed accommodation for more than three children, which provides or enables access to the care and services normally available to children and such additional measures of care, control and treatment as resident children require. I have gone beyond this definition where I attempt to fulfil the wider remit of considering the position of children in care who are placed in institutions other than children's homes.

2.2 Children in care are currently placed in:

- Children's Homes – community homes provided by local authorities, some with observation and assessment, some with education on the premises; voluntary homes; private children's homes;

- Schools – maintained or independent boarding schools, often catering for special educational needs;

- Health Facilities – NHS hospitals or psychiatric units; mental nursing homes;

- Secure Institutions – youth treatment centres, penal institutions, or secure units in local authority community homes.

Information about the number of institutions accommodating children in care is poor, even for the children's homes. There are currently 81 voluntary homes registered with the Secretary of State; we estimate that local authorities in England provide approximately 1,000 community homes, and that there are around 100 private homes.

2.3 Department of Health statistics, compiled from returns made by local authorities, suggest that there were 13,199 children in care in these various settings on 31 March 1990 (the figure excludes children in private homes, for whom a separate return is not yet made). The great majority of these (10,490 or 80%) were in local

Table 2 Children in care in England by type of accommodation

	Percentage	
Type of care	1980	1990
Fostering	37	56.9
Community homes	19.5	11.8
Community homes with education	5.5	1.9
Comm. homes: observation and assessment	5.2	3.6
Vol. homes and hostel	3.8	1.5
Spec. schools/homes and hostel	3.1	2.0
Prison	1.4	0.6
NHS establishments	0.5	0.3
Other placements	23.8	21.3
Total	100%	100%
	(95,297)	(60,469)

authority community homes. There were 1,188 children in care in special schools, 933 in voluntary homes, 204 in health establishments, 337 in prison department establishments and 47 in youth treatment centres (see Table 2).

References

5. Audit Inspectorate (1981) *Inspection of Community Homes, September 1985,* Department of Health and Social Security, London.
6. Audit Commission (1985) *Child Care Report,* HMSO, London.

From: Utting, Sir W. (1991) *Children in the Public Care: a Review of Residential Child Care*, p. 27, London: HMSO.

Document 9
RACE AND CRIMINAL JUSTICE

Black people in Britain

3 Discrimination is an every day experience for black people. In 1984, the Policy Studies Institute (PSI) produced its third report on the circumstances of the British black population. The report states that *'as we systematically compare the jobs, income, unemployment rates, private housing, local authority housing, local environments and other aspects of the lives of people of different ethnic orign ... the circumstances of black people ... continue to be worse than those of white people'*.

4 The PSI report findings were contrary to the expectations of the researchers. They identified three linked problems which contributed to *'a complex jungle of new and old inequalities'*:
'First, it is clear that racism and direct racial discrimination continue to have a powerful impact on the lives of black people. Second, the position of black citizens in Britain largely remains, geographically and economically, that allocated to them as immigrant workers in the 1950s and the 1960s. Third, it is still the case that the organisations and the institutions of British society have policies and practices that additionally disadvantage black people because they frequently take no account of the cultural differences between groups with different ethnic origins'.

5 A disturbing feature is the number of black prisoners in England and Wales, a proportion which has risen for the third successive year. In 1985, the first year for which figures were available, the population of black prisoners was 12.5%. In 1986, the proportion had risen to 13%. In 1987, 14% of the men in prison and 23% of the women were black. Overall black prisoners constituted 14% of the prison population.

From: Dholakia, N. (1989) *Race and Criminal Justice: the Second Report of the NACRO Race Issues Advisory Committee*, p. 27, London: NACRO.

Document 10
PURCHASING AND CONTRACTING SKILLS

2.2 Tensions in Purchasing Practice

2.2.1 Students will need to be aware of the various points along the purchasing sequence, where different interests and agendas are negotiated between government representatives, local authority politicians, relevant officers, community advocates, service users, carers, service providers and practitioners. The subsequent deals, agreements and compromises that are formed from these discussions, will obviously shape and influence the range of possibilities available for working out individual care plans. At least five agendas are identified (...) (below), which produce differing perspectives and tensions in purchasing negotiations and in relation to the different agencies and parties involved. These agendas are economic, managerial, professional, and those of service users, carers and social care providers.

2.2.2 The economic agenda for community care and purchasing may be identified in government concerns outlined in the working brief to Sir Roy Griffiths. Later reports identified a huge rise in social security expenditure on people in residential care during the 1980s (DH 1989). Purchasing of health and social care services is part of government strategy to secure better value for taxpayers' money, to shift away from institutional budgets and remove the **perverse incentives** favouring costly residential and nursing home care. The annual negotiations between central government and local authorities decide upon the funding levels for community care. While (*sic*) local authority has responsibility for planning and providing social care, central government negotiates the provision of the required financial support. Any shortfall of funding has to be resolved by each local authority and its community. Strategies can include all or any of the following: raising taxes, reducing services, charging user fees, narrowing eligibility, depressing market costs, cutting services or standards.

2.2.3 The managerial agenda in purchasing is recognised in the White Paper as making it 'easier to hold ... (agencies) to account for their performance ... and recognising ... that confusion has contributed to poor overall performance' (DH 1989). Along with other government quality assurance requirements like the Citizen Charter (DH 1994) now being developed for public services, purchasing strategy is seen to encourage planning and clear service objectives from which monitoring can be undertaken, so that social services departments can account for their performance. With the implementation of community care, almost all local authorities have established specific client groups and priority groups, from which spending levels can be estimated annually and spending monitored (DH 1993). Departmental budgets can be identified through establishing cost centres, and spending responsibility devolved nearer to the service users both for close accountability of spending and for ensuring cost-effective local resources (Netten and Beecham 1993). The introduction of purchaser/provider separation is designed to influence the pattern of provision in more appropriate ways (DH 1990, para 4.5). A growing number of social services departments are including quality assurance and inspection units in their commissioning and purchasing divisions to monitor performance through complaints procedures, inspection visits and identification of standards. However, an organisational image of clear objective attainment and sound financial management may not easily interact with the complex problems of different localities, ethnic groups and individual views on need. Complaints procedures may focus on individuals, and lack influence upon departments, organizations and resource allocation.

2.2.4 The professional agenda of social work relates to the contribution of ideas from research of case or care management from the 1980s (Challis 1994). This work has demonstrated the importance of comprehensive expert assessment, and continuity of care for people with multiple and long-term care problems. The case/care management models were adopted by the Department of Health in the 1989 White Paper 'to encourage their application more widely' for all identified groups in community care and were fitted into a purchasing strategy. However, the qualifications for the case/care management role were unspecified and suggestions from the Department of Health were that such personnel be drawn from 'a range of backgrounds' and professional groups. In the wake of the attention given by the Department of Health guidance (DH 1991a), the case/care management role has appeared to attract all the elements of power and relevance in the context of community care. Not surprisingly existing and emerging professional groups have developed training and qualifications for the role. Moreover, the varying interpretations of case or care management by respective social services and social work departments have deepened the complexity and uncertainty which now surround the approach. The uncertainty not only bears upon purchasing decisions, it questions how the professional differences, which naturally arise in discussions around the discrete tasks of assessment, care planning, networking, and review, will be resolved. Clear decision making is important as this affects the co-ordination, quality and quantity of care packages. The different options also need to address the various concerns of risk management for all concerned.

2.2.5 The service users and carers agenda Growing pressure has been brought by service user pressure groups to deliver services in a more accessible and relevant way after many years of frustration with poorly resourced and institutionalised services (Disability Unit 1994). Significant sources of influence upon the Government have also been the carers' organizations (Hill 1991). An example of local pressure from both service users and carers identifying their needs, is provided by a black, ethnic and minority group who undertook their own research into Community Care services for black elders (Black and Racial Minorities Interest Group 1993). The above examples demonstrate that in the need identification and local planning lies the potential for service user influence. Bringing service users and carers into the purchasing of services, on their own behalf offers an opportunity for user-led budgets, to enable people to live in their own homes wherever feasible and sensible (Flynn and Common 1992). However, the wishes of service users and carers may often be reasonably or unreasonably at variance to a range of professionals' views in terms of available service providers – or what can be afforded with available finance. Channels for complaints may be ineffective to register concerns or suggestions for improvements. In extreme instances, recourse to High Court action may be the most effective way to bring about change in statutory agencies' practice. Service users and cares from powerful organizations may articulate their needs more clearly than smaller under-represented groups, particularly if the consultancy and representative procedures for local need planning are not yet effective.

Economic or managerial national charities may assume responsibility for a consumer voice – though without sufficient consultation with those they represent – but may also be competing as service providers.

2.2.6 Social care providers' agenda Central government encourages local authorities to extend their range of social care providers in relation to the independent sector (DH 1989). Government policy has incentives for the maximum use of private and voluntary providers alongside good quality public services as conducive to increasing the range of options for consumer choice. A mixed social care sector is seen to develop through the enabling/purchasing role assigned to statutory social services. By dividing off the providers' services, the statutory in-house element is to be encouraged to compete with independent providers. Hence, together, statutory and independent providers are seen as a mixed social care market – a government strategy, to realise a vision of user-led, cost-effective services offering a range of choice. In theory, such individual services can be chosen where need is identified. Specific contracts may be put in place to ensure service users receive services which are innovative, relevant and subject to control through renewal of contracts. Social care providers are concerned that there is a level playing field between independent and statutory in-house provision. There are also questions whether funding and conditions are reasonable, fair and conducive to the ethos of some charity and voluntary agencies or helpful to private providers' service operation.

References

Department of Health (1989) *Caring for People: Community care in the next decade and beyond*, HMSO, London

Department of Health (1994) *A Framework for Local Community Care Charters*, HMSO, London

Netten, A. and Beecham, J. (1993) *Community Care in Action: The role of costs*, PSSRU, Kent

Department of Health (1990) *Caring for People: Community care in the next decade and beyond: policy guidance*, HMSO, London

Hills, D. (1991) *Carer Support in the Community*, Department of Health, London

Challis, D. (1994) Case Management: A review of UK developments and issues, in Titterton, M. *Caring for People in the Community*, Jessica Kingsley, London

Department of Health (1991a) *Care Management and Assessment Practice Guidance: Practitioners' guide*, HMSO, London

Disability Unit, The (1994) *Disability on the Agenda*

Black and Racial Minorities Interest Group (1993) *Community Care: The Black Experience*

Flynn, N. and Common, R. (1992) *Contracting for Care*, Rowntree Foundation, York

Best, D. (1994) *Purchasing and Contracting Skills*, Improving Social Work Education and Training, no.18, pp. 20–23, London: CCETSW.

Document 11
COMMUNITY CARE PLAN SUMMARY 1995/6

Housing and care in the community

Adequate and appropriate housing is a basic component of Care in the Community. Priorities as identified for the Housing Strategy and Investment Programme are: to continue to meet the need for affordable housing for homeless people, overcrowded households and other priority groups.
develop housing options for people with disabilities.
continue the commitment to invest in council homes and maintain these in good condition.
improve the energy efficiency of the housing stock.
reduce empty private sector homes and maintain these in good condition.
promote a positive strategy for improving the condition of private sector homes.

The main service developments are:
The council negotiated 15 one-bedroom flats within housing association developments for a Dispersed Mental Health Scheme. PENTA Housing Agency is providing floating support for tenants. It is hoped that Special Needs Management Allowance (SNMA) will be provided by the Housing Corporation.

There has also been a review of the funding arrangements for adaptations to housing association properties to ensure efficiency and equal access to funds.

A Housing Needs Group has been established to identify the future housing needs of adults with learning disabilities to ensure efficient use of existing resources and appropriate new provision.

Completion of ten one-bedroomed homes for people with learning disabilities on a housing association site in NW2.

A joint initiative to provide 11 places for older people with learning disabilities.

In partnership with the Health Agency, the Family Housing Association is developing a project for people with learning disability resettling in the community.

Developments for next three years
1995/96

Refurbish identified sheltered housing scheme to provide extra care. The feasibility study has been completed and a scheme will be included in the capital programme.

Develop independent housing options for people with learning disabilities.

Ensure that adequate provision is made in the Compulsory Competitive Tendering arrangements for housing management for liaison with Social Services and Health Agencies for people with care needs.

Develop housing options for people with long-term mental health problems and people with learning disabilities resettling in the community in collaboration with the Health Agency.

Implement and monitor the effectiveness of the new housing allocations policies to ensure access to housing for people with social and care needs.

Survey people with hearing impairments to establish the need for specialist housing to combat social isolation.

Develop a sheltered housing scheme specifically for Asian elders.

Review all schemes receiving SNMA to ensure they continue to meet identified needs in Barnet.

Develop a system by which the Agency Services Scheme may be 'commissioned' as part of a package of care.

Establish a joint training package for estate managers, temporary accommodation and social services staff on the implications of Community Care, particularly managing vulnerable and mentally ill tenants, and accessing services.

Develop a scheme of mixed general needs housing including 20 per cent built to 'lifetime' homes specification and ten bedspaces for people with learning disabilities.

Work to ensure sufficient capital and revenue funding is available to keep supported housing affordable for all groups.

Future developments in the field of homelessness include:

During the year there have been a number of setbacks to the provision of the homeless day centre. A site has now been identified. Joint finance for a co-ordinator and an assistant will be sought.

Further council temporary accommodation to be refurbished, and the Croft to include new play provision.

Improve the quality of temporary accommodation and reduce the numbers housed in poor quality bed and breakfast.

Research and implement an appropriate model of supported temporary housing for homeless people with mental health problems.

Review the services available to homeless people resettling in the community.

There will be a Needs Assessment survey of people living in temporary accommodation. This is more extensive than originally envisaged with up to 600 households being interviewed.

Secure additional funding for the Health Visitor specialist post.

Develop a replacement hostel for Barnet Women's Aid in partnership with a housing association.

Develop a refuge for Jewish Women's Aid in partnership with a housing association.

1996/97

Monitor the impact of Compulsory Competitive Tendering.

Continue the welfare adaptation programme for people with physical disabilities.

Ensure appropriate developments to support care in the community are included in the housing association and council's capital programme.

Review independent housing schemes for people with learning disabilities.

Explore models of provision for older people with dementia to live in sheltered homes.

From: *Community Care Plan Summary, 1995/6*, pp. 24–27, London Borough of Barnet.

Document 12
BACK FROM THE WELLHOUSE

Institutional Effects

Social workers operate within a society that discriminates against people on the basis of their particular impairments. The degree and nature of intolerance of a particular impairment will vary, but it will be manifested in a variety of ways which range from a failure to recognise the effects of social and physical barriers on participation into society, to offensive imagery and abuse. Pamela Williams indicates the influence of ageism in the allocation of resources to disabled elders in Paper 2. A forthcoming CCETSW publication will address the combined effect of racism and disablism in services for black disabled people. Disability can therefore be viewed as a social construct and is defined in a previous CCETSW guidance paper as:

'the disadvantage or restriction of activity caused by contemporary social organisation which takes no or little account of people who have impairments and thus excludes them from activities' (Stevens 1991).

One sociological explanation for the basis of disablism focuses on disabled people's association with the means of production in Western Capitalist society. The assumed non-productivity of disabled people finds ideological expression in the notion of dependency (Oliver 1990) (Illsley 1981).

'In the formative years following the industrial revolution, the modern concept of disability became associated with expectations for a life of dependency upon charity and beggary ... Ultimately, this led to the systematic isolation of disabled people from their peers and a form of apartheid evolved which included special residential accommodation, sheltered employment, special transport, and special education geared for leisure rather than for careers in employment' (Finkelstein, 1991, p. 29).

Disabled people should not however be regarded as non-productive. Of the working age population, 3.8% are disabled and are employed, or seeking work. However, one estimate indicates that unemployment rates for disabled people are 2.5 times more than non-disabled people (Barnes 1991).

'Despite the high rates of unemployment in the industrialised world, the majority of disabled people of working age do have a job, and hence are economically productive. In addition, day centres, adult training centres and sheltered workshops make a considerable economic contribution by carrying out jobs that cannot be easily mechanised at wage rates that make Third World workers look expensive' (Oliver 1990).

Negative associations of disability with dependency are however, pronounced within Western culture. Words such as 'invalid', 'dumb', 'handicapped' which are still sometimes used to describe disabled people have other connotations relating to restriction, devaluation and marginalisation. Dependent, menacing, patronising and other images offensive to disabled people have been identified in popular children's literature (Reiser and Mason 1992) and adult films, television and written material (Morris 1991). Some years ago, Wolfensberger identified seven perceptions of people with learning difficulties which devalue and marginalise them, which include 'object of pity', 'burden of charity', a 'menace', and 'sick'. These images remain common in newspaper and other media descriptions of disabled people (Wolfensberger 1975, Barnes 1991). Perpetuation of such images is commonly associated with charity advertising by social welfare voluntary agencies. This has only been slightly modified following protests from disabled people and others (Campbell 1990).

Some professional groups have incorporated principles of anti-discriminatory practice in professional training, most health and welfare professionals operate within agency workplaces where the notions of vulnerability and dependency are inherent in the service statutory responsibilities and the prioritising or 'rationing' of scarce resources.

'Social workers have adopted an ideological position in which the self determination of their clients is paramount. The tasks of enabling and empowering people is seen by many as their main duties. However, the majority find themselves employed by agencies whose perception is somewhat different ... Social workers have found themselves acting as gatekeepers, determining who is most deserving of the applicants for a service, rather than empowering self-determination' (Sapey and Hewitt 1991, pp. 40–41).

There has been some criticism of their perception of disability as a personal problem rather than a social one. This has been described as an 'individual model' or 'medical model' where the problem is perceived to relate to an individual with a sensory, physical or mental impairment failing to adapt to their environment. It is suggested that this perspective should be replaced by a 'social model' where the problem is located within a 'disabling environment' and resolved through the adaptation of the environment to the individual's requirements (Finkelstein 1980, Borsay 1986, Oliver, 1986).

Finkelstein has recently observed that the individual model which accepted that incarceration in residential homes was an acceptable form of care of disabled people, generated a variant deriving from the results of research by Miller and Gwynne (1972). While they accepted to some extent residents' criticism of able-bodied management of residential care they suggested that committal to institutions defined disabled people as 'socially dead' and the problem was to assist residents in their transition from social death to physical death. Their conclusions appalled the group of disabled people involved with the study, which included Paul Hunt. Finkelstein calls this a 'social death model of disability' where disabled people are seen as socially dead, dependent upon others for a 'cure' or to provide permanent 'care'. Wolfensberger has used a similar concept of social 'deathmaking' to explore why health and welfare professionals fail to report abuse by colleagues of disabled people and the co-operation of such professionals in abuse.

It was in part as a result of Miller and Gwynne's research that a number of disabled people in Britain, Paul Hunt in particular, were responsible for generating the social model or what Finkelstein calls the 'social barriers model'. This model involves an integrated living approach to disability services, which is 'environment based' rather than 'health and welfare based'. This involves service providers being redirected from functional assessment to the identification and removal of barriers through the participation of disabled people in mainstream life (Finkelstein 1991).

References

Barnes, C. (1991) *Disabled People in Britain*, Hurst/BCODP.
Borsay, A. (1986) *Disabled People in Britain*, Hurst/BCODP.

Campbell, J. (1990) Cap in Hand, Conference Speech, Unpublished.

Finkelstein, V. (1980) *Attitudes and Disabled People*, Issues for discussion, World Rehabilitation Fund, New York.

Finklestein, V. (1991) 'Disability: An administrative challenge?' in Oliver, M. (ed) *Social Work, Disabled People and Disabling Environments*, Jessica Kingsley, London.

Miller, E.J. and Gwynne, C.V. (1972) *A Life Apart*, Tavistock, London.

Oliver, M. (1986) 'Social Policy and Disability', *Disability, Handicap and Society* 1, No. 1.

Oliver, M. (1990) *The Politics of Disablement*, Macmillan, London.

Illsley, R. (1981) 'Problems of Dependancy Groups', *Social Science and Medicine*, Vol. 15a.

Reiser, R. and Mason, M. (1992) *Disability Equality in the Classroom*, ILEA, London.

Stevens, A. (1991) *Disability Issues: Developing antidiscriminatory practice*, CCETSW, London.

Wolfensberger, W. (1975) *The Origin and Nature of Our Institutional Models*, Human Policy, New York.

From: Stevens, A. (ed.) (1993) *Back From the Wellhouse*: Discussion Papers on Sensory Impairment and Training in Community Care, CCETSW Paper 32.1, pp. 18–21, London: CCETSW.

Document 13
ADVOCACY

We shall see an intimate interplay, even a substantial confusion, between the different terms – for example, between 'self-advocacy' and 'collective advocacy'.

We have looked closely at the developing **independent professional** tradition – the lawyer, the barrister, the ombudsman, increasingly the service-based advocates … What skills do they have? They could easily be tempted into different kinds of imperialism.

The roles of **service professionals** like social workers and psychologists throw up some fascinating dilemmas for advocacy because they usually have so many other conflicting roles. We have looked especially at the whistleblowers, often reviled by the services they seek to change. What should these sorts of professionals do? Can they have any kind of advocacy role without being seen as essentially destructive?

Families have been and are a primary support for people with disabilities, mostly from the female members – mothers and daughters. However, there are no free lunches and they are a source of suffering as well as liberation. The Hollywood film 'Lorenzo's Oil', the story of parents battling to find a cure for their mysteriously sick son, graphically illustrates those complexities.

The fundamental advocacy is that by people with disabilities themselves. To what extent are other forms of speaking out and on behalf of especially and paradoxically if effective – an actual hindrance? How do we balance tasks and processes in advocacy? How can we encourage individuals to recognise their oppression by others who may mean well and **speak up for themselves?** What about those who cannot speak for themselves – some of the dying; those with Alzheimer's Syndrome; those in a coma …? Are there dangers that the other forms of advocacy can drown out the drive for 'speaking for ourselves' and develop other patterns of dependency?

Citizen advocacy originates in this technical form in the United States and has been struggling for a foothold in western Europe over the last fifteen years. It involves a volunteer working with a devalued person, and trying to provide friendship and representation, mainly in the learning difficulties field. Is it simply another form of clever, able-bodied colonialism? Is it just an expensive and pretentious befriending scheme?

Peer advocacy is rapidly expanding and attempts to support individuals who have been or currently are in similar situations as the advocate – for example, a psychiatric patient represents another patient; someone who was disabled in a serious road accident helps another to get through a rehabilitation programme; to rebuild their life. Can peer advocates be effective advocates without being reclientised and reclaimed by the system they once used?

Collective advocacy is an attempt to bring together people who have similar concerns to change legislation; to press government for more resources. It is concerned with political pressure through meetings and lobbying. Increasingly it centres on the disability movement which is very disunited. It struggles to get passed a civil rights Bill for people with a disability. Can that struggle and campaign succeed and how?

Can very stigmatised groups, devalued even within the disability world, like those people with learning difficulties, become genuinely accepted?

As we shall see from this work, there has been a regrettable trend for advocacy to splinter into fragments. It is pulled in so many diverse directions; towards both specialist client groups and the different methods. So in most towns and cities, we have this delicate and fragile advocacy process battling against almost overwhelming odds and concentrated on smaller pieces like, for example, a citizen advocacy project for elderly people fighting other fragments for the scarce resources.

From: Brandon, D. with Brandon, A. and Brandon, T. (1995) *Advocacy – Power to People with Disabilities,* pp. 11–12, Birmingham: Venture Press.

Document 14a
CLUNIS INQUIRY REPORT

1.1 Terms of Reference

1.1.1 The Christopher Clunis Inquiry was set up on 27 July 1993 by the North East Thames and South East Thames Regional Health Authorities. Our terms of reference were as follows:

1. To investigate all the circumstances surrounding the admission, treatment, discharge and continuing care of Christopher Clunis between May 1992 and December 1992;
2. To identify any deficiencies in the quality and delivery of that care, as well as interagency collaboration and individual responsibilities;
3. To make recommendations for the future delivery of care including administration, treatment, discharge and continuing care to people in similar circumstances so that, as far as possible, harm to patients and the public is avoided.

From: Ritchie, J.H., Dick, D. and Lingham, R. (1994) *The Report of the Inquiry into the Care and Treatment of Christopher Clunis*, p. 1, London: HMSO.

Document 14b
CLUNIS INQUIRY REPORT

Recommendations

43.0 General observations

43.0.1 We feel that it is important to emphasise, as many witnesses have reminded us, that the vast majority of mentally ill patients are living safely in the community. Furthermore the vast majority of those who suffer from schizophrenia are also living safely in the community. But there are other patients who are not receiving the care and treatment that they require to ensure that they are safe, and that the public are protected.

43.0.2 We have identified during the course of the narrative in Section IV several deficiencies in the care of Christopher Clunis. It will be self evident how some of those deficiencies may be rectified for the future...

44.0 The principles underlying S117 Mental Health Act 1983 aftercare and the care programme approach

44.0.1 S117 Mental Health Act 1983 and the Care Programme Approach under Health Circular (90)23/LASS letter 90/11 require Health Services and Social Services to provide, in co-operation with voluntary agencies, aftercare services for patients on their discharge from hospital. S117 comes into play when the patient has been detained under the Act in hospital. The Care Programme Approach comes into play for other mentally ill patients on discharge from hospital.

44.0.2 We are concerned that doctors, nurses and social workers who are primarily responsible for providing this aftercare may not fully understand that the principles underlying S117 and Care Programme Approach aftercare are the same. We therefore set out the common principles as we understand them. Although a great deal of very helpful guidance has been published by the Department of Health and others as to the way the Care Programme should work, we are driven to say that we found that the terms in which such advice has been given, was (*sic*) often difficult to understand and couched in unhelpful jargon. We are sure that it is in everyone's interests; that is in the interests of the patient, those who care for the patient, the patient's relatives and the general public, that official guidance should try to be clear and simple. We suggest the following recommendations as a guide to aftercare.

44.0.3 Recommendations
(i) The aftercare needs of each individual patient must be assessed by health and social services before the patient is discharged into the community. Such assessment must take into account the patient's own wishes and choices.

(ii) A plan of care must be formulated for each individual patient, under the direction of the Consultant Psychiatrist under whose care the patient has been admitted.

(iii) The plan must be formulated by all those who will afterwards be responsible for providing any part of the aftercare, so that the plan is made by a team of people who work in a variety of different fields. Such a team for convenience is called the multi-disciplinary team. The aftercare plan must be recorded in detail and a copy of the plan must be given to the patient and to all those who are to provide care.

(iv) The plan of care must fully consider and provide for both the immediate and long term needs of the patient.

(v) The Consultant Psychiatrist with responsibility for the patient must assess, together with the multi-disciplinary team, the risk of the patient harming himself or others.

(vi) Members of the multi-disciplinary team should be aware that aftercare is not provided by medication alone, although it is obviously a useful part of the armoury. There is always a need to help the patient come to terms with his illness and for the patient to have proper contact with those people who will be providing him with aftercare.

(vii) A keyworker must be agreed who will act to coordinate the care that has been planned by the multi-disciplinary team.

(viii) All members of the team should be alerted to signs and symptoms in the patient which may indicate that the patient is likely to relapse. Such signs and symptoms may be identified by the doctors but may also be identified by the patient himself or his relatives or friends. Non compliance with medication should be recognised as a significant pointer to a relapse.

(ix) The aftercare which is provided must be properly coordinated and supervised; it is severely to the patient's detriment if each member of the team acts in isolation. The Consultant Psychiatrist and Care Manager from social services must together be responsible for supervising aftercare.

(x) It is essential that each member of the team who is providing care for the patient responds effectively to signs and symptoms which suggest that the patient is likely to relapse. Help which can be given before a crisis develops is more beneficial to the patient than the care that can be provided once the patient is in crisis.

(xi) When the patient moves from the district where he has previously been receiving care, responsibility for his aftercare should be formally transferred to the services responsible for his care in the district to which he moves.

(xii) Although Health and Social Services often have boundaries and catchment areas which do not overlap, proper co-operation between those who are providing care is likely to resolve any potential problems. Catchment areas should never be allowed to interfere with proper care in the community.

(xiii) It is essential that the aftercare for patients is properly monitored by Health and Social Services.

(xiv) Any area of unmet need which is identified by the multi-disciplinary team must be brought to the attention of the managers of the Health and Social Services.

From: Ritchie, J.H., Dick, D. and Lingham, R. (1994) *The Report of the Inquiry into the Care and Treatment of Christopher Clunis*, pp. 109–111, London: HMSO.

Document 15
BROADMOOR

From 1863 to 1948, Broadmoor was run directly by the Home Office, as with prisons. When the National Health Service was set up, Broadmoor Criminal Lunatic Asylum was handed over to the Department of Health, which promptly renamed it Broadmoor Special Institution. The stamp remained however; the august *Times* took no notice of this change of labels and referred to it as a criminal lunatic asylum till 1953. In 1959, Broadmoor was renamed yet again and became Broadmoor Special Hospital. This time it took *The Times* ten years to refer to it as a special hospital. (3) In 1972, there were plans to re-name the hospital yet again. Sir Keith Joseph, Secretary of State at the time, elected not to do so. But while all this labelling and delabelling was in hand, the political relationship between Broadmoor and government remained the same. It was directly controlled by the Department. Ordinary psychiatric hospitals report to their Area Health Authority, Broadmoor has to justify its policies to the Department of Health which maintains a small special hospitals section. Dr. McGrath has said that he likes that direct relationship because it means he can get decisions from the people in power fast. But, again, there is a feeling that this odd administrative relationship has too many negative consequences. Broadmoor is too close to the Department for the Department to offer effective criticism. The Department does not even employ a full time forensic psychiatrist to monitor what is happening at Broadmoor though it does, from time to time, consult with leading outside experts, especially at the Maudsley. The practice of reporting directly to the Department adds further to the isolation of the special hospital from the rest of psychiatry and to the insularity of its thinking.

The need for effective criticism on Broadmoor is especially obvious because all other hospitals have a board of governors. Their management teams, made up from all the different disciplines, must account to the governors for the way the hospital is being run. The governors are local men and women, usually with time to visit the hospital frequently and who have some sense of local feelings about it. The governors themselves have to account to their Area Health Authority. Without wishing to claim that this system is perfect or always works well, it is not hard to see that it obliges a hospital to justify itself more. It is more likely to scrutinise its own work, its own ideas, its own prejudices – and especially so during a period, such as the 1970s, when psychiatry has been very controversial. Paradoxically, Broadmoor used to have a similar body, its Board of Control. The Physician Superintendent had to submit an annual report to it. (4) The Board forced one Superintendent to stop using solitary confinements to an almost maniacal extent in the 1910's. That was the most evident use of its power but there were others. Yet a consequence of the 1959 Mental Health Act was to abolish Broadmoor's Board of Control.

The ensuing lack of broad accountability for the hospital becomes worrying not least in the Department of Health's apparent satisfaction with the official complaints procedure. In any institution like Broadmoor, patients must feel that it is safe to complain. But both staff and patients argue that there is little point in pressing complaints. If you make a complaint against a nurse, it will be investigated often in effect by his fellow nurses, a Nursing Officer and a Senior Nursing Officer. Two former nurses have alleged that it was not merely difficult for patients to get a fair hearing but also that there was fear of reprisals. In Chapter Four, I outline a number of cases where patients were afraid that making a formal complaint might land them in trouble or delay their hopes of release. Small changes have been introduced recently but there is no independent factor in investigating complaints. The Department of Health does investigate serious allegations but I have already argued that its relationship with the hospital is too close and too uncritical. In the last eight years, according to MIND, the Department has not upheld one complaint.

The Prison Officers Association also believes that the present situation is unsatisfactory. After the *Rampton* programme, made by Yorkshire Television, was screened, the Broadmoor branch of the POA issued a memo to its members, dated 21st June 1979. It noted that the Department of Health was eager to, 'have its collective posteria covered', and warned, '... *we cannot, nor should not, allow ourselves to fall into the complacency that our colleagues at Rampton have been caught up in'*. The memo further argues that the Police should be called in to deal with any allegation of physical ill-treatment. The present system, 'provides a facility for management to cover up crimes or to do the job of the Police for it'. The Prison Officers branch suggest that both are undesirable but adds that if the Police are called in and do not press charges, 'no ill treatment is provable', so, the management will not be able to use its own disciplinary procedures against an accused nurse. The memo adds confidently that if all allegations of ill-treatment had to go to the Police, '*it is unlikely there ever would have been a Rampton allegations programme (with a resultant Police investigation'*. It also advises that there is no way to insure totally against, 'intrusion by outside agencies, adverse publicity and, ultimately, Police investigation. *All we can do is adopt the strongest defence posture'*.

This memo reveals a deep distrust of the management and an obsession with how to outflank complaints. The notion of bringing in the police scuppers the pretensions of the Department of Health to act as judges and makes procedures extraformal. For the police to press a charge, there must be evidence of actual physical assault at least. Callous treatment or neglect, which constitute poor nursing, are not police matters. The memo betrays, in the end, much defensiveness and a certain joy in tactics.

References

3. Hamilton, John (1980) 'The Development of Broadmoor', *Bulletin of the Royal College of Psychiatrists*, September 1980.
4. Dell, Suzanne (1980) 'The Transfer of Special Hospital Patients to NHS Hospitals', *British Journal of Psychiatry*, 136, pp. 222–34.
5. MacKeith, James and Godden, Eric. *A Survey of Special Hospital Patients from S.E. Thames Region* (unpublished import).

From: Cohen, D. (undated) *Broadmoor*, pp. 21–23, London: Psychology News Press.

(Select list from references in book; published by HMSO, London except where stated)

1854   Reformatory Schools (Youthful Offenders) Act
1857   Industrial Schools and Reformatory Schools Act
1882   Criminal Lunacy (Departmental) Commission, *Report of the Commission to Inquire into the Subject of Criminal Lunacy*, Cmnd 3418
1894   Departmental Committee, *Report from the Departmental Committee on Prisons*, Cmnd 7702 (Gladstone Report), Parliamentary Papers (1895), vol.56
1911   Official Secrets Act
1920   Blind Persons Act
1925   Home Office Departmental Committee on the Treatment of Young Offenders (Molony Committee)
1934   Poor Law Amendment Act
1942   Beveridge, W.H., *Social Insurance and Allied Services*, Cmnd 6404
1942   Beveridge, W.H., *Full Employment in a Free Society*, Allen and Unwin, London
1943   White Paper *Educational Reconstruction*
1944   Education Act
1944   White Paper *Employment Policy*
1944   White Paper *A National Health Service*
1944   White Paper *Social Insurance*
1945   *Report by Sir Walter Monckton on the Circumstances which Led to the Boarding out of Dennis and Terence O'Neill at Bank Farm, Miserley and the Steps Taken to Supervise their Welfare,* Cmnd 6636
1946   *Report of the Care of Children Committee* (Curtis Report), Cmnd 6922
1947   Welfare Services Act
1948   Beveridge, W.H., *Voluntary Action: a Report of Methods of Social Advance*
1948   Children Act
1948   Criminal Justice Act
1948   Mental Health Act (Northern Ireland), HMSO, Belfast
1948   National Assistance Act
1951   Committee on Medical Auxiliaries (Cape Committee), HMSO, Edinburgh Committee on Social Workers in the

Mental Health Services (Mackintosh Committee 1951), HMSO, Edinburgh

1957   Percy Commission

1958   Disabled Persons (Employment) Act

1959   Mental Health Act

1959   *Report on Social Workers in the Local Authority Health and Welfare Services* (Younghusband Report)

1960   *Report of the Committee on Children and Young Persons* (Ingleby Report), Cmnd 1191

1961   Criminal Justice Act

1962   Health Visitors' and Social Workers' Training Act

1962   Ministry of Health, *A Hospital Plan for England and Wales*

1962   *Report of the Advisory Council on the Treatment of Offenders* (Advisory Council on the Treatment of Offenders, Non-Residential Treatment of Offenders under 21)

1963   Children Act

1963   Children and Young Persons Act

1963   Local Government Act

1963   Ministry of Health and Welfare, *The Development of Community Care,* Cmnd 1973

1963   *Report on the Prevention of Neglect of Children in their Own Homes* (McBoyle Report), HMSO, Edinburgh

1964   *Children and Young Persons: Scotland* (Kilbrandon Report), Cmnd 2306, HMSO, Edinburgh

1964   Scottish Home and Health Department/Scottish Education Department, *Children and Young Persons, Scotland, Report* (Kilbrandon Report), HMSO, Edinburgh

1965   Home Office, *The Child, the Family and the Young Offender*, White Paper, Cmnd 2742

1966   Home Office, *Report of the Inquiry into Prison Escapes and Security* (Mountbatten Report), Cmnd 3175

1966   White Paper *Social Work and the Community*, HMSO, Edinburgh

1968   Report of the Committee on Local Authority and Allied Personal Social Services (Seebohm Report), Cmnd 3703

1968   Health Services and Public Health Act

1968   Home Office, *Children in Trouble* White Paper

1968   Medicines Act

1968   Social Work (Scotland) Act, HMSO, Edinburgh

1969   Family Law Reform Act

1969   Redcliffe, Maud, Lord (chairman) Royal Commission on Local Government in England 1966-69, vol.1 (Report), Cmnd 4040

1969   Wheatley, Lord (chairman) Royal Commission on Local Government in Scotland (Wheatley Report), Cmnd 4150, HMSO, Edinburgh

1970   Chronically Sick and Disabled Persons Act

1970 Local Authorities (Goods and Services) Act
1970 Local Authorities Social Services Act
1970 Review Body on Local Government in Northern Ireland, Cmnd 540 (NI) (Macrory Report), HMSO, Belfast
1970 Social Services Act
1970 White Paper *Reform of Local Government in England,* Cmnd 4276
1971 DHSS, *Better Services for the Mentally Handicapped*
1971 Guardianship of Minors Act
1971 Misuse of Drugs Act
1972 Committee of Inquiry into the Selection, Development and Management of Staff in Children's Homes Choosing with Care (Warner Report)
1972 Criminal Justice Act
1972 Departmental Committee on the Adoption of Children (Houghton Committee)
1972 Health and Social Services (Northern Ireland) Order, HMSO, Belfast
1972 Local Government Act
1973 Council of Europe, *Council of Europe Standard Minimum Rules for the Treatment of Prisoners,* Strasbourg
1973 Guardianship Act
1973 Local Government (Scotland) Act, HMSO, Edinburgh
1973 Matrimonial Causes etc Act
1973 National Health Service Reorganisation Act
1974 Department of Health and Social Security, *Revised Report of the Working Party on Security in NHS Psychiatric Hospitals* (Glancy Report), DHSS, London
1974 Health and Safety at Work etc. Act
1974 Home Office/Department of Health and Social Security, *Interim Report of the Committee on Mentally Abnormal Offenders,* Cmnd 5678
1974 *Report of the Committee of Inquiry into the Care and Supervision Provided in Relation to Maria Colwell*
1975 Adoptions Act
1975 DHSS, *Better Services for the Mentally Ill*
1975 Home Office/Department of Health and Social Security, *Report of the Committee on Mentally Abnormal Offenders,* (Butler Report), Cmnd 6244
1975 House of Commons, *Eleventh Report from the Expenditure Committee: Children and Young Persons Act 1969* (Social Services Sub-Committee, Chairman R. Short), 2 vols,. HC 534–1, 534–11
1976 Legitimacy Act
1976 Race Relations Act
1976 Supplementary Benefits Act
1977 Criminal Law Act

1977   Wolfenden Report, *The Future of Voluntary Organisations,*
       Croom Helm, London
1978   Domestic Proceedings and Magistrates' Courts Act
1979   Customs and Excise Management Act
1979   Jay Report, *Report of the Committee of Inquiry into Mental
       Handicap Nursing and Care,* Cmnd 7468
1980   Child Care Act
1980   DHSS, *Mental Handicap: Progress, Problems and Priorities.*
       A review of mental handicap services in England since the
       1971 White Paper
1980   Foster Children Act
1980   *Report of All-party Parliamentary Committee on Mental
       Health* (Broadmoor Report), reported in *The Guardian,
       The Times,* 1 August
1980   White Paper *Young Adult Offenders*
1981   DHSS, *Care in Action: a Handbook of Policies and
       Priorities for the Health and Personal Social Services in
       England*
1981   DHSS, *Care in the Community. A Consultative Document
       on Moving Resources for Care in England*
1981   DHSS, *Growing Older,* Cmnd 8173
1981   Education Act
1982   Barclay Report, *Social Workers: Their Roles and Tasks,*
       National Institute for Social Work/Bedford Square Press,
       London
1982   Children's Homes Act
1982   Criminal Justice Act
1982   Local Government Finance Act
1982   Welsh Office, *The Development of Community Care for
       Mentally Handicapped People.* Report of the All-Wales
       Working Party on Services for Mentally Handicapped
       People, Welsh Office, Cardiff
1983   Health and Social Services Adjudications Act
1983   Mental Health Act
1983   Social Security Adjudications Act
1984   Data Protection Act
1984   Food Act
1984   Police and Criminal Evidence Act
1984   Registered Homes Act
1984   *Report to the House of Commons Social Services Committee
       Enquiring into Children in Care*
1985   Child Abduction and Custody Act
1985   DHSS, Review of Child Care Law
1985   Home Office, *Report of the Committee on the Prison
       Disciplinary System* (Prior Report), Cmnd 9641
1985   Prosecution of Offences Act
1985   Review of Child Care Law

1985 Scottish Home and Health Department, *Report of the Review of Suicide Precautions at HM Detention Centre and HM Young Offenders Institution, Glenochil*
1985 Sporting Events (Control of Alcohol etc.) Act
1986 Audit Commission, *Making a Reality of Community Care*
1986 Children and Young Persons (Amendment) Act
1986 Disabled Persons (Services, Consultation and Representation) Act
1986 Drug Trafficking Offences Act
1986 Family Law Act
1986 Public Order Act
1986 Social Services Inspectorate, *Inspection of the Implementation of the Registered Homes Act 1984 Stage 1: the Impact on Registration Authorities*, Department of Health and Social Security, London
1986 Widdicombe Report, *The Conduct of Local Authority Business*, Cmnd 9797
1987 Access to Personal Files Act
1987 Department of Health, *The Law on Child Care and Family Services*
1987 Family Law Reform Act
1987 Home Office, *A Review of Prisoners' Complaints*, report by HM Chief Inspector of Prisons
1987 Social Services Inspectorate, *From Home Help to Home Care: an Analysis of Policy, Resourcing and Service Management*
1987 White Paper *The Law on Child Care and Family Services*
1988 Department of Health and Social Security, *Community Care: an Agenda for Action* (Griffiths Report)
1988 Education Reform Act
1988 Firearms Act
1988 Home Office, *The Parole System in England and Wales*, Report of the Review Committee (Carlisle Report), Cmnd 532
1988 *Punishment, Custody and the Community*, Green Paper, Cmnd 424
1988 Law Commission, *Review of Child Care Law: Guardianship and Custody*
1988 Local Government Act
1988 *Report of the Inquiry into Child Abuse in Cleveland,* Cmnd 412
1988 SSI, *Managing Policy Change in Home Help Services*
1989 Children Act
1989 Department of Health, *Case Management in Community Care*
1989 Local Government and Housing Act
1989 White Paper *Caring for People*

1989   Department of Health, White Paper *Working for Patients*, Cmnd 855

1989   SSI, *Managing Home Care in Metropolitan Districts*

1989   Audit Commission, *The Probation Service: Promoting Value for Money*

1989   Department of Health, *Caring for People: Community Care in the Next Decade and Beyond*, Cmnd 849

1990   Human Fertilisation and Embryology Act

1990   NHS and Community Care Act

1990   Report of All Party Commission on Citizenship

1990   SSI, *Inspecting Home Care Services: a Guide to the SSI Method*

1991   The Registered Homes (Amendment) Act

1991   Child Support Act

1991   Criminal Justice Act

1991   Department of Health, Social Services Inspectorate, *Care Management and Assessment,* Practitioners' Guide

1991   Department of Health, Social Services Inspectorate, Scottish Office, *Social Work*

1991   Department of Health, *Implementing Community Care: Purchaser, Commissioner and Provider Roles*

1991   Department of the Environment, *The Structure of Local Government in England,* DoE, London

1991   Levy, A. and Kahan, B. *The Pindown Experience and the Protection of Children: the Report of the Staffordshire Child Care Inquiry 1990*, Stafford, Staffordshire County Council

1991   Prime Minister's Office, *The Citizen's Charter: Raising the Standard,* Cmnd 1599

1991   Woolf, Lord Justice, *Prison Disturbances April 1990: Report of an Inquiry by the Rt. Hon Lord Justice Woolf (Parts I and II) and His Honour Judge Stephen Tumin (Part II)*, Cmnd 1456

1992   *Policy Guidance to the Local Government Commission for England*

1992   Department of Health, *The Health of the Nation – a Strategy for Health in England*, Cmnd 1986

1992   Home Office, the Department of Health and the Welsh Office, *National Standards for the Supervision of Offenders in the Community*

1992   Local Government Act

1992   Report of the Inquiry into the Removal of Children from Orkney in February 1991, House of Commons ([HC]; 195, 1992–93)

1993   Department of Health, *Diversification and the Independent Care Sector*

1993   Home Affairs Committee, *Juvenile Offenders*, 6th Report

1993 Social Services Inspectorate/Department of Health, *Report of an Inspection of Management and Provision of Social Work in the Three Special Hospitals, July–September 1993*, Department of Health, London

1993 SSI *No Longer Afraid: the Safeguard of Older People in Domestic Settings*

1993 SSI/Department of Health, *Social Services Department Inspection Units: the First 18 Months, a Report on 10 Inspection Units Inspected in 1992/1993*, Department of Health, London

1994 Social Services Inspectorate, *Evaluating Child Protection Services: Findings and Issues*

1994 Social Services Inspectorate/Department of Health, *Social Services Inspection Units: Report of an Inspection of the Work of Inspection Units in 27 Local Authorities*

1994 Audit Commission, *Taking Stock: Progress with Care in the Community*

1994 Audit Commission, *Seen But Not Heard: Coordinating Community Child Health and Social Services for Children in Need*

1994 Criminal Justice and Public Order Act

1994 Department of Health, *Review of the Children Act 1989* (Second Annual Review)

1994 Dews, V. and Watts, J., *Review of Probation Officer Recruitment and Qualifying Training* (Dews Report)

1994 House of Commons Public Accounts Committee, *Looking After the Affairs of People with Mental Incapacity: 39th Report of the Committee of Public Accounts*

1994 La Fontaine, J., *The Extent and Nature of Organised Ritual Abuse*

1994 Ritchie, J.H., Dick, D. and Lingham, R., *The Report of the Inquiry into the Care and Treatment of Christopher Clunis*

1994 Social Services Inspectorate, *Responding to Youth Crime: Findings through Inspections of Youth Justice Services in Five Local Authorities Departments*

1995 Blom-Cooper, L., Hally, H. and Murphy, E., *The Falling Shadow: One Patient's Mental Health Care 1978–1993*, Duckworth, London.

1995 Carers (Recognition and Services) Act

1995 Davies, N., Lingham, R., Prior, C. and Sims, A., *Report of the Inquiry into the Circumstances Leading to the Death of Jonathan Newby on 9th October 1993 in Oxford*, Oxfordshire Health Authority, Oxford

1995 Disability Discrimination Act

SELECT BIBLIOGRAPHY

Adams, R. (1991) *Protests by Pupils: Empowerment, Schooling and the State*, Basingstoke: Falmer Press.

Adams, R. (1994) *Prison Riots in Britain and the USA*, London: Macmillan.

Adams, R. (1996) *Social Work and Empowerment*, London: BASW/Macmillan.

Adams, R. (1997) *Quality Social Work*, Basingstoke: Macmillan.

Adams, R. (forthcoming) *The Abuses of Punishment*, Basingstoke: Macmillan

Adams, R., Allard, S, Baldwin, J. and Thomas, J. (1981) *A Measure of Diversion? Case Studies in Intermediate Treatment*, Leicester: National Youth Bureau.

Adler, R. and Dearling, A. (1986) Children's rights: a Scottish perspective, in Franklin, B. (ed.), *The Rights of Children*, 205–229, London: Blackwell.

Adoption Act 1976

Allen, N. (1992) *Making Sense of the Children Act: a Guide for the Social and Welfare Services*, London: Longman.

Aries, P. *L'enfant a la Vie Familiale dans l'Ancien Regime*, Paris, translated into English as *Centuries of Childhood*, Jonathan Cape, London, 1962.

Arnold, E. (1987) *Whose Child? The Report of the Public Inquiry into the Death of Tyra Henry*, London: Borough of Lambeth.

Bean, P. and Melville, J. (1990) *Lost Children of the Empire*, London: Unwin Hyman.

Beresford, P. and Croft, S. (1993) *Citizen Involvement: a Practical Guide for Change*, London: Macmillan.

Blackburn, R. (ed.) (1991) *After the Fall*, London: Verso.

Blag, H. and Smith, D. (1989) *Crime, Penal Policy and Social Work*, London: Longman.

Booth, T. (1985) *Home Truths: Older People's Homes and the Outcomes of Care*, Aldershot: Gower.

Borrie, G. and Atkinson, A.B. (1994) *Social Justice: Strategies for National Renewal*, Report of the Commission on Social Justice (Borrie Report), London: Vintage.

Bottomley, K. and Pease, K. (1986) *Crime and Punishment: Interpreting the Data*, Milton Keynes: Open University Press.

Bottoms, A.E. (1974) On the decriminalisation of English juvenile courts, in Hood R. (ed.), *Crime, Criminology and Public Policy: Essays in Honour of Sir Leon Radzinowicz*, 319–345, London: Heinemann.

Bowlby, J. (1965) *Child Care and the Growth of Love*, 2nd edn, Harmondsworth: Pelican.

Brandon, D. (1995) *Advocacy*, Birmingham: Venture Press.

Brayne, H. and Martin, G. (1993) *Law for Social Workers*, 3rd edn, London: Blackstone Press.

Brearley, C.P. and Hall, M.R.P. (1982) *Risk and Ageing*, London: Routledge and Kegan Paul.

Brewer, C. and Lait, J. (1980) *Can Social Work Survive?* London: Temple Smith.

Brody, S. (1976) *The Effectiveness of Sentencing: a Review of the Literature*, Home Office Research and Planning Unit, London: HMSO.

Brown, H. and Smith, H. (1992) *Normalisation: a Reader for the Nineties*, London: Routledge.

Campbell, B. (1984) *Wigan Pier Revisited: Poverty and Politics in the 80s*, London: Virago.

Care Sector Consortium (1991) *National Occupational Standards for Working with Young Children and Their Families*, London: HMSO.

Care Sector Consortium (1992) *National Occupational Standards for Care*, London: HMSO.

Carlebach, J. (1970) *Caring for Children in Trouble*, London: Routledge and Kegan Paul.

Carpenter, M. (1851) *Reformatory Schools for the Children of the Perishing and Dangerous Classes and for Juvenile Offenders*, London: Gelpin; reprinted, London: Woburn Press, 1968.

Casale, S. (1984) *Minimum Standards for Prison Establishments*, London: NACRO.

CCETSW Paper 30 (1995) *Rules and Requirements for the Diploma in Social Work*, London: CCETSW.

Central Statistical Office (1982), *Social Trends 13*, London: HMSO.

Challis, D.J. and Davies, B. (1986) *Case Management in Community Care: an Evaluated Experiment in the Home Care of the Elderly*, Aldershot: Gower.

Challis, D.J. and Davies, B.P. (1980) A new approach to community care of the elderly, *British Journal of Social Work*, vol. 10, no.1, 1–18.

Challis, D.J. and Davies, B.P. (1985) Long-term care of the elderly: the community care scheme, *British Journal of Social Work*, vol.15, no.6, 563–579.

Clare, A. (1976) *Psychiatry in Dissent,* London: Tavistock.

Clough, R. (1981) *Old Age Homes*, London: Allen and Unwin.

Clough, R. (1982) *Residential Work*, London: BASW/Macmillan.

Cohen, S. and Taylor, L. (1972) *Psychological Survival: the Experience of Long Term Imprisonment*, Harmondsworth: Penguin.

Cooper, J (1983) *The Creation of the British Personal Social Services 1962–1974*, London: Heinemann Educational Books.

Coulshed, V. (1990) *Management in Social Work*, London: Macmillan.

Croft, S. and Beresford, P. (1989) User-involvement, Citizenship and Social Policy, *Critical Social Policy*, issue 26, autumn, 5–18.

Culpitt, I. (1992) *Welfare and Citizenship, Beyond the Crisis of the Welfare State?* London: Sage.

Darby, J. and Williamson, A. (1978) *Violence and the Social Services in Northern Ireland*, London: Heinemann.

Darvill, G. and Smale, G. (eds) (1990) *Partners in Empowerment: Networks of Innovation in Social Work*, London: NISW.

Davies, M. (1981) *The Essential Social Worker*, London: Heinemann/Community Care.

Davies, B. (1992) *Care Management, Equity and Efficiency: the International Experience*, Canterbury, Kent: PSSRU.

Department of Health (1995a) *Child Protection: Messages from Research*, London: HMSO.

Department of Health (1995b) *Health and Personal Social Services Statistics for England*, 1995 Edition, London: HMSO.

Donnison, D., Jay P. and Stewart, M. (1962) *The Ingleby Report: Three Critical Essays* (Fabian Research Series, no.231), London: Fabian Society.

Doyle, C. (1990) *Working with Abused Children*, London: Macmillan/BASW.

Elcock, H. (1993), Local government, in Farnham, D. and Horton, S. (eds), *Managing the New Public Services*, 150–171, London: Macmillan.

Fahlberg, V. (1981) *Attachment and Separation*, London: British Association of Adoption and Fostering (BAFF).

Farnham, D. and Horton, S. (eds) (1993) *Managing the New Public Services*, London: Macmillan.

Fernando, S. (1991) *Mental Health, Race and Culture*, London: Macmillan.

Fitzgerald, M. (1977) *Prisoners in Revolt*, Harmondsworth: Penguin.

Garland, D. (ed.) *Justice, Guilt and Forgiveness in the Penal System*, Paper no.18, Centre for Theology and Public Issues, Edinburgh: Edinburgh University.

Heidensohn, F. (1989) *Crime and Society*, London: Macmillan.

Henwood, M. (1994) *Fit for Change: Snapshots of the Community Care Reform One Year On*, London: Nuffield/Kings Fund.

Heron, A. and Myers, M. (1983) *Intellectual Impairment: the Battle against Handicap*, London: Academic Press.

Hill, M. (1993) *The Welfare State in Britain: a Political History since 1945*, Aldershot: Edward Elgar.

Hirst, P. (1994) *Associative Democracy: New Forms of Economic and Social Governance*, Oxford: Polity Press.

Hockey, J. and James, A. (1993) *Growing Up and Growing Old – Ageing and Dependency in the Life Course*, London: Sage.

Hoggett, B. (1993) *Parents and Children: the Law of Parental Responsibility*, 4th edn, London: Sweet and Maxwell.

Hollis, F. (1948) *Social Casework in Practice*, New York: Family Service Association of America.

Holman, B. (1988) *Putting Children First: Prevention and Child Care*, London: Macmillan and the Children's Society.

Hood, R. (ed.) (1974) *Crime, Criminology and Public Policy: Essays in Honour of Sir Leon Radzinowicz*, London: Heinemann.

Howe, A. (1994) *Punish and Critique: Towards a Feminist Analysis of Penalty*, London: Routledge.

Howe, D. (1986) The segregation of women and their work in the personal social services, *Critical Social Policy*, issue 15, spring, 21–35.

Hoyles, M. (ed.) (1979) *Changing Childhood*, London: Writers and Readers Co-operative.

Hudson, B.A. (1993) *Penal Policy and Social Justice*, London: Macmillan.

Hugman, R. (1994) *Ageing and the Care of Older People in Europe*, London: Macmillan.

Jamieson, A. and Illsley, R. (eds) (1990) *Contrasting European Policies for the Care of Older People*, Aldershot: Avebury.

Jeffs, A. (1979) *Young People and the Youth Service,* London: Routledge and Kegan Paul.

Jones, K. (1991) *The Making of Social Policy in Britain 1830–1990,* London: Athlone.

Jones, K., Brown, J., Cunningham, W.J., Roberts, J. and Williams, P. (1975) *Opening the Door: a Study of New Policies for the Mentally Handicapped*, London: Routledge and Kegan Paul.

Kahan, B. (1970) The child care service, in Townsend, P. *et al.*, *The Fifth Social Service: a Critical Analysis of the Seebohm Proposals*, London: Fabian Society.

Kahan, B. (1991) *Residential care and education in Great Britain*, in Gottesmann, M. (ed.), *Residential Child Care: an International Reader*, 138–156, London: Whiting and Birch.

King, R., and Morgan, R. (1976) *A Taste of Prison: Custodial Conditions for Trial and Remand Prisoners*, London: Routledge and Kegan Paul.

King's Fund Centre (1980) *An Ordinary Life. Comprehensive Locally-based Residential Services for Mentally Handicapped People*, London: King's Fund Centre.

Knapp, M. (1989) Private and voluntary welfare, in McCarthy, M. (ed.) *The New Politics of Welfare: an Agenda for the 1990s?*, 225–252, London: Macmillan.

Korman, N. and Glennerster, H. (1990) *Hospital Closure*, Milton Keynes: Open University Press.

Kübler-Ross, E. (1982) *Living with Death and Dying*, London: Souvenir Press.

Kuhn, T.S. (1970) *The Structure of Scientific Revolutions*, 2nd edn, Chicago: University of Chicago Press.

La Fontaine, J. (1990), *Child Sexual Abuse*, Cambridge: Polity Press.

Laing, R.D. (1962) *The Divided Self*, Harmondsworth: Penguin.

Le Grand, J. and Bartlett, W. (eds) (1993) *Quasi-Markets and Social Policy*, London: Macmillan.

Lee, P. and Raban, C. (1988) *Welfare Theory and Social Policy, Reform or Revolution?*, London: Sage.

Lipsky, M. (1980) *Street Level Bureaucracy*, London: Russell Sage.

Lister, R. (1991) Citizenship engendered, *Critical Social Policy*, issue 32, autumn, 65–71.

Maguire, M., Vagg, J. and Morgan, R. (eds) (1985) *Accountability and Prisons: Opening Up a Closed World*, London: Tavistock.

Maidment, R. and Thompson, G. (eds) (1993) *Managing the United Kingdom, an Introduction to its Political Economy and Public Policy*, London: Open University, Sage.

Mann, K. (1994) Watching the defectives: observers of the underclass in the USA, Britain and Australia, *Critical Social Policy*, issue 41, autumn, 79–99.

Marquand, D. (1994) No time for giant-killing, *The Guardian*, 24 October, 20.

Marris, P. (1974) *Loss and Change*, London: Routledge and Kegan Paul.

Marshall, T.H. (1967) *Social Policy*, revised edition, London: Hutchinson.

May, D. (1971) Delinquency control and the treatment model: some implications of recent legislation, *British Journal of Criminology*, vol.11, no.4, 359–370.

Mayo, M. (1994) *Communities and Caring: the Mixed Economy of Welfare*, London: Macmillan.

McCarthy, M. (ed.) (1989) *The New Politics of Welfare: an Agenda for the 1990s?* London: Macmillan.

Mearns, R. and Smith, R. (1994) *Community Care: Policy and Practice*, London: Macmillan.

Miedzian, M. (1992) *Boys will be Boys: Breaking the Link Between Masculinity and Violence*, London: Virago.

Millhan, S., Bullock, R. and Hosie, K. (1978) *Locking up Children: Secure Provision within the Child Care System*, Farnborough: Saxon House.

Mishra, R. (1986) *The Welfare State in Crisis: Social Thought and Social Change*, Brighton: Harvester Press.

Mishra, R. (1990) *The Welfare State in Capitalist Society: Policies of Retrenchment and Maintenance in Europe, North America and Australia*, Hemel Hempstead: Harvester Wheatsheaf.

Morris, P. (1969) *Put Away: a Sociological Study of Institutions for the Mentally Retarded*, London: Routledge and Kegan Paul.

Morris, J. (1990) *Our Homes Our Rights: Housing, Independent Living and Physically Disabled People*, London: Shelter.

Morris, J. (1994) Community care or independent living? *Critical Social Policy*, issue 40, vol.14, no.1, 24–45.

NISW (1988a) *Residential Care: a Positive Choice*, Independent Review of Residential Care (Wagner Report), London: HMSO.

NISW (1988b) *Residential Care: the Research Reviewed*, Literature surveys commissioned by the Independent Review of Residential Care (Wagner Report Part II), London: HMSO.

Oliver, M. (1990) *The Politics of Disablement. Critical Texts in Social Work and the Welfare State*, London: Macmillan.

Packman, J. (1975) *The Child's Generation: Childcare Policy from Curtis to Houghton*, Oxford: Blackwell.

Parkinson, L. (1987) *Separation, Divorce and Families*, London: BASW/ Macmillan.

Parry, N., Rustin, M., and Satyamurti, C. (eds) (1979) *Social Work, Welfare and the State*, London: Edward Arnold.

Parton, N. (1985) *The Politics of Child Abuse*, Basingstoke: Macmillan.

Parton, N. (1991) *Governing the Family*, Basingstoke: Macmillan.

Pearson, G. (1983) *Hooligan: a History of Respectable Fears*, London: Macmillan.

Pilgrim, D and Rogers, A. (1989) Radical mental health policy, *Critical Social Policy*, issue 25, summer, 4–17.

Platt, A.M. (1969) *The Child Savers: the Invention of Delinquency*, Chicago and London: University of Chicago Press.

Player, E. and Jenkins, M. (eds) (1994) *Prisons After Woolf: Reform through Riot*, London: Routledge.

Plumb, J.H. (1973) Children: victims of time, in Plumb, J.H., *In the Light of History*, part 2, essay 5, 153–165, London: Allen Lane.

Pollock, L. (1987) *A Lasting Relationship: Parents and Children over 3 Centuries*, London: Fourth Estate.

Pringle, K. (1995) *Men, Masculinities and Social Welfare*, London: UCL Press.

Propper, C. (1993) Quasi-Markets, Contracts and Quality in Health and Social Care: the US experience, in Le Grand, J. and Bartlett, W. (eds) *Quasi-Markets and Social Policy*, 35–67, London: Macmillan.

Pugh, G. (1988) *Services for Under Fives: Developing a Co-ordinated Approach*, London: National Children's Bureau.

RADAR (1994) *Disabled People Have Rights*, London: RADAR.

Raynor, P., Smith, D. and Vanstone, M. (1994) *Effective Probation Practice*, Basingstoke: BASW/Macmillan.

Reiner, R. and Cross, M. (1991) *Beyond Law and Order: Criminal Justice Policy and Politics into the 1990s*, London: Macmillan.

Richmond, M. (1917, reprinted 1925) *Social Diagnosis*, New York: Russell Sage Foundation.

Roberts, M. (1988) *Mediation in Family Disputes*, Aldershot: Wildwood House.

Rodgers, B. and Stevenson, J. (1973) *A New Portrait of Social Work*, London: Heinemann.

Rogers, A., Pilgrim, D. and Lacey, R. (1993) *Experiencing Psychiatry: User's Views of Services*, Basingstoke: MIND and Macmillan.

Rojeck, C., Peacock, G. and Collins, S. (1988) *Social Work and Received Ideas*, London: Routledge.

Russell, D.E.H. (1986), *The Secret Trauma, Incest in the Lives of Girls and Women*, New York: Basic Books.

Rustin, M. (1979) Social work and the family, in Parry, N., Rustin, M. and Satyamurti, C. (eds) *Social Work, Welfare and the State*, 140–160, London: Edward Arnold.

Rutherford, A. (1983) *Prisons and the Process of Justice*, London: Heinemann,.

Rutherford, A. (1992) *Growing out of Crime: the New Era*, Winchester: Waterside Press.

Rutter, M. (1972) *Maternal Deprivation Reassessed*, Harmondsworth: Penguin.

Ryan, M. and Ward, T. (1989) *Privatization and the Penal System: the American Experience and the Debate in Britain*, Milton Keynes: Open University Press.

Satyamurti, C. (1981) *Occupational Survival: the Case of the Local Authority Social Worker*, Oxford: Blackwell.

Saunders, C. (1959) *Care of the Dying*, London: Macmillan.

Scull, A. (1977) *Decarceration*, Englewood Cliffs, New Jersey: Prentice Hall.

Shaw, R. (1992) *Prisoners' Children: What are the Issues?* London: Routledge.

Shearer, A. (1972) *Normalisation?* Discussion paper no.3, London: Campaign for the Mentally Handicapped.

Sim, J. (1990) *Medical Power in Prisons: the Prison Medical Service in England 1774–1989*, Milton Keynes: Open University Press.

Smale, G. and Tuson, G. (1990) Community social work: foundation for the 1990s and beyond, in Darvill, G., *Partners in Empowerment: the Networks of Innovation in Social Work*, London: National Institute for Social Work.

Smale, G. and Tuson, G. (1993) *Empowerment, Assessment, Care Management and the Skilled Worker*, London: HMSO.

Social Services Inspectorate (1991) *Women in Social Services: a Neglected Resource*, London: HMSO.

Solomon, J. (1987) *Holding the Reins: Parents, Children and Nannies in Their Search for Domestic Salvation*, London: Fontana/Collins.

Sontag, S. (1991) *Illness as Metaphor* and *AIDS and its Metaphors*, Harmondsworth: Penguin.

Stedman Jones, G. (1984) *Outcast London, a Study in the Relationship between Classes in Victorian Society*, Harmondsworth: Penguin.

Stein, M. and Carey, K. (1986) *Leaving Care*, Oxford: Blackwell.

Stenson, K. and Brealey, N. (1991) Left realism in criminology and the return to consensus theory, in Reiner, R. and Cross, M. *Beyond Law and Order: Criminal Justice Policy and Politics into the 1990s*, 223–247, London: Macmillan.

Stephens, M. and Becker, S. (eds) (1994) *Police Force, Police Service: Care and Control in Britain,* London: Macmillan.

Stern, V. (1989) *Imprisoned by our Prisons: a Programme of Reform*, London: Unwin Hyman.

Stewart J.D. (1986) *The New Management of Local Government*, London: Allen and Unwin.

Taylor, D. (1989) Citizenship and social power, *Critical Social Policy,* issue 26, autumn, 19–31

Taylor, I., Walton, P. and Young, J. (1973) *The New Criminology: for a Social Theory of Deviance*, London: Routledge and Kegan Paul.

Thomas, T. (1993) *The Police and Social Workers*, 2nd edn, Aldershot: Gower.

Thornton, D., Curran, L., Grayson, D. and Holloway, V. (1984) *Tougher Regimes in Detention Centres*, Report of an Evaluation by the Young Offenders Psychology Unit, Home Office, London: HMSO.

Thorpe, D.H. (1994) *Evaluating Child Protection*, Buckingham: Open University Press.

Thorpe, D., Smith, D., Paley J. and Green, C. (1980) *Out of Care: the Community Support of Young Offenders*, London: Longman.

Titmuss, R.M. (1979) (ed.) *Commitment to Welfare*, London: Allen and Unwin.

Townsend, P. (1962) *The Last Refuge: a Survey of Residential Institutions and Homes for the Aged in England and Wales,* London: Routledge and Kegan Paul.

Twine, F. (1991) Citizenship: opportunities, rights and routes to welfare, *Journal of Social Policy,* vol.21, no.2, 165–175.

Ungerson, C. (1987) *Policy is Personal: Sex, Gender and Informal Care*, London: Tavistock.

Ungerson, C. (1993) Caring and citizenship: a complex relationship, in Bornat, J., Pereira, C., Pilgrim, D. and Williams, F., *Community Care: a Reader,* 143–151, London: Macmillan and Open University.

User-centred Services Group (1993) *Building Bridges Between People Who Use and People Who Provide Services*, London: NISW.

Utting, W. (1992) *Children in the Public Care: a Review of Residential Child Care,* London: HMSO,.

Waine, B. (1992) The voluntary sector: the Thatcher years, in Manning, N. and Page, R. (eds) *Social Policy Review 4,* 70–88, London: Social Policy Association.

Walker, A. (1989) Community care, in McCarthy, M. (ed.) *The New Politics of Welfare: an Agenda for the 1990s?*, 203–224, London: Macmillan.

Walker, N. (1991) *Why Punish?* Oxford: Oxford University Press.

Walton, R.G. (1975) *Women in Social Work*, London: Routledge and Kegan Paul.

Ware, A. and Goodin, R.E. (eds) (1990) *Needs and Welfare*, London: Sage.

Warner, N. (1994) *Community Care: Just a Fairy Tale?* Report of a UK research survey commissioned by Carers National Association, London: Carers National Association.

Webb, A.L. and Wistow, G. (1987) *Social Work, Social Care and Social Planning*, London: Longman.

Weinstein, J. (1994) *Sewing the Seams for a Seamless Service,* London: CCETSW.

Whitehead, P. (1990) *Community Supervision for Offenders*, Aldershot: Avebury.

Whitfield, D. (1992) *The Welfare State,* London: Pluto Press.

Williams, B. (ed.) (1995) *Probation Values*, Birmingham: Venture Press.

Willmott, P. (1978) *Consumer's Guide to the British Social Services*, 4th edn, Harmondsworth: Penguin.

Wilson, D. and Game, C. (1994) *Local Government in the United Kingdom*, London: Macmillan.

Winn, L. (ed.) (1992) *Power to the People: the Key to Responsive Services in Health and Social Care*, London: King's Fund.

Wolfensberger, W. (1972) *The Principle of Normalisation in Human Services*, Toronto: National Institute on Mental Retardation.

Wolfensberger, W. (1994) A personal interpretation of the mental retardation scene in light of the 'Signs of the Times', *Mental Retardation,* vol.32, no.1, February, 19–33.

Woodroofe, K. (1962) *From Charity to Social Work in England and the United States,* London: Routledge and Kegan Paul.

Wootton, B., Seal, V.G. and Chambers, R. (1959) *Social Science and Social Pathology*, London: Allen and Unwin.

Wyatt, G. (1985) The sexual abuse of Afro-American and White-American women, *Child Abuse and Neglect,* vol.9, 507–19.

Younghusband, E. (1978) *Social Work in Britain 1950–1975: a Follow-up Study,* two volumes, London: Allen and Unwin.